We Will Always Be Here

OTHER SOUTHERNERS

UNIVERSITY PRESS OF FLORIDA

Florida A&M University, Tallahassee
Florida Atlantic University, Boca Raton
Florida Gulf Coast University, Ft. Myers
Florida International University, Miami
Florida State University, Tallahassee
New College of Florida, Sarasota
University of Central Florida, Orlando
University of Florida, Gainesville
University of North Florida, Jacksonville
University of South Florida, Tampa
University of West Florida, Pensacola

We Will Always Be Here

Native Peoples on Living and Thriving in the South

Edited by Denise E. Bates

John David Smith, series editor

UNIVERSITY PRESS OF FLORIDA

Gainesville · Tallahassee · Tampa · Boca Raton
Pensacola · Orlando · Miami · Jacksonville · Ft. Myers · Sarasota

This book may be available in an electronic edition.

21 20 19 18 17 16   6 5 4 3 2 1

Library of Congress Cataloging-in-Publication Data

Names: Bates, Denise E., editor.

Title: We will always be here : native peoples on living and thriving in the
South / edited by Denise E. Bates.

Other titles: Other southerners.

Description: Gainesville : University Press of Florida, [2016] | Series:
Other southerners | Includes bibliographical references and index.

Identifiers: LCCN 2015041911 | ISBN 9780813062631 (alk. paper)

Subjects: LCSH: Indians of North America—Southern States—Social conditions.
| Indians of North America—Southern States—History. | Southern
States—Race relations.

Classification: LCC E78.S65 W4 2016 | DDC 975.004/97—dc23

LC record available at http://lccn.loc.gov/2015041911

University Press of Florida

15 Northwest 15th Street

Gainesville, FL 32611-2079

http://www.upf.com

Contents

Acknowledgments

I would like to express my deepest gratitude to the contributors of this collection who generously shared their wisdom, memories, and talents that unfold through the pages of this book. They offer us an important glimpse into both the painful as well as celebratory moments that have helped to shape their experiences as southern Native people. For their patience and generosity, I will be forever grateful. They have each enriched my life in ways that I wish I could adequately express.

This collection is something that I had been considering for some time, but it finally grew some conceptual roots during a trip to give a talk and participate in a panel discussion hosted by the Coushatta Tribe of Louisiana in 2012. As a result, I would like to express my appreciation to Ernest Sickey, David Sickey, and Jeanette Alcon for the lively conversation, inspiration, and support to further develop an idea for a collection that would be regionally focused, and would offer an opportunity for Native people to tell their own stories and share some of their greatest challenges and achievements.

This project was able to further progress thanks to John David Smith, who reached out to me seeking a contribution to the University Press of Florida's Other Southerners series, and to Sian Hunter for helping me navigate through questions and keep everything on track. I'm thankful that the University Press of Florida recognizes that although archival-based research is important to further understanding the southern historical narrative, there is also a need to open up a space for the very people being written about to speak and document their own experiences and construct their own arguments—all in their own words.

Locating contributors to this collection was a process that took on many forms. Although I was able to initially draw from my own existing network, this project would not have unfolded in the way that it did without the assistance and suggestions of Karla Martin, Cedric Sunray, Marcus Briggs-Cloud, Brooke Bauer, Robert Caldwell, Lars Adams, and David Sickey. I would also like to thank Amy Gobert of Elton High School for working with Elliott Nichols (the youngest contributor to this volume) in supporting and encouraging him as he prepared his contribution. You are an example of the type of support system that all young people should have.

Finally, I would like to thank my colleagues at Arizona State University for their support of this endeavor, as well as my family, who serves as a constant source of joy and inspiration. I am a lucky woman.

Introduction

This book is an invitation—one that welcomes you to broaden your understanding of the issues faced by Native people of the Southeast, as well as the many contributions they have made to the cultural, social, economic, and political fabric of the region. From Louisiana to North Carolina—and every state in between—Indians are featured prominently in tourism literature, indicating a rise in popularity for southern states to celebrate their indigenous past and present over the last few decades. Yet even with such acknowledgment that represents a positive shift away from an era where many southern Native people lived in obscurity, it is just not enough. The story of survival in the face of centuries of warfare, discrimination, and attempts at forced removal is a powerful one that appeals to many people; however, the story doesn't end there. In fact, it severely understates the activities that truly characterize the southern Indian experiences of the post–World War II era, which include impressive displays of leadership, tribal nation and infrastructure building, entrepreneurial ventures, and cultural revitalization, maintenance, and evolution.

The second half of the twentieth century was a time of increased visibility and political organization among the South's Native population. Although southern Indians were deemed nearly extinct in a 1948 report issued by the Smithsonian Institution,[1] over the course of just a few decades the region came to comprise the largest percentage of tribal petitions for both federal and state recognition in the nation.[2] Presently, there are eleven federally recognized and over forty state-recognized tribes in the South, with a few dozen other groups vying for a formal political status.[3] These numbers are staggering in light of earlier grim reports. So, what happened? Simply put: the South has always been home to a substantial number of Indian people who essentially existed as an invisible population. Although thousands of Native peoples were removed from their southeastern homes and forced westward in the 1830s, thousands of others remained or later returned. As a result, many isolated themselves from their non-Indian neighbors, while others intermarried with, or developed alliances and garnered support from, the surrounding communities. In some instances this helped in the maintenance of tribal identities within a volatile environment. In others, substantial elements of identity and culture were lost over time. Racial segregation also complicated matters prior to the collapse of Jim Crow. In some areas of the South, Indians were forced into either a "white" or "colored" racial status, denying their identities as "Indian." Other locales, however, did account for their Indian populations through a triracial social system. The lack of consistency in how racial segregation was orchestrated across the region served to further marginalize Native peoples by preventing a clear and accurate understanding of the locations and existence of their populations.

In order to better understand the shift to a more defined southern Indian "presence," we have to first look at the role that federal Indian policy played in the trajectory of tribal development. In the wake of devastating federal Indian policies, such as ones generated during the 1940s and 1950s intended to terminate the federal government's trust relationship with tribal nations,[4] there emerged a new era that gained momentum in the 1970s and was aimed at supporting tribal self-determination.[5] This more favorable political environment reset the stage for Native peoples across the nation by ending tribal termination, supporting tribal nation-building, and establishing a process by which tribes that were either formally terminated or previously unacknowledged can petition for federal recognition. The result of this shift was a massive retribalization. Some of the petitions that were submitted were from tribes that were already organized as distinct communities and who intended to use the opportunity to secure a formally acknowledged political status as a tribal nation. In other cases, previously disparate people—some with dominant Indian identities and others claiming distant descendancy—came together for the first time and formed new communities, developed tribal governmental structures, and petitioned for federal recognition. Although petitions poured in from all over the country, southern Indian people—in large numbers—also used the opportunity to assert their political status as tribal nations, simultaneously challenging a region that largely defined them by race.

Although this is the backdrop from which many southern Indian groups have come to develop—and in many cases, thrive—these shifts didn't emerge spontaneously. Rather, they were the result of the efforts of Indian leaders and activists, as well as non-Indian advocates and supporters, who leveraged the publicity and awareness raised by the Black Civil Rights Movement as well as Indian rights groups in other parts of the country. The political environment was right, and southern Indian people engaged—and continue to do so—in various forms of activism, community organizing, and revitalization efforts, all of which contributed to a change in the direction of southern identity politics. The Southern Indian Movement took on its own unique characteristics across the region and served to generate public awareness, allowed Indian people access to new resources, and inspired the joining or formation of intertribal coalitions that had a hand in influencing federal and state Indian policies.

The incredible political, economic, and social strides made by southern Native people over the last several decades have not gone unnoticed by scholars. In fact, while many are engaged in the important work of investigating the deep history of southeastern Native peoples,[6] a growing body of historical and anthropological literature has also emerged that addresses the twentieth century. *Indians of the Southeastern United States in the Late 20th Century*, *Anthropologists and Indians in the New South*, and *Southeastern Indians since the Removal Era* are scholarly essay collections that offer starting points to better contextualize Indians within the narrative of the New South.[7] The Eastern Band of Cherokees,[8] the Mississippi Choctaw,[9] the Florida Seminoles,[10] the Lumbee of North Carolina,[11] and the Poarch Band of Creeks[12] have each received some focused attention in the scholarship that covers the mid-nineteenth century to the modern era. Additionally, there is other scholarship that looks at specific groups or takes on a broader perspective in the analysis of politics, race, and tribal acknowledgment issues within a southern context.[13]

There are many lessons that we can glean from this scholarship, one of which is that it is impossible to generalize the southern Indian experience, at either the tribal or individual level. "Experience" is deeply personal and cannot adequately be captured through archival research or secondhand information. That very notion is what sparked the creation of this collection, which captures firsthand accounts of historical and contemporary issues in Indian communities across the South—specifically focused on Louisiana, Mississippi, Tennessee, Alabama, Florida, Georgia, North Carolina, South Carolina, and Virginia—in order to generate a better understanding of southern Native identity and perseverance. It serves to enhance and contextualize the existing collections that share the literary voices of southern Native peoples through poetry, plays, and other creative endeavors,[14] as well as beautifully compiled volumes that offer insight into the lives of contemporary Native people that are either focused on a particular southeastern state or tribal nation and serve as keepers of photographs, oral histories, letters, speeches, or other primary materials.[15] What this book sets out to emulate are historical collections that capture testimonials on a national scale, but have traditionally emphasized the experiences of western and Great Plains tribes.[16] These collections offer valuable tools in appreciating Indian perspectives and have made significant contributions to classroom instruction for decades; however, their coverage of southeastern Indians is sparse and unrepresentative. Times are changing, and if the recent endeavor of Matika Wilbur—a Native photographer from the Pacific Northwest who launched "Project 562" to photograph Indian people from all over the country—is any indication, southeastern Native peoples are no longer being left out. In fact, as this Introduction is being written, Wilbur has taken her project to North Carolina and then is off to Alabama as she adds to her growing collection.[17]

The contributions compiled within these pages are heartfelt, honest, inspiring, and, in many cases, controversial. In his foreword to the classic anthology *Native American Testimony*, Vine Deloria Jr. argued that anthologies of personal narratives are intended to offer "the missing dimension in our knowledge," which is the "informality of human experience."[18] That is what this book aims to offer: the human experience as it comes in various forms and through a multitude of voices. Rather than offering a narrow—and singular—perspective on the issues represented here, the contributors offer us a glimpse into their unique experiences, emotions, rationales, and aspirations. The entries come in the form of autobiographical narratives, professional reflections, opinion-based essays, interviews, and speech transcripts. Together, they create a powerful collection of primary sources generated by modern Native people who have all contributed to or witnessed dramatic shifts in the lives of southern Indian people in recent decades.

A few of the contributors are established writers, but most are making their writing debut. They represent varying generations, levels of authority within their communities, professions, and political statuses ranging from belonging to federally recognized tribes, state-recognized tribes, unrecognized tribes, or not holding membership within an organized tribe. This diversity in coverage was intentional in order to get a fair cross section of perspectives. With that said, however, in no way is this collection comprehensive. Not all Southeast Indian groups are represented, nor are all of the issues and challenges faced by southern Indian people addressed. Instead, this book aims to bring its contributors' voices into the larger conversations that are presently taking place across Indian Country focused on such issues as sovereignty, cultural preservation and restoration, education, economic development, and identity politics. Although there are many experiences that southern Native people share with other Native people nationally, the South—both historically and presently—offers some unique advantages and challenges that still need further exploration.

This collection is organized into four chapters that loosely situate the contributions into themes aimed at addressing issues and experiences that southern Native people have faced, and continue to face. Chapter 1, "Growing Up Indian in a Southern Context," sets the historical stage for subsequent chapters by including pieces that strike a balance between fond childhood memories connected to family, culture, and place and painful reflections of racial discrimination and the barriers that Jim Crow policies placed on Indian people. Chapter 2, "The Politics of History and Identity," unveils the controversial issues of tribal resurgence, legitimacy, politics that surround tribal recognition, and the task of challenging dominant historical narratives. Chapter 3, "Cultural Grounding," then moves us into a rich discussion of the role that cultural traditions, worldviews, and language play in the lives of contemporary Indian people. While some cultural elements have endured, others are being revitalized, adopted, or reinvented. The collection then closes with chapter 4, "Moving Forward," which, as its title suggests, includes pieces that embody the visions and hopes of the contributors for their communities in such areas as education, economic development, politics, and health. Even more than their hopes for the future, however, the contributions in this final chapter offer some examples of the work that has *already* been done in each of these areas—work that reflects strong leadership and savvy decision making.

Compiling this collection was an incredible journey. With only a general sense of what the completed volume would look like, it seemed to evolve organically as each new submission unveiled a deeper understanding of the issues that the contributors wanted to share and what they found most important. The enthusiasm to educate and bring a greater awareness to both historical and contemporary southern Indian issues demonstrated a great need—one that I hope doesn't end with this book. The time is right for southern Native people to not just be written about, but for them to also be the authors of their own stories and historical narratives. Coushatta leader Ernest Sickey put it best when he said, "I don't care if it is one line, but people need to hear what Indian people have to say, and in their own words—from the source and from the heart."[19]

Growing Up Indian in a Southern Context

Reminiscing about childhood memories can be both a pleasurable and painful exercise—one that is indulgent and cathartic. The contributors of this first chapter offer us access to some of their lives' defining moments that are deeply personal and, in most cases, being shared publicly for the first time. There was no particular formula or prescribed process from which these personal essays were collected, so they each take on their own unique style and points of emphasis.[1] Collectively, however, they set the stage for subsequent chapters by offering some insight into the important roles of family, culture, and place in the lives of southern Native peoples—many of whom grew up within the context of a racially polarized region that had a profound impact on them.

The pieces within this chapter are more than simple childhood memories. They offer tribute and respect to the authors' ancestors—both from the distant and more recent past. Those earlier generations sacrificed and persevered in order to lay the foundation for their descendants to carry on their cultural lifeways, knowledge, and connection to their homeland. Nanette Sconiers Pupalaikis manages to capture this beautifully in her piece, "The Ballad of the Choctawhatchee River: Ripples from Our Past," through her reminiscing about her Muscogee Creek grandmother's teachings about the importance of the Choctawhatchee River to "their history and their soul." This essay shares an important message that resonates throughout this collection, that although some history and knowledge have been lost over time, Indigenous identity—much like the river—has withstood the test of time.

This resilience is often attributed to the role that grandmothers and mothers played—and continue to play—as matriarchs, protectors, and teachers.[2] In fact, Stan Cartwright, in "Muscogee Lifeways in Central Georgia," credits his great-grandmother for having the most influence on his life through the healing knowledge and lessons that she passed on. Similarly, Patricia Easterwood, in "My Family's Legacy," and Wanda Light Tully, in "Hiding My Indian Identity," both identify with the strength and wisdom of their grandmothers who, like many southern Indian people, were forced to hide their identities from outsiders as a way of protecting themselves. In fact, family, in general, played an important role within an isolated and precarious time, often captured in vivid childhood memories.

Just as much as family and place were significant factors in shaping the context from which southern Indian people grew up in the early to mid-twentieth century, so was the region's race-based political and social structure. Native peoples' experiences were influenced by their location and relationships with surrounding non-Indian communities. Sometimes this meant that they were among friends and supporters, while other times their relationships were defined by instances of discrimination and hostility. Examples range from the Houma of Louisiana encountering "No Indians Allowed" signs in local stores to the nationally publicized case of the Lumbee of North Carolina breaking up a nearby Ku Klux Klan rally in 1958.[3] As difficult as these overt acts of hatred were to address, the role that Jim Crow played on the ability—or inability—of Indian children to gain an education seemed to have the biggest impact of all.

In most areas of the South, Indian children were forbidden admission to white schools. As a result, their choices were limited to not attending school at all, attending black schools, or establishing their own "third-tier" schools, often with the help of missionaries or local school boards, or by tapping into federal Indian funds. The Indian schools, however, were often poorly funded and limited the years of instruction to grammar school, which forced many Indian children to have to complete their education by traveling long distances to Indian boarding schools or integrated schools in other states.[4] "Growing up MOWA Choctaw," by Chief Framon Weaver of the MOWA Choctaw of Alabama, and "The Sacrifices We Made for Our Education," by Chief Kenneth Adams of the Upper Mattaponi of Virginia, together offer a powerful message on the impact that the South's segregated school system had on Indian families and communities. In both cases, Baptist churches had a hand in the development of Indian grammar schools, as well as the facilitation of helping Indian children leave home to gain access to high schools. Sending their children away to be cared for by strangers was extremely difficult for Indian families; however, as Weaver points out, the sacrifice was worth it because the first generation of educated people to return back to their communities became teachers, business people, and community leaders.

Following the *Brown v. Board of Education* decision in 1954, and the subsequent movement toward school desegregation, it became clear that southern Indian communities that developed their own schools were divided on the issue. While some communities, such as the Poarch Creek of Alabama and the Four Holes community in South Carolina, celebrated the closures of their dilapidated Indian schools, others, such as the Lumbee, fought to keep their separate schools that served as community centers and important symbols of identity.[5] Despite the position that any given community took on the issue, and as Chief Kenneth Adams demonstrates in his essay, the desegregation period proved to be a tough transition for those Native people who were often on the front lines of the process. In fact, this is the very same point echoed by Charles "Chuckie" Verdin, author of "Showdown at Bayou Pointe-aux-Chien," who was among the first group of Indian children in Terrebonne Parish, located in southern Louisiana, to encounter severe resistance as they were positioned to desegregate the local white school.

The demographics of the schools may have shifted with the decline of Jim Crow; yet the challenges of racism that many southern Indian people experienced remained and, in some cases, even took on a new dimension. In the next two essays, "Racism in New Brockton, Alabama," by Nancy Wright Carnley of the MaChis Lower Creek, and "One Poarch Creek Family's Educational Journey over Three Generations," collectively compiled by the Martin family, we are given a glimpse into how race impacted—and continues to impact—these authors. From relationships with the local non-Indian communities that are based on confusion or hatred, to educational experiences filled with bullying or misinformed teachers and classmates, these multigenerational reflections offer valuable snapshots of journeys still in motion.[6]

With each new generation come new challenges as well as triumphs. This chapter ends with Ernest Sickey's "We Will Forever Remain Coushatta and We Will Always Be Here" because the message it conveys permeates this entire collection. Like other southern Indian communities, the Coushatta of Louisiana were economically marginalized and suffered from a high level of unemployment. Uniquely, however, their circumstances were further exacerbated when the federal government unofficially terminated them as an Indian tribe in the 1950s. Instead of buckling under the pressures of their circumstances—and defying the predictions of academics that they would disappear—the Coushatta persevered. At the heart of their endurance were community and culture, as well as the ability to exercise some agility as the social and political environment shifted.

From the early years that are represented within the contributions that comprise this chapter to the most recent reflections, one thing is certain: the context in which southern Native people are coming of age today is very different from what it once was. This is, indeed, a good thing. However, as narratives reflecting the childhoods of younger generations deviate from the experiences of isolation, poverty, and racial discrimination, it is imperative that we do not forget what once was and that we continue to celebrate and honor the sacrifices and work of those who laid the foundation for southern Indian people today.

The Ballad of the Choctawhatchee River: Ripples from Our Past

Some of the great days of my youth were spent on the Choctawhatchee River with my grandmother. When I tired of fishing—because Elma Groce never did—I would hop off onto a sandbar to run wild and free until she returned for me. We traveled up and down the river fishing all of her favorite spots. Grandmother loved the river like some women adore fine jewelry. Of course, she never wore jewelry, makeup, or even perfume that I remember. I often observed as she plunged her arms into the muddy water to wash her hands after unhooking a fish. Sometimes she sat a minute longer watching as the river flowed and sparkled through her fingers. As I grew older, I realized that the river was like an old friend, and if it had been possible, she would have spent every day fishing it. It seems many folks in our community hold more than a fondness for the Choctawhatchee River. It is not only an element of their livelihood but a part of their history and their soul.

Elma Groce fishing on the Choctawhatchee River. (Photo Courtesy of Nanette Sconiers Pupalaikis.)

Grandmother pointed out every bend, slough, and lake, and I can still hear her call them by name: Chapman Lake, Blue Hole, Powell Lake, Warehouse Slough, Curry Lake, French Fish Hole, and Horse Shoe Lake. She noted what the current carried along—foam or driftwood—thus predicting whether the river was rising or falling. She paid attention to the clouds and wildlife in order to surmise the weather. She loved to see birds migrate in the spring and fall, and she always knew what flocks were coming and going. Alligators eased off sunny logs to slip quietly into the water, and great blue herons lumbered lazily skyward to find another fishing spot. Deer, turkeys, wild boar, and other animals wandered cautiously to the river's edge, and Elma Groce watched them with tenderness—she knew every tree along the bank and every birdsong.

I sat on her boat and listened to stories of long-gone days. She spoke in simple terms about the complex history of the river—ferry routes, political doings, sober days of trouble, old farm sites and gristmills, the location of a wrecked steamboat, pulp wooding, and the logjam near her favorite boat ramp. She well remembered the coldest winters and the hottest summers, the long days working in cotton fields, and the first dance with the love of her life, Floyd Groce. "In those days folks would celebrate after raising a new barn or harvesting their fields. Some men played fiddles and others played their guitars, and your grandpa and I danced on peanut hulls." Her stories were amusing and always down-to-earth real. Elma Groce was an intelligent woman who had a deep perception of people and life. She awakened with the sun and hastened to the bait bed. I remember the cardinals singing at dawn and Grandmother insisting that even the redbird was calling, *hurry up!*

There were days when we watched as a heavy fog rolled down the river or we would sit out a thunderstorm because Grandmother knew it would pass quickly and there were hours of daylight left to *catch the fish*. She was not easily daunted or discouraged by thunderheads or slow bites. The days were warm and long. She always greeted other fishermen—exchanging friendly words about their luck that day or their family's health. Then they pulled away slowly so as not to churn up the water and spoil her spot. She read the river like some people read a book, always keeping a watchful eye out for snags. Sometimes we made excursions through the backwaters in search of the best fishing place—which changed now and then due to a hard rain upstream. She spoke of everything from her earliest childhood memories to a favorite song she heard at church recently—all with the same intensity and clarity as if it had happened the day before. I listened to endless stories about the great flood of '29 and of outlaws who hid in the woods and fished for survival. There were tales of moonshiners who risked the current to escape the pursing revenuers and of old-time baptisms when the voices of folks singing—*shall we gather at the river*—rose above the swamps and drifted heavenward. She often sang herself as we traveled from one spot to another, and the truth is she had a strong alto voice that blended beautifully with the river's song.

There was one location that Grandmother never failed to acknowledge: "Your grandfather's people lived there," she would say. "His grandmother came up the Choctawhatchee River on a large raft with others from her tribe." She explained how Crissy Ann, a Seminole Indian, had met her Creek husband, Robert Craven, at the place called Bear Pen, where they were married and built their home. I often imagined these great-grandparents hunting and fishing along their beloved river much like their descendants continue to do.

After Holmes County was founded in 1848, Bear Pen, originally known as Hewitt's Bluff, was selected as the county seat. It was later moved to Cerro Gordo and other locations before Bonifay was chosen in 1905. Most historians agree that the county was named after Holmes Creek, which was a primary waterway in that era. However, there is some speculation regarding why the name "Holmes" was given to the creek itself. Some believe that it was called after a Creek Indian Chief who had taken an English name, but other scholars insist that it was named after Thomas J. Holmes, an early settler in the region.

The Choctawhatchee River begins in southern Alabama and flows approximately 140 miles south into northwest Florida. Native Americans lived and thrived throughout our region and along the riverbanks prior to the first appearance of the Spanish conquistadors and the British conquerors. The *Milan Tapia* journal, a bibliography that was printed in 1693, refers to the river as Chicasses—a term that applied to the Chatot Indians who lived near the river at that time. From 1764 to 1781, a Scottish surveyor, George Gauld, was consigned by the British to chart one of the first manuscripts of the Gulf of Mexico and parts of west Florida. Gauld was captured at the Siege of Pensacola in 1781. He was taken to Havana and later New York, and then finally returned to England, where he died soon after. In his manuscript dated 1769, Gauld referred to the river as Chacta-hatchi. Later Roman maps from 1774 and 1776 recorded variations of the same name. It is believed that Chatot was likely a synonym for Choctaw, and the river may have been named for them. If so, Choctawhatchee simply translates to "river of the Choctaws."

Early records indicate that other clans also dwelled along the river. Some of these Indigenous tribes have faded, and their names are long forgotten. Though we have little knowledge of their customs, it is impossible to forget their existence because the landscape is still rich with their artifacts. Many changes have occurred from the time of the first people to the present. And yet the river seems unchanged—endlessly winding and cutting her path through the lives of a changing world, while memories along with history dissolve like sandbars with the flow of time. An era has gone, and a new generation now wades into the water.

Perhaps it is inevitable that every generation moves farther from the banks of their ancestral home. Nevertheless, some things cannot easily be undone by a forever-changing world that now offers high-tech entertainment with river sports that can be enjoyed online. My youngest brother once visited me when I lived in Tennessee. I had never seen him ill. However, after making the drive he came straight into our home and collapsed on the couch. He was in bed for the first twenty-four hours of his vacation. When I asked, "Dean, what is wrong and why are you sick?," his reply was simple and real. "I have traveled too far from the river—I think it is my lifeline." Once I assured him that there was a beautiful river nearby and ancient Indian grounds to investigate, he became adventurous again and could not be restrained from exploring the woods and river. Surely, some part of our heritage is embedded into our genes or simply breathed into our soul. I have had the fortune to travel the world, but I have not found another home. The call to return to the Choctawhatchee River and the wild and wonderful clan that I call my family is too strong.

Editor's Note: This essay was previously printed in the *Geneva Reaper* (Geneva, Alabama) and the *Holmes County Advertiser* (Bonifay, Florida).

Nanette Sconiers Pupalaikis is a freelance writer who has lived many places throughout the United States and abroad. Her earliest memories are of stories told to her by her father and grandparents—all Muscogee Creek descendants.

Muscogee Lifeways in Central Georgia

My Muscogee great-grandmother was the one with the most influence on my life, through her daughter—my grandmother. They led a very secluded life, living along the Flint River and in the mountains of central Georgia. My great-aunt told me that when great-grandmother moved into the Cove (mountain range of the Flint River), she was known simply as the "Indian Woman" and the locals came to her for healing. My other great-aunt had told a similar story years earlier, but not with as much detail—that great-grandmother was a "conjurer" and could "heal" was her story.

Her daughter, my grandmother, had a huge hand in raising me. For whatever reason, I was taken into the mountain range of a place called the Cove (just south of what is now Woodbury, Georgia). I went along to explore, was shown old home places (our first home was actually a log house built around 1850), picked berries with my grandmother, was taught to hunt quail and deer, fished baskets in the Flint, ran and fished trot lines, slept on the ground with bare essentials for days at a time, and fished for sucker fish during their spawning season. I was also taken to caves that my father knew of and told that they were used to hide out in times of need. I walked behind my grandmother as she plowed and threw down soda (fertilizer) as she and my dad planted, and I watched my dad build boats of sawed boards and then seal them with pitch. I was even a patient of my grandmother when I was sick and received Lord knows what kind of salve when needed, but I do remember tobacco being a big one for bee stings—which were frequent.

House brooms were made of broom sage, and "yard rakes" were bundles of sticks tied together. Grandmother lived within walking distance of the Flint, and everything caught was cooked, including the fish heads. It was better not to ask what was being eaten, just eat and be thankful. Outhouses were the toilets, and no one thought anything about it. Funny thing, names seemed interchangeable. I didn't know my dad's real name until I was ten or so. Everyone called him "Junebug." My grandmother was called either Willie Lou or Middie Lou, she answered to either. Granddaddy was called "preacher." My grandfather was a master weaver of baskets, bottoms and backs for chairs, and even a few fish baskets. This puzzled me a little because I often thought this was primarily a woman's chore. His baskets were mostly of white oak strips that he cut by hand using a knife, and sometimes a drawknife. Granddad did some weaving with cane. Again, he cut the cane into usable strips. Grandmother did it all—plowed, churned butter and buttermilk, and milked cows for the "regular" milk. When we tagged along, she would shoot the milk from the cow right into our mouths. She thought it was funny. It was warm, but tasted good. Every move on the farm was done according to the phase of the moon.

What was perhaps one of the most important lessons in my life was learning about "Rain Crow." I believe "Rain Crow" to actually be a mourning dove, although some research states that there is actually a bird known as the "rain crow." Sitting on my grandmother's porch, we could hear the bird off in the distance singing its low mournful cry. Grandmother and Dad would say, "That is the rain crow and in three days, it will be raining." More often than not, rain would follow. This was such an important part of my life that I refer to my youngest granddaughter as "Rain Crow." Nowadays, I do not hear the rain crow very much. When I do, I am a child again . . . sitting on grandmother's porch, watching her rock to and fro, and saying, "You hear the rain crow? In three days, it will rain." I am now teaching my grandchildren these things, but I rarely hear the rain crow anymore.

Editor's Note: These memories were originally recorded through a project conducted by the Perdido Bay Tribe and funded by The Able Trust. Stan Cartwright's full story was previously printed by Don Wells and Diane Wells in parts 4–6 of "Hiding Your Indian Culture" in *Smoke Signals* (July–December 2013).

Stan Cartwright is of Muscogee and Cherokee descent and a fifth-generation resident of the Cove, in Meriwether County, Georgia. He has a master's degree in education from the University of Georgia and has spent thirty-seven years serving people with disabilities. He currently is the transition coordinator for the Meriwether County School System and a coauthor of Strong Fox, a book inspired by the stories of his father to empower children to concentrate on their strengths rather than perceived weaknesses.

My Family's Legacy

As a child growing up, my maternal grandmother told us quite often that she was half Indian. Her mother, Nicey Cooper, was full-blooded Cherokee. Her father was full-blooded Irish. My grandmother was forced to change her name legally in the white man's court, from "Tinnie Belle" (Tiny Bell Cooper), her given Indian name, which was after the lily of the valley, to "Theresa Price," a white name, for the purpose of owning her own home. It was not acceptable for an Indian to buy a home at that time. Mom's dad, Walter Cullen Jones, was Creek, but we don't know much about him as he died when she was two years old.

Grandmother taught us Indian ways in a subtle manner. She made Indian camp skirts for us to wear to school with rows of rick-rack sewn on them. When we asked about a particular plant we saw growing in her yard, such as mullein, she would say, "That isn't a plant, that's medicine." Today I grow my own medicinal plants. She also taught me to cook hoecakes. Hoecakes are wonderful and different from western-style frybread, which is made in smaller pieces and deep-fried quickly. Grandmother's hoecake is made in a frying pan as one big cake, basically one big fried biscuit and so yummy for breakfast with tomato gravy when you wake up hungry.

On my father's side, my grandmother, Linnie Elizabeth Jackson, was Creek, Choctaw, and Scottish. My grandfather, Edward Napolean Emmons, was Creek and English. Neither of my paternal grandparents spoke of their lineage. I do not know if they were ashamed or afraid of the government, but they managed to teach us Indian ways just the same. Watching my grandmother, I saw how she lived the matriarchal ways of the Creeks. I saw how strong she was, physically and mentally; how hard she worked; and how she taught and led the family. I also saw how gentle she could be, which is very important.

Grandmother was every bit the matriarch of her family. At a very young age, I challenged her. I don't believe either of us actually won that challenge, but we both had great respect for each other after that. I believe she saw a leader in me at that young age, a person who would stand up for myself and my family. She knew I was learning from her. Grandmother was a very hard woman who taught us strength. She also taught me to cook. I think most of all she and my dad taught me to show great respect for the elders. This is the Indian way.

The "Old Home Place" is what my dad and grandparents called their home in Alabama between Toxey and Butler. It was 385 acres deeded to my grandmother's great-grandfather, Jesse Jackson, after the Indian Removal (Trail of Tears). This was the place where he and his family went to hide and avoid the trail. Later, when it was all over, the land was deeded to him as a family reservation for the purpose of having a Creek village. The village was complete with a longhouse, a cookhouse, family homes, and a school.

It was called "Old Bogaloosa" after the river that ran through it. Later, when the railroad crossed the lower valley, it became known as "Jackson Spur." Jackson was my grandmother's family name. It is called Jackson Spur to this day.

There was a school there on the land until 1855 when it was closed and moved to Pushmatha, a nearby town. At that time, Jessie Jackson moved his family into the log cabin that had been the school. He raised his family there, and his son, Lewis, raised his family in the same cabin, and his son, Jordan, after him. Jordan was my grandmother's father. My grandmother, Linnie Elizabeth Jackson, grew up in the old log cabin with a dirt floor. I remember walking down the dirt road by the house with her. She would point into the woods where the old log cabin was falling down and tell me that was the house where she grew up. Since then, the old cabin has fallen down and the woods of nature have taken it over.

After my grandmother married my grandfather, Edward Napolean Emmons, they built a wood plank house with a wraparound porch just down the dirt road from the old schoolhouse. That is the house we spent all our weekends and holidays visiting when I was a child and teenager. After I married, I took my husband and daughter there. Over the years, that old house became the "Old Home Place" to me as well. It was the house where my dad grew up and I grew to love.

Down the hill behind the house was an artesian well where the family got their water. At that time there was no running water in the house. The family farmed and hunted on that land until my dad was grown, and then all but one cousin moved to Pensacola. My father's cousin lived there until he died, and then the house stayed vacant for a while. That house still stands today, and I still love to visit. It is now being restored by a family who intends to move into it.

My grandmother's family lived on that land for five generations. When we visit, we can still feel the energy of all the generations that walked it before us. It is truly a spiritual experience to walk that land today.

Editor's Note: These memories were originally recorded through a project conducted by the Perdido Bay Tribe and funded by The Able Trust.

Patricia Easterwood grew up in Pensacola and is of Cherokee, Creek,
and Choctaw descent. She married at the age of nineteen and became
a professional seamstress as taught by her Cherokee grandmother. She
now owns her own alterations business. As a member of the Perdido
Bay Tribe of Lower Muscogees, she serves as a board member and
teaches Native crafting techniques at their cultural center in Pensacola,
sharing cultural traditions every chance she gets.

Hiding My Indian Identity

It always bothers me to look at an old map of tribal locations in the United States and not see Cherokees represented in northern Alabama. It is almost like we don't exist. The Creeks are there in the southern part of the state, but the Cherokees are left off.

Although this bothers me, I understand why we are overlooked. Indian families, such as mine, in the area were very careful not to talk about who they were or where they came from. In fact, we were instructed not to tell anyone we were Indian. My family lived way up in the mountains and got up into the caves when the soldiers came to move Indian families during the Removal period. Later, they made their way back down to settle into log homes or work in fields. When I was a kid, my maternal grandmother and grandfather told us to tell people we were "white" because they were afraid that the same thing would happen to us again if the government discovered that we were Indians. As a result, we were always careful and my grandparents were very suspicious of outsiders.

My grandfather was born in northeastern Alabama in 1884 to Cherokee parents. As the baby of the family, he was spoiled. He said that when he was a child, he was petted and he was going to be petted all his life. I don't know how my grandmother put up with him. My grandmother was born the same year, and in the same area, to Cherokee and Irish parents, but was orphaned at a young age and had a hard life. The two of them met while working in the fields of neighboring farms. They met one day at the end of a work row and then began talking this way. After a while, a romance developed. They married in 1902 and went on to have twelve children, eight girls and four boys.

My grandfather eventually acquired some land where they lived in a lit-

Wanda's grandmother, Martha King Hendrix, outside of her home wearing one of her aprons that has become a major part of Wanda's childhood memories. (Photo Courtesy of Wanda Light Tully.)

tle log cabin. I have vivid memories of my grandparents sitting side-by-side on the front porch of that log cabin with my grandmother tucking her arms into the folds of her beloved apron—the same apron she used to dry grandchildren's tears or wipe their faces. When I was young, I thought she wore it for us kids to use as a hand towel. Her apron was also used to carry eggs, baby chickens, vegetables, fruit, and wood for cooking.

My grandma never went anywhere, not even to the country store. She kept a garden, cooked, cleaned, and had babies. She raised her children and helped raise many of her grandchildren, including me. I don't remember hearing her raise her voice to anyone. She also used to doctor us. She treated coughs with turpentine and sugar, colds with onions and garlic, and earaches with smoke that she would have someone blow into our ears through cupped hands. She was wise, mischievous, and absolutely beautiful. I have so many fond memories of my grandma, who often sang or made up her own poems. Today, I really wish I would have written them down, but I guess I always thought she would be around. She almost never wore shoes and always wore a big sunbonnet, long dress, and, of course, her full apron with a bib and deep pockets to carry her sweet snuffbox and peeled wood toothbrush.

Grandma was the best cook I have ever known. She always had biscuits, corn bread, and a pot of pinto beans made in case anyone was hungry. The family could help themselves to the food any time of the day. Almost every Saturday afternoon Grandma made a batch of large cookies that she called "tea cakes." All the family sure did love those cookies. I watched as she removed flour, sugar, lard, and other ingredients from her pantry. I don't remember her using any type of measuring device, everything was from memory. She poured all of the ingredients into a wooden bowl and mixed them with her hands. She tasted the mixture and added new ingredients as needed. After another taste, she would smile at me and say, "Now these cookies will be good!" She didn't roll out the cookies, but she would dust her hands with flour and pinch off a cookie. This is how she also pinched off the batter for biscuits. Grandma's oven had no regulation to keep the temperature adjusted evenly, so she would sit nearby to watch. Now and then she pressed the cookies with her finger until she knew they were done. Sitting with Grandma in the kitchen as we listened to the fire snapping and crackling in the oven while smelling the aroma of fresh-baked tea cakes was one of the most delightful events of my young life.

My mother, who was the second oldest of the twelve kids, didn't talk much about her youth, but talked about how she and her sisters cut lumber for railroad cross ties, with a two-man saw, to sell to L & M Railroad. She also talked about how all the kids had to work hard in the fields to pick cotton. Granddaddy saw to it that all of his kids worked hard. At the age of two years old, the babies were given a twenty-five-pound sack to use for picking cotton. If he caught up with his older children, he would knock the children on up the cotton row so that they would speed up and then he would yell at the babies to "get on up there!"

In 1922, my mother left home at the age of thirteen, and it was thought that she got married at that young age (to whom, I don't know), and then went on to continue making her way as a cotton picker, and then a waitress and a cotton mill worker. It wasn't until 1930 that she met my daddy and went on to have my brother Junior and me.

My birth created quite a story within the family. I was born on a straw pallet and only weighed about three pounds. Mom said that I was so small that she could put my head in a teacup. She also said that I was born with a "hood over my head," which was really the membrane sac. This was special because it meant that I was prone to having visions and seeing things that others don't. I was named Wanda Bell Ila Louise Light. Daddy named me "Wanna Bell," but Mom later changed it to "Wanda." Daddy said that "she had to get fancy!"

My daddy talked about being Indian more openly than my mom and grandparents. He used to tell me that when he was little his parents always made him walk in ditches to get to his grandmother's house so that the Creeks wouldn't steal him. He was taught that some of the Creeks would take Cherokee children, so he had to be careful.

As far back as I remember, I was taught about different remedies. For example, I used to get bad nosebleeds, so my mom used to hold a cold spoon or pair of scissors down my back against my bare skin. She also used to treat it by placing a cold nickel directly under my nose, between the upper lip and gum. I was also taught that if you want it to rain, that you kill a snake and hang it from a tree. One day Junior and I killed a water snake and hung it from a tree. Well, it rained and rained. After about three days, we thought we should go take that snake down. The snake was gone, and it quit raining that day! We were glad someone had taken it down, or did the old screech owl get it? We were afraid to tell Mom that we made it rain. We never did put another snake on a tree.

I had no supervision as a kid, so I roamed the woods a lot. I could sing or holler whatever words came into my head, as loud as I liked, and no one could hear me. I would locate a spot where sunlight filtered through the branches to play. In the summertime I would sweep a clean place under the fresh-smelling tall pine trees as large as a house. Then I would divide the space into three or four rooms by raking pine needles into lines to make invisible walls. For furniture, I used different amounts of pine needles to make a couch and a chair. I had to be careful not to rake up a snake. I had one orange crate that I used for a table, and I cut up a coffee can to build a fire in. Sometimes I boiled some water and cooked an egg on top of the can. When I went into the woods, I tried to have a safety pin with string wrapped around it pinned to my clothes in case I wanted to go fishing. I could always find a stick to make a pole, and then I would catch a grasshopper or dig up worms for bait. I cleaned and washed the fish in the creek, and I took the fish home to cook for the family.

One of our neighbors grew watermelons, and Junior and I would often take watermelons from his patch without asking. If we got hungry while out wandering in the woods, we would thump the watermelons to determine the best one. We would pick a ripe one and let it drop. When it burst open, we would eat only the heart with our bare hands, letting the juice run clear to our elbows. The owner of the patch was nice about it, and when I got older I even worked for him. I picked his cotton for 25 cents for every 100 pounds that I collected in a toe sack that I dragged behind me. I also pulled turnips for the same farmer. We would bundle and tie them with twine and then throw the bundles to someone standing on the back of the truck who would stack them neatly. I was usually the one to catch the bundles, and sometimes the boys would throw the turnips hard to see if they could knock me out of the truck, and often I was. You may have heard the old saying "I didn't fall off the turnip truck," meaning "I am not that dumb." I don't know how dumb I am, but I have fallen out of the turnip truck many times!

I guess I had a taste for adventure. Often, I would put on my only good yellow dress, and Junior and I would go hitchhike. Someone would always pick us up, but mostly soldiers who were going on maneuvers cross-country in army trucks. We knew that if we showed our thumbs to the army trucks, they would pick us up and then let us out about 30 miles away. I don't know why anyone would pick up two young children, but they did! I know God had to have been looking out for us because we always managed to find the train that ran by the back of our house. We would wait until it stopped and hide in one of the open boxcars. When the train would get close to our house, we would anxiously wait for the sound of the train slowing down to make a curve. We would then get in position to jump toward the front of the train, or we would get sucked under it. We did this many times, and we always got back before Mom got home from work.

My grandma's house was right across from what we called "Colored Town." Just as you crossed the road there was a bridge, and on the other side of the bridge was the black store run by an old gray-haired lady. She was very nice to us. She had a row of jars filled with penny candy that she sold by the piece. After Junior and I spent all our pennies on the candy, she would give us an extra piece and say, "Now you little childrens had better get on back across the bridge." There was a church close to the store that we often hid outside in the bushes by the church window and watched the service. They would get so excited praising God. The windows and the doors were open because it was hot, and they used paper fans. You could hear everything. We would stay for a while, but made sure not to get caught. I don't know what would have happened, but what I do know is that it was exciting to watch them not be ashamed about who they were as they all gathered together on those hot Alabama days.

Looking back at some of these memories that I have as a child, I realize that some memories are good and some are bad; yet they all helped to shape my life. As a Cherokee child growing up in Alabama, I had very little education, and I mostly only associated with my brother and cousins. Outside of my family, I didn't have a congregation of people like those who went to the black church on the other side of the bridge. I was isolated, and, as I was taught, I didn't dare let anyone know that I was Indian. I finally got over that as I grew older, moved away, and had children and grandchildren of my own. Although my own mother continued to avoid all discussion about our history right up until her death, I made it my mission to teach my children and grandchildren to be proud of who we are. It might have been something that I was denied, but it certainly doesn't have to be their fate.

Wanda Light Tully presently lives in Sulphur Springs, Texas, and enjoys documenting and sharing her family history with her children, grandchildren, and great-grandchildren.

Growing up MOWA Choctaw

One of my favorite things to do when I was a kid was ride on my daddy's shoulders and neck. He was my idol. We did a lot of things together during my first seven years. He was a big fan of movies and after the drive-in movie theater opened in McIntosh, Alabama, we went as often as he could afford to on a logger and construction worker's pay. In those days we didn't have electricity throughout our community, but we got it as soon as the electric lines reached our house. We didn't have a TV in those days either, but we would sit for hours at a time listening to my daddy's favorite radio shows.

We would go in the woods to get firewood, and he always took his gun in case a deer or some game appeared while we were gathering lighter wood knots and box faces for firewood. The last thing I did with him was take our heater pipes to the welding shop to have them braised so they would not separate. He was killed in a hunting accident the next day. My entire world changed after that.

That's when I realized how strong a woman my mother was. She really stepped up and made sure my brother, two sisters, and I always had food and clean clothes for school and church. The trips to the movies were not as frequent after my father died, but we still got to go some. I remember my uncles taking us several times.

My mom married my stepdad after a while, and she finished building the new house she had started with the help of Baker Reed, her maternal grandfather. He was our guardian angel from the time my dad passed until his death in 1966. My mom's dad was also one of my heroes, and I spent a huge amount of my childhood at his home as well. He raised four children as a young widower with the help of their aunt Evelyn Reed, who took care of them while he was away working in log camps. They did an awesome job.

I started school at Reeds Chapel School at age six. It was an all-Indian school when I started and remained that way most of my twelve years. Only one white child was enrolled as far as I remember, and that must have been sometime around 1959 or 1960. There were no black children. From the time it was first established until it closed it remained predominantly Native American.

The Indian schools in Washington and Mobile Counties were central meeting places for my people. Unlike the black community, we did not use churches for political and community organizing. I think the reason was that white missionaries often served as pastors of one or two of the Indian churches, and they did not wish to encourage us to exercise any kind of independence. They even taught in our schools some, but did not participate in many community activities.

Reeds Chapel School was located in the community where I grew up, and Bilbo Creek crossed two of the roads that led to my community. A big branch crossed the other entrance and flowed into Bilbo Creek just a few yards from where it crossed the road. Whenever Bilbo Creek would get out of its banks after a storm we were unable to have school for two or three days because the teachers and most of the students were blocked by high water. The county finally paved two miles of Topton Road in 1962, which solved part of the problem.

We always got hand-me-down books from the white schools, and sometimes from black schools too. We were given used balls, bats, and other sporting goods from white schools if they were available. The only time we ever got anything new was when we raised the money to purchase it ourselves. If we didn't have enough textbooks, the teachers had to write lessons on the blackboards.

Reeds Chapel School only taught grades one through eight for a long time. Students who wanted a higher education had to go to Indian boarding schools in Louisiana and Oklahoma. Bacone College in Muskogee, Oklahoma, started as a high school and two-year college. Acadia Baptist Academy in Eunice, Louisiana, was a church-run Indian boarding school. George Marion Reed was the first one of our tribal members to go to Acadia Baptist Academy, and Priscilla Murphy Reed was the first to go to Bacone High School and College. Many of my people went to these schools over the years. We have had two or three go to Haskell Indian College in Kansas as well. Beginning in the 1930s, through to the present time, MOWA Choctaw students continued to enroll and graduate from Bacone College. Unfortunately, Acadia Baptist Academy fell on hard times and had to close.

Bacone College has been great for my tribal members, providing an opportunity for Indian students from very poor families that could never afford to send their kids to college in Alabama. Indian students never had an opportunity to be admitted into the white colleges in the Jim Crow state of Alabama anyway. Many of the friends we've made over the years have been in a position to come to our aid when needed. Bacone alumni from southeastern tribes are now leaders in their communities, and some are members of the new organization called the Alliance of Colonial Era Tribes (ACET).

Lucile Reed graduated from Wayland Baptist College in Plain View, Texas, and she came home and started teaching in Reeds Chapel School.

She was later joined by Pricilla Reed, Nola Reed, Bennett Weaver, Tempress Reed, Annie Weaver, and Gallasneed Weaver. We had a majority Choctaw faculty, and the progress of our student body really improved. Gallasneed Weaver became principal at Reeds Chapel School in the 1970s, and he was not only able to keep it open, it flourished under his leadership. Bennett Weaver was vice principal, and the two made a great team. They were also pastors of Indian churches and leaders in our community. They both played a key role in writing a new constitution for our tribal government.

Besides the Reed Chapel School, there were other schools established within my community. Calcedeaver is the Indian school in Mobile County. It was established after the Mobile County School Board combined three Indian schools into one and combined the three names to come up with "Calcedeaver." The earliest Indian school in Mobile County was established in 1835 by the federal government. It was one of the schools that became part of Calcedeaver. I suppose that makes Calcedeaver the longest continuous operating Indian school in the state of Alabama and one of the oldest in the country. Weaver School, Shady Grove, and Cedar Creek are the three schools that eventually became "Calcedeaver," and today the school's student population is 95 percent Native American.

In the 1920s, the Southern Baptists saw a need to send a missionary to work with our people, and a young woman from Virginia named Martha Walden was given the first assignment to work with us. She did an excellent job working with our Choctaw ministers, and she also taught in one of our schools. As a result, the Southern Baptist Association created the South Alabama Indian Mission Field. They purchased forty acres of land from one of the Native American landowners and established the Southern Baptist Indian Assembly Camp on what is now County Road 96 between Mt. Vernon and Citronelle, Alabama. This was done in the 1940s and was guided by the leadership of Dr. Frank Belvin, the brother to the Chief of the Choctaw Nation in Oklahoma, and a missionary named Dr. Round.

The Baptist missionaries were influential in getting our students enrolled in the Baptist Indian boarding schools and Bacone High School and Junior College. The first missionary previously mentioned, Martha Walden, was quite a woman. She was able to keep a Choctaw inmate from hanging after traveling to Montgomery by train and convincing the governor to commute his sentence. I was fortunate enough to meet her about a year before she passed away. She left money for the Martha Walden Choctaw Scholarship Fund in her will.

The work of the Baptist missionaries—as well as those who ran the Reeds Chapel School, Weaver School, Cedar Creek School, and the Calvert School—really made a big difference for the Choctaw people. Life was a daily struggle after the turn of the twentieth century. Very few people could read or write, and most barely spoke any English. Because of the impact of these schools, we were able to better understand the notes and loans we had to sign for basic needs such as seed, fertilizer, plows, farm animals, tools, and groceries. One by one, tribal members realized the value of having some education.

Since the MOWA Band of Choctaw Indians adopted our new tribal constitution in 1978, tribal leaders have been elected by the tribal membership. The community members have slowly begun to see the advantage of having educated elected officials, as opposed to voting for someone based on personal relationships. The newly elected leadership wasted little time in getting our tribe state recognition and a seat on the Alabama Indian Affairs Commission. We also established the MOWA Choctaw Housing Authority, applied for and received funding from President Reagan's block grant programs, and created vehicles for economic development.

As I look back on the accomplishments of our tribal members, I see where the success of our tribe really began to happen as a result of having access to an education. The first generation of Choctaw teachers had their students enter the job market, go on to college, open new businesses, and get politically involved as we work toward the future.

Framon Weaver has been the Tribal Chairman of the MOWA Band of Choctaw Indians since 2011, a position he previously held from 1978 to 1984 and then from 1986 until 1995. He is a Vietnam veteran who also joined the Teamsters Union and drove trucks on construction jobs, worked for the Olin Corporation, and eventually operated his own trucking business. He is the father of seven and grandfather of four.

The Sacrifices We Made for Our Education

As a young boy growing up in the 1950s in King William County, Virginia, one of my first memories is seeing most of my older brothers and sisters leave home so that they could go to high school in other states. At that time, I did not know the reason why they had to leave, but I later came to understand the role that racial segregation played. Although white and African American children had local high schools to attend, Indians did not.

There were ten children in my family, and every one of us started off attending Sharon Indian School. Until 1952 it only went through seventh grade, and then after that time it began to extend into the higher grades, but no one ever graduated from there. You had to go elsewhere if you wanted to finish high school.

Sharon Indian School first started in either 1917 or 1918. It got its name because some of the members of Sharon Baptist Church helped in the building of the school. It was not an Indian church, but a white church, although some of the local Indians attended that church at one time. Indian education wasn't a big priority in the Commonwealth of Virginia, so the Sharon Indian School was basically a one-room building with one teacher. The original building was replaced in 1952, but still had limited space.

Sharon Indian School, King Williams County, Virginia. (Photo Courtesy of Kenneth Adams and the Upper Mattaponi Indian Tribe.)

According to some of the folks who have already passed on, there was another Indian school that came before the Sharon Indian School. It was in operation in the late 1800s for a short period of time and was fairly close to where the school is now. In looking back to some of the old folks that I knew who have since passed, and who were kids during the late 1800s, some of them could actually read and write. Not very well, but I was told that there was another school that they went to. There was a request made by the local school superintendent to the Bureau of Indian Education in 1892 to help support the Indians of King William County, so perhaps this earlier school was a response to that. There was also a response that was filed from that request, which indicates that there was a school; however, there is absolutely no documentation about that at all. What knowledge we have about that school now is all through oral histories. There is only one person who is still living who has any information at all about that, my aunt Eunice, who was born in 1924. She told me that there had been a school in the late 1800s, and she actually told me where it was located, at a place called the Oakes. This was maybe three-quarters of a mile from what became the Sharon Indian School.

After attending Sharon Indian School, my next-to-oldest sister, Nora, had to go live in another county about 45 miles away with a Chickahominy Indian family, as the Chickahominy school taught at least one year higher than Sharon Indian School. The following year, just after I was born in 1947, she had to travel even farther away from home when she went to Bacone High School and College in Oklahoma. At one time, Bacone was actually a grade school through high school. Then, in the 1950s, they had their last high school class. Bacone College is the oldest institution of higher learning in Oklahoma. It was established initially for the Five Civilized Tribes and is located in Muskogee. The land that the college was built on was provided by the Creek Nation, so most of the students were from eastern Oklahoma. Over time, that changed, and there have been students at Bacone from over 140 tribes. They came from all over the country, and Indian students from Virginia started attending shortly after World War II.

So, my sister went there for one year, and then she went to live with a family in Michigan to finish high school. The way that came to pass was through a pastor from Indian View Baptist Church, which was right next to Sharon Indian School. That particular pastor was at Indian View for a while and then went on to become a pastor in Michigan. While he was in

Michigan, he talked to some of the local families and arranged for kids in my family and others to reside with them so that they could attend high school. My sister later went on to study nursing in Detroit, becoming a registered nurse.

Not having access to a local high school also caused me to not really know my oldest brother, Wesley, who left home when I was a little kid. Wanting an education forced him away. He traveled to Bacone in 1952 and started his first year of high school, continuing for three years, and then entered the first of two years of college at Bacone, attending a full five years in Muscogee. Many years later he told me he worked in the dining facility for all those years to help support his costs at Bacone. By the time he turned eighteen, he was in the National Guard, with at least two weeks of training every summer, cutting the time he could be with his family in Virginia. His Guard time also helped him with his costs for college. After his graduation with an associate's degree, he entered the U.S. Army, serving in combat in the Dominican Republic in the early 1960s and then in Vietnam in 1968 and 1969. By 1965, I was in the U.S. Air Force, and since I didn't grow up with my brother, when I went to visit him in 1970, it was almost like walking into the home of a stranger. It was awkward. That is part of the story that I told when testifying on the federal recognition process before the Senate Indian Affairs Committee and the House of Representatives committee in 2002. I tried to make them understand how traumatic those types of experiences were for Indian families. In fact, when my eighty-eight-year-old mother listened to the testimony, she sobbed when hearing that story.

My next oldest brother, Howard, like my sister Nora, also went to live with a family in Michigan when he was only about fourteen or fifteen years old to get a high school education. He had such a bad experience that he left to join the Marines when he turned eighteen years old and was able to leave, not finishing high school. When I tried to talk with him about that time, he was hesitant to talk about those years, as it brought back to him some bad memories. I have heard someone say he was treated almost like a slave. I do not know many details, as he refuses to discuss that time.

My next oldest sister, Emily, also left home in the early 1950s to attend high school in Michigan. She graduated in 1957, went to Bacone College that fall, and stayed through the spring of 1958. Her reason for not going back was because she was tired of being poor and away from home. I recently took her back, and she visited with several of her classmates. She said it was the best trip she had ever taken.

Two of my sisters, Sally and Louise, actually went to the prestigious Virginia prep school called Oak Hill Academy. Sally describes it as a very difficult year that she spent there. She ended up leaving and didn't go back. I'm not sure exactly why, but in looking back, it was hard for all of us kids to leave home, and it took a lot of adjustment. Later, she did go on to have a very successful career. The seventh of nine boys and girls, Louise also went to Oak Hill for her senior year, and I am told she graduated with honors.

The last three brothers and sisters, who include me, my younger brother Ben, and our sister Carol, all graduated from the nearby King William High School. Ben and I were the first of a group of seven or eight Indians from Sharon Indian School to attend the previously all-white high school. Indians went there before African Americans did. I guess they figured that it was an easier transition to get us in there first and then to bring the others in. There were two of us who started there as seniors, and the rest were juniors or sophomores. In 1965, one other student and I were actually the first Indians to graduate from a public high school in King William County. In discussions with the others who first attended, I don't think we ever felt really welcomed with open arms. There were some kids who really ostracized us and a handful who really talked to us in an almost normal way; yet we always felt that we weren't fully welcomed.

In 2012, I attended a dinner with most of the graduating class of 1965, which was the first time being with them in a group setting in forty-seven years. For years, I decided not to attend any reunions, but finally relented and enjoyed the evening. One thing that was very odd at the reunion was that when we took a group picture at the end, one of the folks said to me, "Well, you were always one of us." And I said to myself, "If I was always one of you, you would not have to say it."

Since my father did not complete the first grade and my mother only went through the eighth grade, the mere fact that several of their sons and daughters attended college, despite not being able to attend high school at home, is quite an achievement. However, they had to sacrifice tremendously, with their children leaving home after barely becoming teenagers, living with strangers, and having the only communication being through letters delivered by the postman. I can barely imagine the sacrifice they made. They had no money to send them and relied on many others for assistance.

This is only a minor part of the issues our family faced. I could write an entire book on our educational experiences, but it all starts with Sharon Indian School. The same teacher who taught my mother in the early 1920s also taught her sons and daughters until 1964, retiring when the school finally closed in 1965. Today, the building is used as the Upper Mattaponi Tribal Center. It isn't a very large building, given that there were only about thirty-five or forty kids there at one time, but we use it now as a tribal meeting place and on occasion we have events there. It is on the National Register of Historic Places, and since the reservation schools were all state-run schools, it is the only Indian public school that is still standing in the state of Virginia.

Kenneth Adams is Chief of the Upper Mattaponi Tribe of King William County, Virginia. He is actively involved in lobbying Congress for federal recognition of Virginia Indians. He also serves as chairman of the Board of Trustees of Bacone College and as a member of the Board for Preservation Virginia and the Virginia War Memorial Educational Foundation.

Showdown at Bayou Pointe-aux-Chien

I was raised in lower Pointe-aux-Chien (PAC) in southern Louisiana, which is the boundary line between Lafourche and Terrebonne Parishes. The lower end of PAC is an Indian community, while the upper end is white.

The first school in our community was started by Baptist missionaries who opened up a school and church. They used some French and some English in the schools. My first language was French because our people had adopted the language of the French and Cajuns. French is still a dominant language in my community for people in my age group and up.

The people of Terrebonne Parish didn't want us to go to school with the white kids. There were two buildings put on a barge on Bayou Lafourche and then brought to Pointe-aux-Chien and offloaded to be used as an Indian school. In the mid-1960s, I went there for first and second grades. For my third year of school we were sent to the upper PAC school where the white kids went. On the first day, the white people of upper PAC surrounded the buses. I was so young, so I don't remember much, but I remember that day.

They did not want us Indians to go to school with their kids. We could see people around and we were trying to figure out what was going on. Some of what I know is what the adults had explained to us afterward, but I remember people around the bus talking and yelling. At that age, I didn't really comprehend what was happening. They were yelling for us to "get out" and "go back home." A couple of them even had signs.

After what seemed like a showdown, Reggie Dupre, who was the local constable, tried to keep the peace and calm the situation down. He told the group if they didn't let the Indian kids get off the bus, the parish would bus in black kids. I don't believe he was prejudiced against us because he had good dealings with the Indian community. He had a small shipyard and a store, and everybody went to his store. He was just trying to keep everybody calm. The crowd eventually settled down and let us get off.

Charles "Chuckie" Verdin followed in the tradition of his grandfather, father, and uncles and became a commercial fisherman (shrimping) following high school. By 2000, he owned four offshore shrimp vessels working the Gulf of Mexico and along the East Coast. With the decline in shrimp prices in 2003 due to imports, he began shrimping part time, and started also working on boats catering to the oil field. In 1999, he was elected as Tribal Chairman of the Pointe-Au-Chien Indian Tribe, which has since been recognized by the state of Louisiana and Terrebonne and Lafourche Parishes. They are still hoping to one day meet the criteria for federal recognition.

Racism in New Brockton, Alabama

This is about my daddy, John Nadirs Cornelius Wright, also known as Neal or Nadirs. He was born on November 24, 1921, in the Yellow River Swamp in Covington County, Alabama, and died on October 9, 2008, at his son's house in Geneva County, Alabama. His children, Nancy Wright Carnley and James Cornelius Wright, as well as his daughter-in-law, Melissa Wright, and great-grandchildren (ages four, five, and nine years old) cared for him in his last days while fighting cancer. As the youngest of nine children, three of my daddy's siblings had already crossed over. He grew up living in the swamps, where he had to hide while hunting and fishing.

When he was seven years old, his father, John Wright, passed away at the age of sixty-five. As a result, my daddy went to work farming, logging, turpentine gathering, and trapping to help support his mother and the rest of his family. Around the age of ten years old, his job was in the timber business blowing up tree stumps (fat lighter stumps). One time when he lit the fuse to the dynamite to blow up the tree stumps, another worker was setting off my father's dynamite sticks without his knowledge, and he ran directly into the blast. A piece of the stump hit him and caused him to lose the back of his calf, his vision in his right eye, and gave him several other wounds on his body.

In 1942, governmental officials came and told his mother, Nancy Wright, that she was on government land (the Conecuh National Forest) and that she must move from there. This was the land they had survived on for generations, and where they kept from starving by eating pine tree bark at times, fought outlaws on the run, and laid their loved ones to rest. My daddy's family came to Covington County from Barbour County to get away from the outcome of the Indian Removal Act. We heard our grandmother say many times to not say anything about being Creek Indians because when they found us before, we could only take what could fit on a wagon when we got away.

Our grandmother and her two sons, J.D. and John Wright, moved to New Brockton, Alabama (Mule Town), which is located in the center of Coffee County. Here, they became familiar with racism and discrimination. Soon after getting into town, they tried to sell their wagon for rent, but ended up selling one of the two mules they had in order to have enough for four weeks' rent. The wagon alone should have covered the rent, with cash left over, but because they were Indians, they were cheated.

The "Bottoms" became their home for many years. It consisted of six black tar–covered houses with no electricity until around 1968, and no indoor plumbing until 1973. Until around 1975, their house and yard sometimes flooded with sewage from the high school during heavy rains. Everyone who lived in these houses was Indian and had very little education. I never have understood how someone could ask for rent on these houses, which is where we lived until the early 1990s. We eventually bought the "Bottoms" and the lot where the houses sat for $3,000.

One of my father's first employers owned a pulp wood company and sawmill and had a reputation for not paying his workers of color. After working the first week, Daddy only received half of his pay. When he asked the owner about it he was told that it would be made up in the next week's paycheck. The next Saturday, after standing in line for his check, he was surprised to find that he did not have a check at all. He did not get paid for any of his work. Daddy had never had anyone not pay him for working before, so he set out to tell his boss that he better get paid by noon on Saturday. The African Americans who worked there told Daddy that the owner and his nephew carried ax handles to beat people who questioned them or talked back. Fear kept the sawmill operating. In spite of what he learned, my father went looking for the owner uptown to ask about his pay. The owner told him to meet back at the sawmill to work this out. Daddy was sitting on a stack of lumber when the owner showed up with his nephew and rest of his family. The owner drove up, got out of his truck, and said, "You are not getting more pay unless you work like the rest of these niggers do, but my nephew and I are still going to teach you a lesson about respect." At this point the owner grabbed an ax handle from the back of the truck. My daddy responded by pointing a gun at the owner's wife saying, "I'm going to shoot your wife first, then your son, and then your nephew so you can watch them die before I kill you. I want you to see them die first." Needless to say, he paid Daddy. Then, Daddy said, "What about them over there? You can pay them too now." Everybody that was owed money got paid. After this episode, the sawmill closed and Daddy never went back.

That wasn't the last time my daddy had to stand up for himself and his family. When I was in the ninth grade, regardless of what quality of school work I turned in, I got an F while the white students got an A. The terrible thing was that a lot of these students would copy from my test papers. One day, I got one of my classmates to let me have her paper. When I got home I had to always give my papers to my grandmother or mother so they could read them to my dad who could barely read. Well, I made sure that they saw that my answer sheet was the same as the other person's sheet. After that, Daddy went to the school, and when he did not get an answer from the teacher, he went to one of the school board members. My grades went from Fs to As and Bs in that teacher's class. I never had that problem again.

Even in recent times, some of the town's residents continue to be racist toward American Indians. In 1995, it got so bad that the U.S. Department of Education's Civil Rights Division was contacted and, through an investigation, found New Brockton High School guilty of discriminating against my daughter, Elizabeth Carnley, because she was an American Indian. Other students regularly gathered around her making war-whooping sounds or hand motions imitating guns or tomahawks. They said such things as "the only good Indian is a dead Indian." Elizabeth even received several injuries as a result of this bullying. Once, one of the male students took a pencil and stuck it in her ear to imitate an Indian cartoon that had been on the night before where the Indian was walking around with an arrow going through his head. She was even strip-searched by some of the band students who claimed to be looking for money. The school officials always used the same old responses: "Children will be children" or "You know how boys are." The band director even made Elizabeth play what the other students called "junkie junk instruments" rather than what she wanted to play. Once the Civil Rights Division completed its investigation, things changed for the better. The students' behavior was brought under control, and the war whoops, tomahawk motions, and anti-Indian clothing and sayings were prohibited. Elizabeth was even allowed to begin playing the bass drum in band. Shortly after, many of the students who bullied her resigned from the band, and several teachers and school administrators retired or resigned as well. During this time, my car and home were vandalized.

In March 2004, the MaChis Lower Creek Indian Tribe of Alabama's archive building was destroyed by arson. The fire destroyed out-of-print books and genealogical records. It took the arsonists three attempts to burn the building and contents completely. Instead of trying to find the criminals, the local police department accused my family of setting the fire. We could not drive anywhere without the police stopping us and asking questions about where we were going or coming from. So, I started walking from my house to the tribal office. One day my daddy and I were walking and the police stopped us and asked where we were going. We simply replied, "Walking." They followed us to the office and sat across from us in the parking lot of the First Baptist Church. I had to contact the Alabama attorney general to stop the racial profiling and police harassment. They have never found who set fire to the building.

I will end with one more example of the types of troubles Indian people here have to endure. Recently, the tribe's Chief attended a funeral; some of the area's non-Indian elderly people slid across the pew and spread their arms to keep him from sitting down. Then, after he left and sat in the very back, the little group slid back to sit as a group again. I wonder what is going to happen in the afterlife if they still insist on segregating people into different spaces. One thing is for certain, racism is still alive and well in Alabama.

Nancy Wright Carnley holds a degree in nursing. She also serves on the Tribal Council of the MaChis Lower Creek Indian Tribe of Alabama and represents her community on the Alabama Indian Affairs Commission.

One Poarch Creek Family's Educational Journey over Three Generations

"We didn't have a lot, we worked
with what we had to get what we got."

Together my grandmother, grandfather, dad, aunt, sister, and I would like to share our experiences in school. When these stories were written in April 2014, my papa, Otha, was eighty-four years old; my mamaw, Marie, was seventy-eight years old; my aunt Pauline was fifty-six years old; my dad, Nathan, was fifty-four years old; I (Karla) was thirty years old; and my sister, Kaci, was twenty-seven years old. We represent three generations of Poarch Creeks who grew up and went to schools in Escambia County, Alabama.

"We went to school for a little while,
but most of what we know we learned in life."

Otha and Marie both grew up in the small Indian community of Headapeada (Head of Perdido), which is now where our tribal headquarters are located. They both started school in first grade. Papa's first school was a one-room schoolhouse with one white teacher and first-through-sixth-grade Indian students. In 1939, four Indian schools were combined into the Poarch Consolidated School for Indian students in the first through sixth grades. This school was built by and located in St. Anna's Episcopal Church, and the county provided the teachers. Papa explained that when he went to school, "they would work me instead of teach me so that I could earn things for my family." As the oldest child of a single mom, he had to work to earn money to help support his mom, brothers, and sisters, which was much more important than anything he could learn in school. Papa "went" to school until the sixth grade but never learned to read or write. He said that the Board of Education didn't really want Indian people to learn. "They didn't care what we did as long as we didn't learn anything." Papa worked most of his life and today still tells stories from his many jobs. His favorite job and stories are from working as captain of a tugboat. He said the boat is where he got his education. He worked very hard learning the waterways by using a tape recorder and having his brother-in-law help him. Papa said, "I learned more with that thing, on the river, than I learned from anything."

In the early 1940s, by the time Marie started school, the Indian school had moved to another building, the Pickrell House. Mamaw said it was a three-room schoolhouse with six grades, two grades in each room. Only Indian students went to this school, and all of the teachers were white. There was an outdoor bathroom and a lunchroom that was built off of St. Anna's Episcopal Church. She had to walk to school every day. In the late 1940s, that school was closed, so Mamaw attended sixth grade at a school in the nearby community of McCullough with white and Indian students. For seventh grade, she went to the white high school in town until she got pregnant with her oldest child, quit school, and got married to Otha in 1952. Mamaw said, "I learned a lot from women older than me about things such as cooking, quilting, canning, and many other things."

"Stay in school because we didn't have the opportunity to go."

Pauline and Nathan's schooling began in first grade at Poarch Consolidated School, which they referred to as "the Poarch School" or "Poarch Elementary." This was a first-through-sixth-grade Indian school in their community of Headapeada that had one classroom and one teacher for each grade. All of the students were Indian, and the teachers and principal were white. During this time, this school was often the gathering point for the three surrounding Poarch Creek communities: Hog Fork, Headapeada, and Poarch Switch.

Both my aunt and dad transferred to a white elementary school in town in third or fourth grade because their mom believed they would get a better education there. In 1969, a court order required the state of Alabama to desegregate schools. So in 1970, many schools in the state were closed, and students were reorganized or rezoned for different schools. At this time, the Poarch Consolidated School was closed, leaving no school in any local

Martin family. The photograph was taken in their home in the late 1960s. Left to right: (back row) Otha Martin, Marie Martin, and Lamar Martin; (front row) Nathan Martin, Pauline Martin Wilson, and Nelson Martin. (Photo Courtesy of Otha, Marie, and Karla Martin.)

Indian community. This directly affected both Pauline and Nathan. As a middle schooler, my aunt went to the only middle school in the area, which was located "across the railroad tracks" in the black community in town. My aunt remembers being in school for the first time that all races were put into the same place. She remembers the racial tension and a lot of riots that broke out at school. As a fourth grader, my dad went from a predominantly white school in the white part of town to a predominantly black school with a few Indian students in a black community outside of town.

My dad and aunt both continued to go to desegregated public schools: seventh and eighth grades at the middle school, ninth and tenth grades at the junior high school, and eleventh and twelfth grades at the senior high school, which is where they both graduated. Because their mom didn't drive and their dad worked off on a tugboat, they rode the bus to school until they were able to drive.

Race was a central part of their experiences in school, town, and the surrounding communities. They went from all-Indian schools, to a segregated white school, and then to desegregated schools. By the time my aunt and dad were in high school, "everybody sort of mingled together, started liking one another, and getting along." However, many things in school were organized around two racial categories: black and white. Racially, as Indian people, they remember being considered "popular" because they weren't in either category and could move between all races in ways that others couldn't at this time. They also remember being placed into the white category for school contests and their classmates "getting mad we were picked as class favorite and stuff like that 'cause most of the time it would be the Indians and the whites (in a category together), 'cause they didn't say white, black, and Indian, it was black and white and we were considered white."

Both Pauline and Nathan went through the tribe's government-funded Comprehensive Employment and Training Act (CETA) program to learn a trade and get an education past high school. Pauline explained, "Whenever I went to go work at the hospital, CETA paid for me to work there one year to get a trade. Then when I went to work at the nursing home, they paid for me to take this course to be a certified dietary manager." Nathan shared, "When I was in ninth grade, I went to trade school two nights a week for four hours. They paid us minimum wage through the CETA program. That's how we earned some money, but at the same time, I was in cabinet making and you learn a trade too." He played football for three years while he was in high school, so he had to continue taking classes at the trade school after he graduated to finish his degree. Pauline became a dietician and Nathan a cabinetmaker, both using these skills their entire lives as Pauline worked as a dietician for a nursing home and Nathan as a general contractor and owns his own construction company.

"Go to school and get your education. Can't nobody ever take that piece of paper away from you. You earned it."

Both my sister and I started three-year-old kindergarten at First Baptist Church and went straight through school until we graduated with our graduate degrees. Our town was small, but between the both of us we managed to go to almost all of the schools in town, with the majority of our time spent in public schools. My sister and I had somewhat similar, yet extremely different, experiences in school.

Our family always supported and encouraged us to do our best. Our mom always said, "Girls, you never know what is going to happen and you have to learn to be independent . . . to take care of yourself." Our mom worked in the day, went to college at night, and also had a family, which we saw was hard on her. She told us, "You don't want to have to be like me and miss out on part of your childrens' lives to go to school, so go to school now while you're young with no kids."

As with the other two generations, race was a major part of our schooling experiences. Throughout school, we identified and were recognized as Indian. My first memory of "being Indian" in school was in kindergarten when our class had to stand up and be counted by race, gender, and lunch status. I also remember struggling in elementary school with reading, so the Indian aide at our school pulled me out of class and helped me with my reading skills. In every grade, K–12, my sister and I both remember calls over the intercom saying "all Indian students report to the lunchroom or library," which is where they would give us announcements about programs or services for Indian students. Kaci remembers, "During math class my teacher was talking about fractions and people thought it was funny to take our blood quantum to teach us about fractions. When the teacher did this lesson it was teaching people about blood quantum and how to factor what other blood quantum we would need to make our children be on the tribe's roll. This really irritated me during the class, but of course the teacher didn't like me so I didn't say anything during that time."

While we were recognized as Indian students, the school often treated "Indians" as a race in between white and black. For example, in high school we were both chosen as homecoming maids/queen. Every year students elected one white and one black homecoming maid for each class. There was no official discussion about how people should be categorized, but we both remember people asking us what category we would be in. The unwritten rule was that if you weren't black, you were put into the white category. Often times, at least half or more of the "white" maids did not self-identify racially as white.

Both of us graduated from the one public high school in town, the same high school that our mom, dad, aunts, uncles, and cousins graduated from. After graduation, I attended and graduated from the University of Alabama with my bachelor's degree in elementary education. Then, I went to the University of North Carolina at Chapel Hill on a scholarship and earned a master's and Ph.D. in education: culture, curriculum, and change. After graduation, Kaci went to Shelton State Community College for a year and then transferred to the University of Alabama where she graduated with her bachelor's and master's degrees in social work.

At college, we quickly realized that we were a part of a very small population of Native people, which actually pushed us to try our best to make our family and community proud. My sister and I were usually the only Native person in all of our classes and the first Native person most students and teachers had ever met. Unfortunately, that meant that Native people or perspectives were not discussed in the majority of our classes, and when they were, we were usually the ones teaching or answering all of the questions.

Graduate school was a lot harder on both of us as Native women. We both remember being frustrated when students would believe professors,' books,' and museums' information about Natives instead of our own experiences and knowledge. We have similar memories of getting angry, crying, and wanting to quit our programs because of the ignorance and mistreatment that we endured from professors. My sister vividly remembers a policy class where her professor only discussed black and white issues. Her professor's solution to including more perspectives was to call on Kaci to "give me the Indian view on this subject," tell her she could teach a class about Native Americans, and then fail her on an opinion-based test "where my opinion didn't match hers." I have blocked out many of the comments from my own memory, but the experiences that have stuck to my soul are those where my knowledge, identity, and ability were questioned. Comments were made to me like, "All Indians live in tepees," "Indians can't read or write so how would they answer a survey," and "You need to stop being a one trick pony and talk about other things besides Indian stuff."

Unfortunately, my sister and I have too many examples that end with negative feelings and emotions. Some of our experiences ended with us getting angry that our professors were allowed to attack and demoralize us because we were Indian, while other experiences ended with us reporting our experiences to the administration to demand actions be taken against these professors. We both graduated from our programs with the support of amazing family, friends, professors, and peers. However, our experiences show that while educational institutions have come a long way, they still have a long way to go in learning about Native people and supporting Native students.

Despite the challenges we faced, my sister and I earned our degrees and have returned to the tribe to work for and contribute to our community. Kaci currently works in human resources at the tribe's casino, where she supervises the Wardrobe and Wellness Departments. I am the Tribal Cultural Director. I work with our staff and board to plan and implement cultural events and classes that teach our history and culture to members of the tribe and the larger community.

"We have come a long way, but have a lot more work to do."

From segregated one-room Indian schools in the 1940s to graduate degrees in the 2010s, our family has gone through a long educational journey. Living in a small community in the South, race has shaped all of our experiences. Having the opportunity to attend school is something that our tribal community spent a long time fighting for. Our experiences and journeys tell many stories, but the one that my family wants to pass on is the pride that we have in each other for our accomplishments. Our stories show a history of how educational experiences have in some ways changed yet in other ways have remained the same for Poarch Creek people over three generations.

This story is written by three generations of the Martin family.
They were all raised in southern Alabama and are deeply connected
to their tribal Poarch Creek community.

We Will Forever Remain Coushatta and We Will Always Be Here

When I was eight years old, my father had me write my first letter to a U.S. senator asking him about how the Coushatta people might get help from the federal government because we didn't have any housing, running water, jobs, or medical programs. We didn't have anything and lived in extreme poverty. We were just a community of people who were living in Allen Parish, Louisiana, striving to survive. Unemployment was critical. Several of our men who went and fought in World War II came back to a community that was still the same as far as poverty and unemployment. What few jobs were available were in the logging industry, which was fading fast. There was also some employment available to the tribal members in the local farms, but farming is cyclical and these were only seasonal jobs. So, we had to survive through whatever means we could without any public assistance of any kind. I remember a lot of the tribal people going hand fishing in the bayous nearby to catch fish so they could eat. As a group, they would go jump in the bayous and either catch a turtle or a fish. Those types of survival skills existed in the community when I was growing up.

Prior to this time, back in the 1930s, the Bureau of Indian Affairs (BIA) did come into the community and offered a little bit of technical assistance to us in the way of health care. They also provided a BIA school that went from the first through the sixth grades. This changed when the Eisenhower administration came into office in the 1950s and they decided to get out of the Indian business. As a result, they decided to pick on a number of tribes within the country who they thought were "right and ready to be assimilated" into the mainstream and went about enacting a policy of Indian Termination. Those are the words they used against the Coushatta. This was interesting because the older people in the community don't remember anyone coming to ask them if we were ready to be assimilated. They had no clue what that even meant. No one came to do a head count or to talk to us; yet they were ready to take over our destiny.

The Choctaw Agency in Mississippi was the BIA agency responsible for overseeing the Coushatta and the Chitimacha. One day in 1953, they came to the community with a resolution saying, "If you sign this, you will be left on your own and you will no longer have to deal with the federal government. You will be free to do what you want just as anyone else in the non-

Indian community." The old people met at the school and decided that they didn't even know what all of that meant. They didn't understand termination, and they didn't understand what it meant to be released from federal wardship. So, they decided not to sign it and returned the resolution back to the Choctaw Agency.

It turns out that even though the Coushatta never did sign the resolution saying that they wanted to terminate themselves, the BIA ignored their rejection of it and automatically cut off the few services that were provided to the tribe, which were the basic health care and the school. They just walked off. They shut the school down and cut off the few dollars that they were giving toward health care, and they left without an explanation and never came back. Nobody said, "You are terminated. You are no longer going to get services. You are no longer a tribe." They just walked away. The federal government assumed that the Coushatta didn't know any better, so they just walked off without any legislative enactment of termination, such as they did with other tribes like the Menominee or a few other tribes across the country that were terminated legislatively through House Resolution 108. As a result, the Coushatta sat there for about twenty or twenty-five years not knowing what really happened. People questioned why our school was no longer funded or why we were no longer getting health care.

The BIA also ended the trust status of the 160-acre reservation that was a piece of land stuck in the middle of the community. This land was divided up between two Coushatta families, and that was the end of the trust land. No one knew what happened exactly except that these two families had it divided into two 80-acre tracts. They didn't know what was going on, so they just took the land. The community just continued to live on the land as before. Fortunately, the Coushatta tribe has a different lifestyle as far as land ownership, so it didn't really have a large impact. Also, many families lived on privately owned land within the community that they had acquired under the Homestead Act in the early 1930s. Later on, unfortunately, because of the lack of knowledge of how the system worked, a lot of the Indians lost land due to the fact that they didn't know they had to pay taxes on it. A major timber company came on the scene and bought up a lot of land around the community due to their nonpayment of taxes. This was a tough time, but many families still do maintain private ownership of land that they acquired through the Homestead Act.

This is why we started looking into reconnecting. My father was very interested in learning more about what the federal government was about and wanted me to get involved. This is why he had me write a letter to a senator at the age of eight, and why he continued to encourage me as I got older to get involved in the community. My whole life I heard him say, "The Coushatta could do better. The Coushatta should be able to gain employment. The Coushatta should be able to get educated." He always talked to the old people in the community about organizing or doing something to bring in employment. He also talked about the future of the community and thought about what our young people will be facing in twenty or fifty years: Will we even still be here? Will we still be speaking Coushatta? Will we still be practicing our medicine? Will we still have our medicine people?

That is how I was groomed and trained. I also had role models to look up to because even though the tribe struggled to survive, five or six Coushatta people graduated from high school in the late 1930s. I've always been impressed with that, and I really admired those people. In spite of all the hardships and poverty—and I've heard stories that they barely had shoes and clothes—they still made it through high school. I was also inspired by other Indians around the country even though I was hardly exposed to anything outside of my own community. We would go visit the Alabama Coushatta in Texas, and that was about it. We were impressed with them because they were our neighboring tribe and they had federal assistance and housing. They had things going on for them that we didn't have, and they still continued to be very strong culturally. Their old people made sure that their language, culture, and history were very strong.

My community also maintained a strong sense of culture, and it was important that we stayed together. They fought battles, such as diseases, and they maintained their medicine, history, and language. One thing that I always used to hear from the old people was, "We don't ever want to lose the language or our identity. We don't want to lose that we are the Coushatta people. No matter what happens, we are not going to go away. We will forever remain Coushatta, and we will always be here." That was what I heard growing up, and I'm happy to say that even though changes have come about, the Coushatta are still thriving.

I was fortunate enough to live in two worlds: one is Choctaw, from my mother's side, and the other is Coushatta, from my father's side. So, I grew up speaking both languages in the same household and understanding both cultures. While my father wanted me to get involved in the community, my mother wanted me to be a minister. They were constantly battling over what I should be when I grew up. In the end, my father got his way.

When I first got started, some of the old people would talk about their vision to move beyond our present status. They heard about tribes living in Oklahoma and how they lived under better conditions because they had help from the federal government. They also went back to the story that they had always heard about our people signing papers generations ago so that the government would help us. They never knew what they signed, but I'm sure they were talking about treaties that made promises for things that never came to the Coushatta or any other southeastern tribe. The old people also asked me to find out why the BIA walked away in 1953 without saying anything. Some of them still remembered that they had refused to sign a piece of paper, which of course was the termination resolution.

Although the federal government ceased to see us as an Indian tribe, that didn't stop an influx of academics from coming to our community. Many of them were anthropology and archaeology students from Louisiana State University and other nearby institutions. They would come to Coushatta and do what I would jokingly refer to as "measuring heads to make sure we are Indians." They would come and say, "Well, based on what we have seen and heard, there will be no Coushattas in twenty or thirty years. This is because the tribe is so small, and they are either going to die away or be assimilated into another tribe." They would go on with all of this historical stuff that they read in order to learn about us, but they never came and actually sat down with a Coushatta family and really asked about their history, their lifestyle, and what they envisioned for the future young people. Instead, what a lot of them did was go back to the university and write what their vision of the future of the Coushatta people was. Those are the sort of things we faced. We would all laugh when they would leave in their beautiful new cars and go back to their campuses, and we would never hear back from them. That was one of my biggest aggravations because there are many times when people would want to come interview me and spend about two hours of my time asking all types of ridiculous questions and comparing us to tribes elsewhere in the country. They asked me questions like, "Why don't we live in tepees? And why don't we ride horses?" Well, they had no understanding of Southeast Indians, so this line of questions was very typical. To them, they thought Indians should be running around half naked chasing buffalo and deer. They were so disappointed that I wasn't sitting in my office with my face painted and feathers all over.

Even so-called linguists would come in and do studies of our language and do comparative analyses with other languages. Three students from some university came in one time, and they asked me to "say something" and then poked a microphone in my face. I didn't know what they wanted me to say! I felt like they wanted me to perform for them. Other academics even had the nerve to come in and say, "Well, you aren't saying that correctly." Who are they to say that I'm not saying that correctly!

After a while we just told these people to stay away and leave us alone. We told them that we don't want to be written about, or studied, or measured. We just wanted to be left alone because "if you cannot write what we are expressing to you as Coushatta people, as Southeast Indian people, then we don't want you here." I actually told people that because it was very difficult for me to sit there for two hours, or half a day, talking to some academic that had their own interpretations of what I should be as an Indian. I think this is a very important point that needs to come out because history has not been in our favor to start with, and then we are approached by people who have knowledge about certain things, but no clue about anything that has any relevance to our particular community. They come in with their own perceptions about what I should be doing, what I should look like, what I should be wearing, and how I should be talking. We have a different message than what they wanted to impose on us.

I don't think we have even reached the peak of telling our story from the Southeast. Whatever made the headlines in the past was about Indians in the Southwest or other places where there was supposedly high populations of Indians. The major story that we used to hear about regarding Southeast Indians is when the Lumbee of North Carolina ran off the Ku Klux Klan in 1958. Other than that, Southeast Indians didn't get much news coverage.

Fortunately, in recent years things have changed in a positive way as more people have started expressing what they want written. I think we are better prepared now than we ever were. Academia is shifting, and what was once annoying to me is changing. I think the shift is occurring because of some of the forums that we are participating in at universities that serve to better educate people about Southeast Indians. The tide has turned where we are able to tell our story the way we want it to be told, and academics are supporting Indian people and working with tribes in areas like linguistics. Also, Indian people are beginning to assume more responsibility as more young people are going into academia and expressing their own views on Indian rights. In Coushatta, we have a lot of young people going into universities, and some are becoming lawyers, doctors, and professionals. Hopefully they will contribute back to the Coushatta community at some point in their lives. At the same time, I hope they go out into the world and tell the story that the Coushatta want to tell.

When I was growing up, I used to look at the eighty- and ninety-year-old people in my community and be just amazed at how they made it this long and with so much against them. We were always on the move, we were always the target of something, but yet we lived to be quite old while living off the land, teaching our children, and surviving in ways that no one could ever understand. I used to think about how that was possible, and now I understand that it is a gift. As Indian people, we have a gift to survive. We are in tune to the world, and we are always teaching the next generation. Growing up, I was taught a lot of things that still work today. I don't think the Internet could replace that. Neither can emails, high-flying jets, or supersonic aircraft. Nothing would ever replace what I have in the Coushatta people and what they have in themselves. That can never be replaced.

Ernest Sickey (Turkey Clan) is a member of the Coushatta Tribe of Louisiana, where he served as Tribal Chairman for twenty-six years and led the successful effort to have his tribe officially re-recognized by the U.S. Secretary of the Department of the Interior in 1973. During the 1970s, he served as Louisiana's first Deputy Commissioner for Indian Affairs and as the first Director of the Office of Indian Affairs, and he established the Inter-Tribal Council of Louisiana. He has a half-century of experience in local and national Indian affairs.

The Politics of History and Identity

The massive southern tribal resurgence of recent decades has generated a politically charged environment, one characterized by a flurry of newly recognized tribes at the state and federal levels. This has fueled lively debates over issues of tribal membership, recognition processes, and authenticity. Further complicating matters are the diverse circumstances in which Indian groups find themselves— ranging from closely knit and culturally vibrant to scattered and politically disconnected. Additionally, some groups have a long relationship with their non-Indian neighbors who have consistently accepted and acknowledged their Indian identities, while other groups were deemed racially ambiguous and not formally recognized as Indians over the last century. Several factors culminated to take their toll on southeastern Indian people, many of whom were severely impacted by disease and warfare, pushed to relocate, went into hiding, or intermarried with other Native or non-Native groups. As a result, each southeastern Indian group—as well as individuals of Indian descent—has its own unique historical circumstances from which it has emerged into the present. Although several of these issues were addressed in the previous chapter, this second chapter serves to expand the discussion by addressing the roles that Native people play in challenging dominant historical narratives that serve to undermine both their historic and contemporary presence in the region.

The contributions to the first half of this chapter are devoted to the Chowanokes of North Carolina. As one of the most populated Algonquian tribes living along the coastal banks of the Chowan River at the time of English contact, like other Indian groups subject to the traumas of colonialism, the dominant historical narrative eventually lost track of them as many either succumbed to disease or intermarried with other groups. Although it would be tempting to dismiss the Chowanokes as merely occupying a space within North Carolina's deep history, Marvin T. Jones, in his essay "A Rebirth on the Chowan," sets the record straight in proclaiming that "we are not extinct." In fact, the Chowanokes serve as an intriguing case study of a group that has engaged in a modern tribal resurgence process that has many political implications. For Jones, the documentation and preservation of his ancestors' history—conducted by the Chowan Discovery Group that he founded—help to assert the Chowanokes' continuous presence in the region. Other contributors to this chapter, such as Shoshone Peguese-Elmardi ("Speaking for My Ancestors") and Lars Adams ("From Cherokee to Chowanoke: Discovering the North Carolina Algonquians"), have also joined in this movement to advocate on behalf of their unbroken—yet transformed—ancestral history, while simultaneously defining their own modern Indigenous identities through the preservation of family stories, enhanced by rigorous research and discovery.

In addition to engaging in a historical revival that served to feature the Chowanokes more prominently within North Carolina's public history, the Native peoples of the area also began to organize themselves politically as disparate groups of Indian families came together under umbrella tribal governments. This is a trajectory seen throughout the region beginning in the 1970s. Although this shift created many new opportunities, it also proved challenging as political infighting and efforts to gain recognition often overshadowed efforts to ensure a strong community base. In "The Chowanoke Indian Resurgence," which is the transcript of an interview conducted by

Lars Adams with longtime Meherrin-Chowanoke Nation leader Doug Patterson, we gain a deeper appreciation for how this once-deemed "extinct" group of people are living and thriving today and how they are working to rebuild their nation-to-nation relationships—first with the state of North Carolina and then with the federal government.

While tribal revitalization and nation-building across the Southeast are progressively alerting the larger public to the modern presence of Indian people, the inclusion of Native perspectives within historical narratives is also beginning to bring greater depth to our understanding of the past. As former Southern Historical Association president Theda Perdue acknowledged, "Indians provide us with an opportunity to examine different experiences and perspectives in the history of the South, ones that do not follow the standard narrative but instead promise both to challenge and enrich it."[1] This is, indeed, what Chief Kenneth Adams sets out to do in his piece, "Jamestown 2007: A Native American Perspective." Adams both challenges and enriches the popular understanding of the founding of Jamestown, Virginia, in 1607 by addressing the impact this had on the area's Indigenous people. He previously wrote this piece as celebration preparations were under way to commemorate the 400th anniversary of the founding of Jamestown, which is often marked as a pinnacle time in the nation's history as English colonists braved the foreign terrain while laying the groundwork for what would later become the United States. Adams brings a more somber perspective to the period, reminding us that the story for him—as well as other Virginia Indians—is one of "sorrow and pain." It was not the beginning of the end for Virginia Indian people, as typically depicted, but it was the beginning of hard times. Adams appeals to the reader to acknowledge the injustice in the situation and commemorate the founding of Jamestown by also properly recognizing those Native peoples who were impacted by supporting the formal recognition of their descendants who—like the celebrated English colonists of Jamestown—survived and persevered under difficult circumstances.

The manner and degree to which Indian identity endured across the Southeast is complex—determined by both internal and external forces over the generations. While tribal histories and cultural identities primarily existed loosely and privately within families, the "tribal resurgence" during the second half of the twentieth century enforced a more formalized way of thinking about these issues and thus further pointed to the problems posed by southern racial politics. Jim Crow left a legacy that went beyond limiting Indian access to education and other public spaces; it reinforced the denial of Indian identity in areas of the region dominated by a system entrenched in a biracial form of thinking. As a result, many Indian people were identified with false or misleading racial identifiers on legal documents, such as birth certificates or drivers' licenses.[2] The rule of hypo-descent, or the "one-drop rule," which classified anyone with any known African ancestry as "negro" or "colored," further complicated matters for some communities who, although maintaining strong Indian identities like the Lumbee of North Carolina, the Houma of Louisiana, or the MOWA Choctaw of Alabama, also had deep histories of colonization and intermarriage.[3] Still, others found that the only way to survive was to attempt to pass as "white." This "powerful hold that Jim Crowism had on the lives of Indian people" is at the crux of Hodalee Scott Sewell's piece, "Eastern Creeks and the Persistence of Identity." Although racial segregation complicated the lives of Indian people, Sewell argues, this didn't prevent groups like the Creeks of Alabama, Georgia, and Florida from secretly maintaining their oral traditions, ceremonial practices, and identity. He positions the elders—many of whom participated in an oral history project in 1996—as "a powerful authority" on the endurance of Creek identity.

In spite of enduring Indigenous identities within families and larger tribal groups, the lack of documentary evidence—whether in the form of colonial documents or documents generated during the Jim Crow era—has been one of the biggest challenges southern Indian people have faced in recent years. In fact, this divisive issue has caused some groups to splinter or restrict tribal membership in their efforts to increase their chances of obtaining state or federal recognition. Lack of "proper" documentation has also blocked many Indian people from becoming members of existing recognized tribal nations. Using government documents to identify "authentic" Indian people is full of ironies; however, it is also a way of protecting already scarce resources both within and across tribal nations from potentially fraudulent claimants. It is not an issue one can easily take a side on because, as Tony Mack McClure points out in his piece, "To Be or Not to Be a 'Wannabe,'" there is a great deal of misunderstanding around Indian identity and how it should be determined. McClure, who himself is an authority on Cherokee genealogical research, offers some insight into the purpose of the Cherokee historical roles and the exclusionary nature of some of the rules associated with them.[4] Although he accepts why these rules are in place—even though they impact him personally—he also argues that they should not be the basis for determining Cherokee authenticity. Government documents—or blood quantum, for that matter—are problematic determinants of Native identity because they don't penetrate peoples' complex and nuanced connections and experiences.

In the final contribution to this chapter, Cedric Sunray, in "Jim Crowfeather in Indian Country," continues the discussion by addressing identity as a "social and cultural experience." Central to his argument are the misconceptions that surround the MOWA Choctaw of Alabama who, despite not being federally recognized as a tribal nation, are headquartered on a state-recognized Indian reservation (of which there are only a few in the country) and have had many of their community members attend Indian boarding schools during the Jim Crow years (a history generally associated with federally recognized Indians). Yet despite some of their parallel experiences with federally recognized tribal nations, they have been denied federal recognition. There is a great deal of recent scholarship on the problems that the federal acknowledgment process poses in providing what Klopotek deems, in his recent book on Louisiana tribes, a "uniquely explicit, public, and potent arena for the dramas of identity to be enacted."[5] For the MOWA Choctaw, Sunray surmises, their "drama of identity" was determined by factors that were economic and racialized, rather than on the merits of their documentation.

Indian identity is a difficult thing to define. Is it based on tribal membership? Belonging to a federally recognized tribe? Being raised to speak your language or see the world through an Indigenous worldview? Is it something you can just decide to adopt one day based on vague ancestral connections? The contributions within this chapter touch on each of these questions, offering some "food for thought" and—hopefully—encouraging the adoption of a more complex perspective. Gone are the days when declarations were made that Indians no longer populate the Southeast. Instead, it is time to address the public's growing interest by offering Native historical perspectives and educating people about the diverse and unique challenges of today's southeastern Indian people.

A Rebirth on the Chowan

Northeastern North Carolina is a coastal plain with plenty of rivers, mostly the slow-moving kind. My parents and I were born within 4 miles of one of the largest of those rivers, the 50-mile-long Chowan. In most North Carolina histories, the Chowan is hardly mentioned, perhaps because the larger of its two towns, Winton, has only 800 people.

The time when the Chowan River had a deeper meaning to a large number of people was over 400 years ago. It took some passing words from my mother and a few decades for me to discover the story and meaning of that time. My mother told me that we were descended from an Indian leader named John Robins. It was one of those things I filed away and didn't give much thought to at the time, but would later discover the implications.

On a summer day in 1963 when I was eleven years old, two teachers and my mother took us to Roanoke Island along North Carolina's Outer Banks. To leave our county, we traveled across the Chowan River Bridge in Winton. Just before reaching the bridge, we passed a silvery highway marker. That day, as in many days before and since, I would read its brief text: "LANE'S EXPEDITION—Ralph Lane and a group of English colonists explored the Chawanook Indian Country and the Chowan River, 1586, north to this vicinity." The so-noted expedition was the beginning of my region's written history.

As we continued on our trip, our two cars went farther east to the Outer Banks on the Atlantic Ocean. We first visited the Wright Brothers' Memorial at Kill Devil Hills and took lunch in our cars—we were all "colored" and so we chose to spare ourselves any restrictions that would have soiled our day. Mr. and Mrs. Brummell, my mother, my brother, my sister, and a neighbor continued back toward the mainland to visit the Elizabethan Gardens—the first English expeditions happened during Queen Elizabeth I's reign. I saw two more markers when we arrived on Roanoke Island: one noted the English expeditions of the 1580s—it was connected to the Winton marker. The other noted the birth of the first English child in North America.

As evening approached, we were allowed into the outdoor theater where the annual summer drama, *The Lost Colony*, had been running since 1937. It is still running. There was not much I remembered about the play, since I was just eleven years old, other than the disappearance of 115 English colonists who were left on Roanoke Island in 1587. The disappearance is still an unsolved mystery, but I realize that my ancestors must have known what happened to the vanished colonists.

Twenty-three years before the founding of the Jamestown colony, the English explored North Carolina looking for areas to settle and to raid Spanish ships. A year later on a second expedition, they rowed up the Chowan and encountered the Chowanoke people (although they are listed as "Chawanook" on the present historical marker). The Chowanokes were the largest of the Carolina Algonkian groups. The capital of Choanoac was estimated to be larger than the Winton of my time. Ralph Lane's expedition reported that there were nineteen other Chowanoke towns and villages along the Chowan.

In less than 200 years after Lane's report, as a result of colonization, it was officially reported that the Chowanoke population dwindled to two families. By then, the Chowanokes lived on America's first reservation, and its remnants soon passed into white ownership. Yet within two generations, both families expanded through intermarriage with uncounted Chowanokes and other people to attain a rebirth by 1800. Despite this rebirth, however, they were declared an extinct people. Being outnumbered, the "extinct" Chowanokes kept their existence to themselves and passed on the heritage for the next two centuries.

I was born as part of the unspoken growth of Chowanoke descendants. Like so many of my relatives, I have gone through more than one identity while holding on to the family ties given to me.

After the freedoms gained from the civil rights movement, Indian descandants along the Chowan River began to assert their Native American identities, and my area now has two organized Indian groups: the Chowanokes and the Meherrins. The tribal names of both groups were unknown to me as I was growing up, but this new awareness may have prompted my mother to tell me about John Robins. After that moment, two decades passed before I acted on her information. She died during that time.

Now, the last ten years have been remarkable for the Chowanoke memory. It took only online research to find that John Robins was indeed a Chowanoke leader from 1734 to 1754, and that he was one of the two remaining Chowanoke family heads. I came to realize that the Robins/Robbins family was well documented from John's time to today.

Families that I have long known, like my mother, also began to assert their Chowanoke ancestry and pooled their efforts to bring the Chowanoke heritage into the open. This spurred me to research further by going over documents, maps, observations I made during my past canoe and fishing trips, and books.

A book published by a New York professor, Michael Leroy Oberg, became very dear to me. *The Head in Edward Nugent's Hand: Roanoke's Forgotten Indians* is about the Carolina Algonkians encountered by the English expeditions to Roanoke Island and the Chowan River. Oberg takes the viewpoint of the Carolina Algonkians. Of the numerous books and articles about that time, only Oberg has written about the seven Carolina Algonkian groups and how they coped with the new and dangerous strangers.

Oberg wrote of the English taking hostages, including a Chowanoke ruler and his son—perhaps they are my relatives, even direct ancestors. He goes on to cite the burning of towns, the unexplainable and devastating diseases the English brought, and, ultimately, the beheading of the ruler of Roanoke Island. This ruler was the first to host the English, to befriend them. I learned how the seven Carolina Algonkian groups belonged to a world that communicated and traded among each other, and how they would pass on information about the deeds of the English, especially the beheading in 1586.

The group that comprised the Lost Colony arrived at Roanoke Island in the summer of 1587. The ships that brought them departed weeks later, and little has been learned about the colony since. I have heard and read many stories about the lost English. Many people have asked me about my thoughts on the fate of the Lost Colony. What is never included in the questions and tales is the declining state of relations between the English and the unmentioned Carolina Algonkians. The arrival of the Lost Colony, unlike the arrivals of the previous two expeditions, was viewed as the coming of an enemy force that would bring more mass illness, destruction, and death. From Oberg's narrative, I imagined that the small English enemy was attacked and the survivors were absorbed. Perhaps the Chowanokes were involved. Most certainly, they knew the truth about the disappearance that is frequently called "America's Greatest Mystery."

On Roanoke Island, August 2013. Marvin T. Jones with one of his nominated markers, the North Carolina Highway Historical Marker for the town of Dasemunkepeuc. There, the English beheaded the ruler of the Roanoke Indians. (Photo Courtesy of Marvin T. Jones, assisted by E. Laverne Jones.)

Just as I did as a child, I continue to travel across the Chowan River Bridge, past the silvery highway marker that, like the others, told nothing about the original people. Oberg's book inspired me to make new highway marker nominations for three Carolina Algonkian towns so that the area's Native peoples will be remembered. As a result of these efforts, these towns now have their own markers. Two of the towns disappeared as a result of English violence. Dasemunkepuec, one of the two towns, was even the site of the beheading that figures much into Oberg's book title and theme.

The first of the three markers that was installed was for Choanoac, the capital of the Chowanokes. Choanoac was not destroyed, but was eventually abandoned. It left plenty of evidence for the archaeologists to piece together its history. On the day of the marker dedication, I was able to bring the Robbins and Bennett families together since they were part of the two main surviving Chowanoke families—as well as other Chowanokes and white and African American supporters together. This was an inspiring event that allowed me to build upon the history that my mother shared with me.

More recognition of the Carolina Algonkians' past and present is to come. Earlier I wrote of how the Chowanokes once lived on America's first reservation across the river from Choanoac. Since losing the land and being declared "extinct," there was no tribal land-base. However, in 2014 the Chowanokes bought back 150 acres of what was once our reservation land, which has given us a piece of our history back.

There remains one last story here. In 1586 or 1587, a map was made of the North Carolina coastal lands that the English explored. The original map is in the British Museum in London and frequently reproduced. A blank patch covers one part of the map. The patch covers land at an important water crossroad where the Chowan and Roanoke Rivers empty into the Albemarle Sound. Four Carolina Algonkian groups bordered each other there. When planning the Choanoac marker dedication, I began to wonder about that featureless patch—it was too important of an area not to pursue more details about. A year later, it was announced that the outline of a fort was identified under the patch. As I expected, the authorities began speculating whether the Lost Colony visited and used the fort. As a result, archaeologists are working to locate the fort. Once again, however, no one is consulting the Carolina Algonkians. My take is that there was no fort there, perhaps only the proposed location of a fort. The Chowanokes, Moratocs,

Weapemeocs, and Roanokes would not have allowed it. Not after what happened the year before.

If scholars would consult with the descendants of the Carolina Algonkians living in the area, they might just be able to learn more about the area's history and gain a deeper understanding of our perspectives. We are not extinct. In fact, we are once again gaining ground and have an exciting future ahead of us.

Marvin T. Jones is a documentary media producer in Washington, D.C. He founded the Chowan Discovery Group (chowandiscovery.org), whose mission is to document, research, preserve, and present the 430-year-old history of landowning mixed-race people of the Winton Triangle in northeastern North Carolina. He crosses the waters of the Chowan River monthly.

Speaking for My Ancestors

The young girl stood in front of the mirror in the bedroom of the tiny apartment she shared with her mother. She glanced hard at her reflection as it stared back at her. The seven-year-old girl asked the image in the mirror, "Who am I? Where did I come from?" She wondered what her purpose was here. As her mother entered the room you could see the amusement underneath the stern glance she gave. The vigilant and curious seven-year-old stood erect in front of the mirror refusing to move until she got an answer. "Mom . . . who are we and where do we come from?" The mother finally spoke, "We come from Indian people. Our people were already here long before others started coming to America from other places." The girl then asked, "What happened to those people . . . our people?" "Many of them died long ago, but we are part of them. I am here and you are here." Following this conversation, there were many more questions over the years and visits to their ancestral homeland in the small North Carolina town near the South Carolina border where their family resided. The faces of family members were reflective of an ancient people that once thrived and had a great and viable history. A people that had survived hundreds of years of physical, cultural, and historical genocide, warfare, slavery, and miscegenation would have their place. These ancestors could no longer speak. That seven-year-old girl in the small apartment looking at her reflection in the mirror was me. I would someday become a voice for my ancestors.

I often wondered about our people, my ancestors many generations before me as far back as our DNA could take us, before the arrival of Europeans to the shores of America. What story would my ancestors have to tell? I loved listening to stories told by my mother and her sisters about our family lore, including more recent tales about their "Indian uncle Frank." He lived with them in an old wooden house at the edge of a small North Carolina town. There were many other stories and histories, yet they are omitted from America's mainstream history books and educational resources, leaving us forgotten or not "Indian enough." While much focus was put on Native Americans out west, or those residing on reservations, remnant Native peoples and their descendants like my family who had dwindled in numbers or merged with other Native or non-Native groups are overlooked and ignored. Survival is all we had. We had to survive like the Native people who were forced onto reservations. In fact, my ancestors lived on some of the first reservations in the Carolinas.

Throughout high school and college I found ways to integrate the broader Native history, as well as the history of my people, into whatever curriculum we had. I often found myself doing presentations, reports, or crafts that focused on my Native ancestry. I worked to enlighten my fellow students and teachers alike, particularly since many teachers left out certain aspects of Native history or gave a biased view of our culture and people. This often contributed to the misunderstanding that is prevalent in America today. My history is not part of the war bonnet–wearing Indians portrayed by the media and on television. All Native people did not live that way. It was appalling to me that one person or a group of people could destroy or alter another person's history, yet preserve their own. Ancient Roman philosopher Marcus Tullius Cicero (106–43 B.C.) really inspired me by his perspective: "To be ignorant of what occurred before you were born is to remain always a child. For what is the worth of human life, unless it is woven into the life of our ancestors by the records of history?"

One must understand, and other Native peoples must also take note, that southern Native peoples were among some of the first people to be in contact with Europeans. It is true that many of our western Native peoples engaged in long years of warfare against European encroachment to prevent losing their lands. Yet some of our battles had begun long before, since

Shoshone's great aunt and one of the ancestors for whom she now speaks. (Photo Courtesy of Shoshone Peguese-Elmardi.)

not all Native people in the southern part of what became the United States were willing to let our lands be taken so easily. In fact, as early as 1643 my Chowanoc ancestors, who resided in the northern part of North Carolina at what is now called Bennett's Creek, fought the British in a battle at Weynock Creek. Our people once again fought the British settlers in 1675. The battle was harsh, and the Chowanoc initially prevailed, but the British settlers were able to get reinforcements and defeat our people. Though our people were left decimated and our lands were taken, some of the Native families still thrived. I am one of their descendants. As it was told, our family was able to make their way south with Indian traders. They settled into small separate communities near plantations on the edge of the North and South Carolina border. They eventually became itinerant farmers settling on land given to them. Indian women became midwives, and later some Indian families owned cotton farms. They interacted and intermarried with other Native remnant groups from over in the Pee Dee region. Some whites and slaves were absorbed into our bloodlines as well. There was a very old Indian trading path that stretched through Anson County into the Pee Dee region. The Pee Dee Indians were one of the tribes that lived along the Pee Dee River where my grandmother would often take us fishing.

The Pee Dee region has a very long and interesting history. One of the earliest known settlements in America was located in this area. It was said to be the first settlement within the borders of the United States. It was even older than Jamestown. Believed to be located at or near the mouth of the Pee Dee River, a Spanish explorer and colonizer named Lucas Vasquez de Ayllon settled there with galley slaves of African, Arab, and Berber descent. The Native people of the area became very suspicious and uncomfortable and soon attacked the Spanish settlement. Along with this attack, the slaves also revolted. This was one of the earliest recorded slave revolts in America. The slaves of the Spanish were taken in by the Native peoples, and the surviving Spaniards were chased off the land where they headed to the island of Hispanola, which is the present-day Haiti and the Dominican Republic.

I took my first-born son to many Native events over the years and passed along any knowledge I have learned from my mother about our history. When my second son was born, I repeated the same ritual. I engrained both boys with the knowledge of their Native history and culture. Since we lived in New York, we often took trips back to the Carolinas to community gatherings, events, and powwows, all in remembrance of our Native forebears. One memory that touches me deeply is a time when my two sons, some elders, and others stood on the banks of the Chowan River in North Carolina where the villages of our Native ancestors lived over 500 years ago. Marvin Jones, also a Chowanoc descendant and historian, spoke at the gathering. I have never felt such pride and honor as the history of our people was told. We reflected on the voices of those long-dead ancestors, and this is something that my children will have the honor of carrying with them for the rest of their lives.

I enjoy speaking and writing about my experiences as a modern-day Native person as often as I can. When I travel the world, I try to find opportunities to correct the historical amnesia that has become part of American history and break down misconceptions and stereotypes about modern-day Native Americans. In addition to working to educate people, I also dance for my ancestors as a woman's traditional dancer in competitions and host craft tables at events, such as my son's school harvest festival where I explain the origin, history, and meaning of such items as dream catchers, and answer many questions to further break down stereotypes. To be Native, one has to keep one's identity and culture alive by being a part of one's community. It has been a rewarding experience, and I have been received very well. I enjoy attending cultural events and powwows in order to meet other Native peoples from various tribal nations. Even though we live on the same continent, there is still much Native people have to learn about each other and their histories. This saddens me. I will emphasize to anyone that my ancestors have always been here. Native peoples covered the continent, not just a specific geographical area, before America was ever discovered by Europeans.

I am thankful for my mother and elder Olivia for being the keepers of our ancestors' knowledge and for passing this down. Like other southern Native peoples, my ancestors' voices were suppressed and their identities obscured as land was taken away and records destroyed. I will tell the correct history, my history. I will rewrite it if necessary. I am the resurrection of those voices. I speak for my ancestors.

Shoshone Peguese-Elmardi is a Chowanoc descendant and member of the Pee Dee Indian Nation of Beaver Creek. She studied cultural anthropology, with a focus on world indigenous cultures, and is presently a genetic genealogical consultant and researcher.

From Cherokee to Chowanoke: Discovering the North Carolina Algonquians

When I was young, my parents would tell me about my Cherokee grandparents. I suppose they thought it would be difficult to explain that these "grandparents" were at least several generations back and no one really knew specifics. The way they talked about them as "grandparents," though, made me feel close to them and fascinated by them. It made me want to meet them and find out more. I was only seven or eight at the time, but I was fiercely proud of this Cherokee heritage and would frequently tell people that I was "part" Cherokee. Usually they would then ask, "Which part?" to which I would jokingly point at my elbow.

As I got older I became increasingly curious about my heritage and began asking more people in my family questions, but the more I asked, the less specific things seemed. It turned out they weren't even sure we were Cherokee, and I found several stories from different family lines pointing to several different tribes, including the Sioux and Mandan. My father's and grandmother's love of history brought me vivid accounts of the heroes of the past, like Tecumseh and Sitting Bull. All this time, my family's frequent trips out west brought me to visit the Navajo people, the Oglala Sioux, historical sites like Cahokia, and several powwows that brought together people from multiple tribal nations. All of it touched me deeply and made me wish I knew more of the true story of my background.

As an adult with young children, I wanted to pass on this heritage to them. But I wanted to give them real specifics—actual and true family stories. I wasn't trying to force an Indian identity on them. I didn't even identify particularly as Indian myself, but it was important to me that they understood their background as deeply as I wanted to understand my own. So, I began genealogical research in earnest, and thus began a journey of several years. Immediately, I found some intriguing clues. My great-grandmother and her brother left behind an audio recording, memoirs, and genealogical notes in some dusty folders that my grandmother loaned me. Through them, I finally found out some specifics on where at least one line of Native heritage came from. Following this bread-crumb trail, I found an old book that mentioned this line of my family as being "half breed Indian" and knew I was on the right path. This was the first independent piece of evidence I had found that confirmed our family stories, so I found new energy to see it through. After some discouraging roadblocks, I finally found the mother lode of documentation from tidewater Virginia, in the form of Bible records, land deeds, and government certificates, all confirming that my ancestors were in fact Algonquian people (and African!) living in the area of the Great Dismal Swamp between Virginia and North Carolina.

I couldn't stop myself there, however. This was fascinating. It meant that the family stories were all true and that this had been at least part of our identity since the very beginning. But as fascinating as it was, there was so little information out there about Native communities in North Carolina. I looked north to the Powhatans of Pocahontas fame that surrounded Jamestown and found volumes of information on them, but on the south side of the Great Dismal Swamp at the North Carolina border there was practically nothing beyond the first contact period. Even worse, from what I was reading at the time, there were no North Carolina Algonquian nations remaining. "Extinct," they called them. But, I thought, while they were severely reduced by war and disease, nothing as dramatic as the Trail of Tears removed all the people. The history books simply ended their history with the sale of their land, but did not pursue these families as they struggled to cope with colonial society. I knew there had to be others, probably a lot of others, like me out there who descended from these people. I created a website called the "Chowanoke Descendants Community" as a kind of beacon for anyone out there who identified the Chowanoke as their ancestors. It wasn't long before I was contacted by several people. More and more have trickled in ever since.

But more important, scattered descendants found on the Internet were not the only people I encountered. True, intact communities of North Carolina Algonquian people still exist in their traditional homelands and are thriving. They are not without challenges, however. The nation that I have had the most intimate contact with was formally called the Meherrin Indian Tribe, the closest related contemporary nation to my ancestors, but when I first contacted them, divisions within the nation were tearing them apart. Earlier in the mid-twentieth century, Wayne Brown, a Meherrin, was inspired by his heritage and strong family history. By taking out newspaper advertisements, he invited "all Indian people" of the Roanoke-Chowan region to gather together for reorganization. The response was immediate and impressive. Local communities of Indian families had been informally connected with each other by kinship ties for over a century from multiple historical tribes and were eager to affiliate under an organized tribal government. After a period of reorganization, they were recognized as the Meherrin Indian Tribe by the state of North Carolina in the 1970s. The majority of the tribe, it seems, were Chowanoke descendants, but lived under the Meherrin name when they were recognized.

In the 1990s and early 2000s, the Meherrin minority, under Chief Wayne

Andrew Jackson Robbins, born in 1848 near the Chowan River, was a member of a growing ethnic enclave in the Roanoke-Chowan area of North Carolina known today as the Winton Triangle. His great-great-grandfather, John Robbins, was among the last Chowanoke "Chiefmen" mentioned in official government records. (Photo Courtesy of Marvin T. Jones.)

Brown, wanted—understandably—to stay as Meherrin. The Chowanoke group, under Chief Thomas Lewis, favored a name change to reflect their history. I became as involved as I could. I wanted to give back to the community of people who gave me my heritage. I spoke with people on both sides of the fence and tried to find common ground, but soon found that the issues went deeper than just a name change. As an outsider at the time, trying to get overly involved would more likely than not make me lose the good standing I was trying to build. Eventually, the split between the two nations was complete following a lengthy court case, and I was, and continue to be, squarely on the side of the Chowanoke Nation. I continue to hold the Meherrin, and Wayne Brown, whom I had the honor to speak with, in great respect. But I had established some very friendly connections in the Lewis camp and found the Chowanoke people's historical records to be particularly compelling, as I will explain. Besides, they were *my* heritage group, not the Meherrin. Still, I have hopes that one day both groups can work together with mutual respect as sister nations.

Research

As an independent researcher studying the North Carolina Algonquian people, I continue to find no limit to research possibilities. My earliest contributions have had to do with colonial warfare, but more recently I found a series of ethnic enclaves created by the sale of the final reservations the most compelling. By the end of the eighteenth century, only a few communities of Chowanoke, Hatteras, Mattamuskeet, and perhaps some Neusiok and Yeopim remained from the dozen or so chiefdoms that originally populated the coastal plain. Once their reservations were sold from the middle to the end of the eighteenth century, a series of multiethnic families connected by kinship created ethnic enclaves of people in a process called ethnogenesis, in which two or more peoples from different cultures combine to form a new culture not quite recognizable from either parent culture. I find this process in North Carolina to be very similar to the Métis communities of Canada (recognized Indian/white communities created during the fur trade). In contemporary communities, an Indigenous renaissance has occurred in which Indian identity and culture have been revitalized. What exactly were the social factors that caused historically "other free" families to either retain or reject an Indian identity in the face of the loss of tribal land? I feel that the North Carolina Algonquians provide outstanding case studies that can answer this and many other questions, especially regarding identity issues.

Most tribal entities in North Carolina recognized on the state level have little hope of gaining federal recognition because of the way records were kept in early American history. In census records, one had to be either white, black, or "other free," making many assume that Indian families were really African American. And because severe population loss in the face of disease, war, and the Indian slave trade caused many historical tribes to coalesce on the frontier prior to the keeping of consistent colonial records, the exact tribal affiliations of the founders of these communities have left a tangled and confusing web of information. In the case of today's

Algonquian-descended groups, such as the Chowanoke Indian Nation and Roanoke-Hatteras Tribe, however, there exists excellent documentation of individuals recorded as Indian people from specific tribal nations that can be traced directly from community founders to modern descendants, so that the history is unbroken and difficult to dispute. This is possible because the Algonquians were the first to be inundated by colonists. So while they were also decimated at an earlier date than most others, this process of acculturation was much better recorded. That is a major reason why I am so attracted to their study. They provide excellent examples that can serve to benefit the history of tribal nations statewide as well as elsewhere in the Southeast and along the Atlantic coast.

Issues for Modern Tribal Nations

I began my journey as an outsider, but the more I have gotten involved with the Chowanoke Indian Nation, the more connected I feel to the Indian communities of North Carolina and elsewhere in the region. What I have observed as the biggest threat to Indigenous sovereignty and unified strength can be summed up in one word: politics. As noted earlier, I began to be involved with the Chowanoke at a very stressful time for the community as political infighting between tribal leaders and issues regarding tribal identity tore one nation into two. In the case of the Chowanoke, this might not have been preventable as there were two different historical nations trying to operate under one name. It may have even been for the best, but this is not always the case. In other cases, such as the North Carolina Tuscarora Nations, many splinter groups have arisen out of political infighting. The same might be said of the Pee Dee groups of South Carolina who have split apart into many, often rival, groups. These groups are relatively small in population. Others, like the Lumbee, have managed to stay incredibly well organized and unified even though they have a population of many thousands. It doesn't take a genius to see that the splintering into rival factions is very unhealthy for Native political strength. What is needed are common goals that can bring opposing groups together, thoroughly organized tribal governments, and established means of resolving internal conflicts. It appears to me that the best-organized nations have had the least amount of political infighting, or if there is, at least there are established means of internally resolving these conflicts.

Of equal harm is a pecking order among first nations in regards to whether they are recognized by the American government, either on a state or federal level. Federally recognized tribes, in general, haven't gotten along with state-recognized tribes, and neither group has a good record of accepting nonrecognized tribes into the community of first nations. In some cases there are good reasons for this. The Cherokee Nation of Oklahoma, for example, has made a campaign out of exposing "fraudulent" state-recognized and nonrecognized tribal entities that bear the Cherokee name. Having visited the websites of some of these nonrecognized nations, I actually can understand their case; there do appear to be many "online tribes" out there who will mail people a membership card for a fee without requiring documentation or having any kind of historical Indian community. That said, this is incredibly harmful to genuine Indian communities throughout the Southeast and elsewhere who aren't yet recognized. There is often an attitude that these communities only want to cash in on benefits afforded to federally recognized tribes, but I personally have not met a single American Indian who has this as a motivating factor. From my perspective, at least in North Carolina, these communities just want the legal right to call themselves Indian without being looked down on, and the ability to carry on government-to-government relations with the United States. It's about the cultural pride of recognized nationhood.

What I propose, for the sake of the many nonrecognized and state-recognized first nations of America, is a nongovernment entity that exists for the purpose of recognizing Indian communities. Such an organization could evaluate local Indian communities with the understanding that some are better documented than others, but those that are fraudulently hawking membership cards would be exposed, and those representing genuine local communities could be freed from isolation and political bias. I admit the concept needs refining, but I feel that the political hierarchy created by suckling at the power teat of the Bureau of Indian Affairs has caused more harm than good. This is not to say, of course, that Indian communities should cease to apply for federal recognition, as this is vitally important for sovereignty and political empowerment, but whether or not a community is recognized should not separate Indian Country into "haves" and "have-nots." It is time that all communities of Indian people give forgiveness for past differences and work together as sister nations for the common good.

Lars Adams is a full-time independent researcher, novelist, and student from the greater Chicagoland area. He has founded the research website "Chowanoke Descendants Community"; published several peer-reviewed essays on North Carolina and Virginia Algonquians, who are among his ancestors; and presented his research on Chowanoke ethnic identity and cultural transformation at DePaul University. He continues to be involved with the Chowanoke Indian Nation of North Carolina and currently is engaged in a book-length study of the Third Anglo-Powhatan War.

The Chowanoke Indian Resurgence

Lars: I'm here with tribal councilman of the Meherrin-Chowanoke Nation, Doug Patterson. I'm going to ask a series of questions here, to deal with the Meherrin-Chowanoke Nation, where you've been, where you are, and where you're going. So, let's start by going way back. What historical Indian nation or nations are the Meherrin-Chowanoke descendants of?

Doug: Primarily, the Meherrin and Chowanoke. Currently, most of our members are of Chowanoke descent.

Lars: I had heard, according to some older accounts, that the Meherrin and Chowanokes seem to have faded out of existence or moved away. How would you respond to that?

Doug: I guess that would depend on what your definition of "fading away" is. If you were to say that there are no descendants of the Meherrin and Chowanoke, that would be false. Many people seem to think that if a tribe does not have a reservation, then they are not Indians. Historically, groups who either sold or somehow lost the last of their lands were considered extinct, even though the people were still there. An example of that is the Nottoway Tribe of Virginia. The "supposed" last Nottoway man [William Lamb] died around 1962, but actually, he was not the last of the Nottoways. He had family, relatives, cousins, etc. A book or an article saying a group is extinct is ridiculous. As long as people have children and descendants, the tribe exists. They don't disappear. Just because you don't have a land base doesn't mean you don't exist as Indians. The same goes for the Meherrin and

Chowanoke. Did they lose the land they had? Yes, they did. Did they disappear? No. But in the eyes of the non-Indian population, they are considered to be extinct as a nation because they have no reservation. Most Indian groups did not choose to lose their lands. Especially with many eastern groups, the land was taken. To obtain these lands, the settlers had to operate under the guise that there were no more Indians there. This was the case with both the Meherrin and the Chowanoke.

Lars: It sounds like there was a lot of pressure on these Indian communities. How was it that you were able to retain your identity under these pressures?

Doug: Well, when they lost their lands, they became a people unto themselves. People who nonetheless remained a cohesive political unit. They had their own stores, their own businesses, their own churches, and their own schools. So regardless of what they were called, they were always considered something different than the surrounding populations. They were viewed as a different type of people. They married within themselves, and these practices remain consistent to this day. It has been that way from the time that they lost their lands to the present.

Lars: Okay, so now let's fast-forward to the twentieth century. A lot has happened legally and socially that has allowed for the recognition of Indian communities who had previously had to operate under the radar. Could you describe the process of reorganization that the Meherrin people underwent?

Doug: I think, prior to recognition, the Indians in and around Hertford County were initially organized by Wayne Brown. From what I understand, he put an ad in the local paper to organize the Indians in the area to become part of the Meherrin Indian Tribe.

Lars: Now at this time you were called simply the Meherrin Indian Tribe, is that right?

Doug: Yes.

Lars: Why is it that you changed the name, and how was it done?

Doug: When the group was recognized, if you read the legislation, it was for all the Indians in the surrounding areas. A lot of people have different opinions about that, but for whatever reason, it didn't differentiate between any type of Indian, at all. So, if you are

Chowanoke or Meherrin, for example, you were included. I'm not sure what the original intent was, but that's how it was written.

Lars: I assume that after time went by, at some point, some members of the then Meherrin Indian Tribe found out they actually had Chowanoke roots. Is that the reason for the initial name change?

Doug: No, that's not true at all. The Chowanoke descendants always knew they were Chowanoke. It wasn't something that just started or anything like that. When it comes to tracing family ancestry, I have no emotional ties when looking at research. I try to remain objective to what the truth is, and what is actual and provable. If something that you believed is shown to be different than what you originally thought, you have to be disciplined enough to accept it. You go where your research goes, regardless of what you wish to believe. I mean you'll have a lot of people who will say, "Hey, my grandmother was an Indian." And most likely they'll say that she was Cherokee or Blackfoot. And they believe that. They believe that because that's what they've been told by their parents and grandparents, but in most instances it won't be true. Usually there is an underlying truth. They may be of Indian descent, but simply got the name of the tribe wrong.

Lars: I can relate to that.

Doug: Right. It's not that they're not Indian because, usually, there's always an underlying truth to the story. But you have to follow it. You can't develop an emotional tie to a set idea.

Lars: And is that because you feel it's a more accurate reflection of the group history?

Doug: Definitely. Many times, when you begin in one direction, it's very hard emotionally to let it go. The thing about it is, like the process of federal recognition, a government agency has no emotional ties to you, or any group. So they look at what you send, and look for flaws in your work. There's probably 400-plus people with letters of intent. The most important thing is that you have one chance to go through the recognition process. If you mess up, you don't get another shot. If you submit a petition, it really needs to be sufficient. This is an area that's really important to the Meherrin-Chowanoke. It's so important that the group was willing to sacrifice many things to reach for higher goals. As Indian people, one of the most important things you can give to your children and grandchildren is federal recognition and to be able to function in a nation-to-nation relationship with the federal government as a political entity. This is very important.

I've seen a lot of blogs out there that say we never existed. You'll see a lot of that. The Meherrin were a historical tribe and the Chowanoke were a historical tribe. How could anyone think that if one is Algonquin and the other Iroquoian that they did not comarry, commingle, or coexist? If they married non-Natives, why would it seem impossible for them to marry other Indians? The Chowanoke were thrown together with Iroquoian groups at different points in history, like the Tuscarora. The Nansemond, another Algonquian tribe, were integrated into the Nottoway, an Iroquoian tribe. The fact that they were of two different linguistic stocks did not matter. Now as for historical tribal names, a great number of tribes today have variations of historical names, but all are Indian. Look at the names of most North Carolina tribes. Many of those names are not historical names, but they are still tribes. The fact of the matter is, most existing tribal names are not names that the tribes called themselves. Tribes evolved today, as they have always done, into branches. It is the way it has always been in one way or another. There are even different Cherokee tribes. There are numerous Chippewa tribes in Michigan, all with different modern name variants. I think what's important is what tribes call themselves.

Lars: So now, with several different blogs and websites reporting on the Meherrin-Chowanoke, it seems there are two different groups. Was this name change the sole reason for the split, or were there other factors involved?

Doug: Some may say so, but there were other factors as well. If you were to go to the Bureau of Indian Affairs website and search for "Meherrin-Chowanoke" or "Meherrin Tribe," what you will see are two letters of intent and one petition that were submitted by different people. I would think that any reasonable person would come to a conclusion that this would create an issue for any group even though this happened in the early 1990s. Another point that I want to clarify is that many current blogs and websites provide incorrect information. Now this is very important because I've read blogs that state that Chief Thomas Lewis, or other individuals, changed the name of the tribe without their consent. That is absolutely false, and it should not be continued to be spread like that. It was not individually or unilaterally done. The name was changed as a result of a tribal vote. It is very important that we clear up this misconception.

Lars: Okay, so, it seems to me that there has been a lot of strife between the two groups. I understand there was a drawn-out lawsuit and a recent court order. Could you elaborate on the legal proceedings of the lawsuit and what does all this mean?

Doug: I've seen a lot of blogs that state that a judgment was made in the litigation. That also is not true. There was no decision made by the judge. He made no ruling. That is the truth. He allowed the groups to compose a consent order, which included a vote.

Lars: So what went on with that vote?

Doug: A vote was held. And from what I understand, those that ran for office did so unopposed.

Lars: And this was a vote on who were to be the leaders of the tribe?

Doug: Yes.

Lars: Okay, so at this point you are operating totally separate from the Meherrin Nation, right?

Doug: We are the Meherrin-Chowanoke.

Lars: And at this point, I understand, that there is legislation in the works to recognize the Meherrin-Chowanoke Nation by the state of North Carolina. How is that progressing?

Doug: I don't know if you've been watching the news, but the legislators are pretty tied up down there with some national issues. The Recognition Legislation of the Chowanoke Indian Tribe will be revisited. We are looking forward to the next legislative session. It should also be included that various tribal members have recently purchased a 146-acre tract of the former Chowanoke Indian Reservation, on which a living village will eventually be reconstructed.

Lars: Well, we all look forward to that.

Doug: You know, what the Meherrin-Chowanoke want is simply to go their way. The governing body wants to concentrate on the membership. The Meherrin-Chowanoke are also focusing on remaining a cohesive unit and gaining federal recognition.

Lars: Is the way the Meherrin-Chowanoke are attempting to be recognized different from the way other North Carolina Indian communities have been recognized?

Doug: In North Carolina, the Commission of Indian Affairs has existed for roughly forty-two years without recognizing anyone. The first tribe recognized were the Meherrin. There was no petitioning process for any of the other grandfathered-in groups. Later, once a formal process was put into place, the Occaneechi Band of Saponi submitted a petition for state recognition. They were denied, and engaged in litigation as a result. Afterward, a judge ruled that they should have been recognized based on their petition, and did so. They became recognized in 2002. Legislation, or other avenues of recognition, should always be an option for groups depending on their individual and specific circumstances. I would seriously caution any unrecognized group against opposing legislation, as it might be their only avenue to be recognized. In addition, it would be very disingenuous for one group to seek recognition—either state or federal through legislation—and at the same time ask another group to follow a petitioning process.

Lars: It sounds like you have your plate pretty full. Other than getting federal recognition and concentrating on tribal members, are there any other future goals of the Meherrin-Chowanoke Nation that you would like to elaborate on?

Doug: We are engaging a few federally recognized groups on future projects, but will make future announcements as time goes on.

Lars: Okay.

Doug: You know, the thought of Indian people engaged in hostility against each other is a very disturbing thing. Federally recognized tribes holding down state-recognized tribes and state-recognized tribes holding down unrecognized tribes is a very unhealthy way for Indian people to exist. At some point, all these groups are going to need each other.

Editor's Note: This originated as part of an interview with Meherrin-Chowanoke Nation Tribal Council member Douglas Patterson conducted by Lars Adams on September 9, 2013, and appeared on the website "Chowanoke Descendants Community."

Doug Patterson has held some form of tribal office with the Meherrin-Chowanoke Nation since about 1996, including being a former commissioner for North Carolina's State Commission of Indian Affairs. It is important to note that the tribe has recently changed their name to the Chowanoke Indian Nation. Patterson has been *involved in Native research for over twenty-five years and sees his research interests as mirroring his profession in law enforcement. He has worked at all levels, including the local, state, and federal levels. He loves his work and looks forward to seeing the vision of federal recognition be obtained by his deserving and well-documented tribe.*

Jamestown 2007: A Native American Perspective

Jamestown 2007. Say those words aloud to any Virginian and you are almost sure to get a response. Say those words aloud to any Virginia Indian and that response could be anything from outright disgust to statements like, "This is an opportunity to tell our story." I must say, I have strong feelings of sadness surrounding the Jamestown Anniversary celebration, but yet welcome the opportunity to let Virginia and the world know the whole story about what truly happened to Virginia Indians. I feel sadness because

Chief Kenneth Adams of the Upper Mattaponi Tribe of King William County, Virginia. (Photo Courtesy of Kenneth Adams and Betsy Barton.)

the story for me, and many other Virginia Indians, is a story of sorrow and pain—a story of growing up in a society where Indian culture had almost been completely destroyed.

I grew up in rural Virginia with three separate school systems: the segregated system we all know about, plus a totally separate system for Native Americans. The Sharon Indian School typically had thirty to forty children from grades one through seven. As children got older, sometimes the grade level would reach as high as the tenth grade, but because of this grade limitation, no one ever graduated from the Sharon Indian School. Therefore, most of the adults could barely read or write. Fortunately, those dark days are years behind us now, and, for the most part, Indians in Virginia are treated with dignity and respect.

The process of getting to this point started at Jamestown in 1607, and now we are rapidly approaching 2007, the 400th anniversary of its settling. When the English settlers first reached Jamestown, conflict with Indians began almost immediately. Of course, the Indians could not possibly want these people invading their homeland. Would you? Today, we have private citizens patrolling the United States border with Mexico to help keep out illegal aliens. To the Virginia Indians, the first British settlers were illegal aliens. The British government finally sent enough people to take over all the land, which the Indians owned, and in the process of the wars that followed, 90 percent of an entire human race of people died. I cannot believe that this was the desire of God Almighty. After all, "For God so Loved the WORLD," and that world also included the Indians.

Our leaders talk about our nation being founded on Judeo-Christian principles. Yet the loss of life, liberty, and land experienced by many Native Americans was in direct violation of these principles. In 1607, there were hundreds of Indian villages along the waterways of Virginia, and now, sadly, on those same waterways there are only two: the Pamunkey and the Mattaponi.

The first treaties with the Indians were written at Jamestown. The first treaties with the Indians were broken at Jamestown. The pattern of broken and dishonored treaties, which began at Jamestown, continued westward to the Pacific Ocean. A broken treaty is nothing more than a broken promise, and even today, promises made by the United States government with the Indians of this land are not being honored. Many of those promises that were made through treaties have been affirmed by the United States

Supreme Court for over 200 years. Some would say those treaties are ancient history. Would those same people say the Bill of Rights is ancient history? Is the Declaration of Independence ancient history?

Today, several of the Virginia tribes are attempting to get historical recognition from the United States government. For those tribes, it is the proper thing to do. For some representatives who oppose that process, they don't seem to care about the broken promises of the recent past. They care not that the Virginia General Assembly voted almost unanimously for this recognition. They care not that the people have spoken and asked for those representatives to help make this recognition a reality.

Where were those politicians as my older brothers and sisters actually had to leave the Commonwealth of Virginia to get a high school education? Where were they when my father struggled to sign his own name because of broken promises? The process of my family having to leave the Commonwealth to get an education is part of the legacy of broken promises to the American Indian. It is time to rectify those failures of the past and encourage *all* congressmen representing this Commonwealth to join in the process of appropriate federal acknowledgment of Virginia's first citizens. Once that happens, and when Jamestown is once again mentioned, much of the sadness in my heart will be buried with our ancestors. Our ancestors will never experience the hope that America promises, but they will understand that the Circle of Life that impacts all Virginia Indians is under repair.

In all, 562 Indian tribes in this country have a nation-to-nation relationship with the United States government, and the Virginia Indians should not be continually treated as undeserving of the same relationship. Virginia Indians were the first in America to have permanent and sustained contact with English settlers and still are not properly recognized as those 562 other tribes are. Is that going to be another sad legacy for this Commonwealth? In the wars of the twentieth century, Virginia Indians fought and died for this land in support of the Constitution of the United States, even when they were being denied constitutional rights at home.

The time is now to right this wrong. We should have the same equality of relationship with the federal government that federally recognized tribes have, with no abridgement of any right under the Constitution of this nation. We have fought and died for that equality, and I, for one, believe any fair-minded Virginian would support that recognition for the Commonwealth's Native Americans. We are proud of being both Indians and Americans. We have waited far too long, and the commemoration of Jamestown 2007 will be incomplete and disheartening without appropriate and unabridged recognition of Virginia tribes.

Editor's Note: This essay was originally published in *Cooperative Living* in June 2005 as planning was under way to commemorate the 400th anniversary of the founding of Jamestown in 1607.

Kenneth Adams is Chief of the Upper Mattaponi Tribe of King William County, Virginia. He is actively involved in lobbying Congress for federal recognition of Virginia Indians. He also serves as chairman of the Board of Trustees of Bacone College and as a member of the Board for Preservation Virginia and the Virginia War Memorial Educational Foundation.

Eastern Creeks and the Persistence of Identity

I, like many Eastern Creek Indians from south Alabama and north Florida, come from families who were split in the 1830s, with part leaving for the sunset on "the trail where they cried," and others remaining in a social limbo that would make them strangers in their own land within a generation. The children and grandchildren of the Creek and other Indian people who were able to avoid removal lived their lives in the tumult of the Civil War years, as their grandchildren came of age in the economically depressed and racially stratified South of the early twentieth century. This was a raw and rugged place, with little contact with outsiders or trust of strangers. The South languished in its own stew of racial strife and bigotry, even as other parts of the country opened up and moved forward. Despite the horror of the removal of the Creek Nation, and the ensuing decades that followed, pockets of Indian people continued to be scattered across the southland, struggling to adjust to a new order—one where their identity was now in question.

The Civil War, which unfolded thirty years after the Removal period, did little to help the situation for Native people in the South. Most were socially invisible in the emerging reality of the post–Civil War racial order. The evolution of identity in conjunction with race happened quickly during the postwar years. Thousands of people who had previously been slaves crossed the color line and became "white."[6] Before the war, one's status as free or slave would have dictated important aspects of a person's treatment by others, as individuals and communities. After the conflict, a new emphasis on racial appearance took hold, with those who had darker complexions casted as "mulatto" or another similarly racialized category.

This reorientation of racial identities was complex, and many of the remaining Creek and mixed-blood families struggled to find a foothold as the prewar binary social structure of slave-versus-free faded into a more appearance-oriented means of defining race. With this situation, the Indians who lived "among the whites" in lower Alabama, in southern Georgia, and in the Florida panhandle began to withdraw into small endogamous settlements in the remotest of areas.[7]

In a 1921 publication, W. E. B. DuBois argued, "The discovery of personal whiteness among the world's peoples is a very modern thing—a nineteenth and twentieth century matter, indeed."[8] This seemed to be the case in the lower South where "whiteness" and "otherness" locked into a struggle that produced dozens of court cases regarding the identity of Indians. The Catawba, Lumbee, Eastern Cherokee, Creek, and Mississippi Choctaw all felt the pressure of being forced into the "colored" class in the eyes of the law and social opinion. The racial environment faced by persons of color during the dark days was harsh and limited. Richard Wright captured the sentiment well in his novel *Black Boy*, where one of the characters expressed, "the pressure of southern living kept me from being the kind of person I might have been."[9] For Native peoples, survival meant relying on fellow community members as well as their own internal strength as they negotiated the racial slippery slope they found themselves on.

In the South of the late nineteenth and early twentieth centuries, knowing one's place was a looming and ever-present part of the social fabric of the rural communities where the grandchildren and great-grandchildren of those who had not been removed or assimilated lived. In the aftermath of the *Brown v. Board of Education* decision in 1954, C. Vann Woodward wrote that "there is more Jim Crowism practiced in the South than there are Jim Crow laws on the books."[10] This was especially true along the area of the border of the panhandle of Florida and its neighboring states. Several communities of Indians and mixed-blood peoples, who had been well established since before the Civil War, were negatively impacted by racial segregation practices. These settlements suffered economically, and they were stripped of the fairly certain and accepted status—an "in-between" identity that they held before the conflict. In Jackson, Calhoun, Holmes, Walton, and other Florida counties, many of the Indian settlements were defined as "colored" within social and legal contexts by the white power structure, and the complex dynamics within and between families in these settlements were tested as each generation responded to the new challenges these decades brought.

When some families could pass as "white" by moving away from the Indian settlement, they would do so, while others stayed and maintained ties with kin and suffered the social stigma that came along with it. As the geographer Steven Hoelscher put it, this externally defined identity that impacted many of the mixed-blood and Indian families was "a central theme in the historical geography of the American south and other places marked by geographies of exclusion: how a dominant group was able to create a culture of segregation that extended well beyond the boundaries of its legal apparatus."[11] The powerful hold that Jim Crowism had on the lives of Indian people who were unable to pass as "white" proved difficult, yet it was constantly in flux and being remade in response to evolving social realities.

The heavy endogamy among the mixed-blood and Indian settlement families intensified during the Jim Crow years as people further isolated themselves. This resulted in the continuation of a strong oral tradition that revealed unique lifeways embedded with rich social memories. Stories of ancestors who lived in the Carolinas passed from the first generations to settle in Florida by the Lumbee migrant families, such as the Oxendine, Jacobs, and Porter families of Scott Town and Blountstown, Florida. These stories were threads in a fabric of survival, a tapestry of place and identity. Similarly, family traditions in lower Alabama and the Pensacola area of Creeks still recounted the courage and fortitude demonstrated by their ancestors in order to survive and "avoid being took out to Oklahoma." These stories were still prevalent in the 1950s, more than a century after the witnesses were gone.

Many of these stories, and the memories that they were created from, were shared during a Community Oral History Project conducted in 1996 as part of the Florida Tribe of Eastern Creek Indians' petition for federal acknowledgment. These oral histories were conducted in private in consideration of the individuals' appearance in order to eliminate prejudice of those who did or didn't "look Indian," as well as to discourage judgment of the position of the family that they came from regarding their status in the hierarchies within the small settlements' social ladders, which old-timers called the "Old Heads." The habit to be selective in the exercise of historical memory was not remiss among the people of Hog Fork, Bell Creek, Poarch, Scott Town, or Scotts Ferry. As the families of the original migrants branched out across the panhandle over several generations, some continued to marry within the cluster of interrelated families and stayed in the safety and security of the small settlements, while others married local whites and became a part of the local mainstream population in town.

"I only went to town maybe three times before I was twelve years old," one elder recalled of her childhood in the 1920s.[12] The avoidance of social situations that could lead to community members appearing on equal footing with local African Americans was an important aspect of how the community saw itself, despite local whites' view of them. "Uncle Hugh Oxendine would always walk when he would come to town, and even when white people would try to pick him up, he wouldn't take the charity," Mrs. Sallie would say of "Uncle Hugh," who was reputed to be the "last full-blood Indian" alive in Woods in the 1940s by several elders who participated in the Community Oral History Project.

What is accepted as the truest version of the past, as remembered by various elders, is a powerful authority at work in the family lines, even after several generations of activity within the larger movement to reassert the historic communities' identities. As George Orwell wrote in *Nineteen Eighty-Four*, "Who controls the past controls the future; who controls the present controls the past,"[13] and this control of the narrative concerning the tribal past would not be without fierce contention in the century after the Civil War. The various perspectives on race, disagreements on tribal origins, community identity, and the social structure and leadership of the presegregation-era settlements became a political football in the struggles of the late twentieth century. The tension is in clearly defining the nature of the Indian settlements before their reorganization and, in some cases, dispersal in the 1960s; however, in the decades leading up to the twentieth century, the small, inwardly focused settlements of Indians scattered across the Gulf Coast were places of family, work, and acceptance in an otherwise hostile world. The Indian communities of the Mississippi Choctaw, MOWA Choctaw, and Poarch Creeks in Alabama—as well as the scattered settlements of Eastern Creek and Lumbee in south Georgia and the panhandle of Florida—survived socially through reliance on one another, and physically through, among other things, subsistence farming, fishing, and turpentine work.

My own family members began to network with others who were reaching out, making connections and glimpsing new horizons that had been unavailable before. Beginning in the 1950s, the Indian Claims Commission made attempts to compensate Native peoples for the unjust seizures of land that had occurred in the past. The Creek Nation, like many others, was awarded funds, which courts ruled applied to Creek people in the East as well as in Oklahoma. When the Eastern Creek land claims payment was organized, many thousands stepped forward to file. Those who could read assisted those who couldn't in trying to gather their hard-to-come-by genealogical documents. Tribal Council meetings among the "Creek Nation East of the Mississippi," as it was then called, brought together Indian people who had formerly been reclusive and nonpolitical.

By 1970, the feeling of a brighter future and a sense of Indian pride was felt all over south Alabama and north Florida, as throughout the country. My cousin, Chief Andrew Ramsey, found a seat on the Florida Governor's Council on Indian Affairs, along with leaders from the Seminole and Miccosukee tribes. I, myself, as a twenty-something-year-old, attended meetings at the state capital, as well as in Washington, D.C., representing the interests of our community. Many other family members also stepped forward to contribute to the struggle. My grandmother helped with cooking for tribal meetings where our options as a "tribe," rather than just a "community," were discussed. In time, we had limited success as some of our people who were previously part of the "Creek Nation East of the Mississippi" divided into smaller groups and sought recognition. In particular, those in Escambia, Monroe, and Baldwin Counties of Alabama secured federal recognition as the Poarch Band of Creek Indians, and Creek people descended from Chief McIntosh living in South Georgia became state recognized. Yet despite this progress, many communities continued to struggle for political acknowledgment. As a young man, I used to talk with elders and kinsmen at Green Corn Dances about what we faced. I became even more fired up by the situation when I became a teenage father. It made me want to fight harder so that my son, Harjo, wouldn't know the challenges faced by my grandparents. At times, anger clouded my mind and put fear in my heart. Auntie Mary Francis Johns would tell me in the quiet evenings during the Green Corn Dance, "Don't worry, we will get there." In time, I pursued my education, graduating from the university with my sociology degree. This was just as my son graduated high school and found his own place in the struggle along with his Cheyenne/Arapaho wife. Our thoughts are always with the elders who strived before us for equality.

Whatever the challenges of the past, today the people who are inheritors of our ancestors' struggles are finding their voices, working to restore community institutions, and implementing language and cultural preservation efforts—all of this alongside much-needed economic development. The Eastern Creeks of Alabama, Florida, and Georgia are finding the twenty-first century a time in which society around them is changing once again. By focusing on the strengths of the past and local ancestral struggles, a pathway into the future is being revealed, and lived.

Today, when I look at the social landscape that I saw through young eyes thirty-five years ago, either at community meetings with my grandparents

Stomp Dance, 2004. (Photo Courtesy of Sallie Kever and Hodalee Scott Sewell.)

or through exposure to tales of a century ago when their grandparents were young, I see that so much has changed in the big wide world, yet not really. It seems that when I travel back down the same dirt road to the Green Corn Dance grounds, and hear those same ancient songs in the night's breeze, smell the same *sofkee* cooking, or see the same tired, but peaceful, faces in the early morning light after a night of stomp dancing, I know very little has changed. We are still here, we are still together, and we are still struggling. Before I leave our little settlement to go back to my pursuit as a graduate student in academia, I always stop by the graves of Emma Hill, Hugh Oxendine, Corva Jacobs, Mathias Porter, Tom Scott, and the other heroes from my grandparents' stories of a darker time when the strength of heart was all that they had going for them, and I feel the ancestors riding with me into the future challenges. When I see my own son circling the Green Corn Dance fire in the moonlight, I know they rest peacefully knowing we will endure. In this circle of generations, I am completed. In this great wide world, wherever I find myself, they are with me.

Hodalee Scott Sewell is Eastern Creek/Cheraw. He is originally from Blountstown, Florida, and a member of the Bird Clan. He coauthored The Indians of North Florida *with his cousin, S. Pony Hill, in 2010 (Backintyme Publishers). He presently works in research and advocacy for Native American and hybrid peoples of the South and East.*

To Be or Not to Be a "Wannabe"

It's up to each individual to decide!

There are many people, especially in the southern United States, who grew up with family traditions of having Cherokee blood. I am one of them. So were both of my parents, maternal and paternal grandparents, and even farther back as far as various family members have ever been able to officially document. It's a part of our lives that most have always been extremely proud of. And every generation has had at least some members who have always made sure that this honored tradition would never die. I'm also one of those! Yet we are among a growing populace of Americans with documented Native blood who, to some federal tribal members, fall into a negative area of recognition. While the names of some of our ancestors and other relatives appear on several of the older historical Cherokee rolls, the fact that they are not listed on what are accepted as the "final" Dawes Commission rolls seems to present a problem. Today, it seems that more than ever registered "card-carrying" members of the three federally recognized Cherokee tribes view most who are not one of their own as "wannabes" or "fake Indians!" Why?

To bona fide Cherokee descendants who are not registered members of a federally recognized tribe, nothing is more insulting or degrading then being dubbed a "wannabe!" This is especially true when we recognize there are many in our society who actually deserve such a curse, because for purely self-serving reasons, they continuously masquerade and falsely represent themselves as Indians of some tribe. But those are authentic "wannabes" and are not the subject of this discussion.

My remarks pertain to the multitude of people in this country who *are* authentic Cherokee descendants. Yet through misinformation, a lack of understanding, or a refusal to accept undeniable historical facts by some Cherokee tribal members, indeed even some of their elected leaders, many bona fide descendants are often also pegged as "wannabes" or "fake Indians."

I came to realize that many such slurs were used especially for those who organized as social groups or newly created "tribes" seeking recognition in states where they reside. But for the purposes of this discussion, I have omitted those types of entities.

Why?

For a few years in the 1990s, I actively participated in some of these groups acting solely as a Cherokee descendant offering cultural advice and historical training. But much to my dismay, I soon came to realize that many of the people in some of the groups I dealt with were really of questionable authenticity and did not actually deserve any type of recognition! To be fair, however, I did meet some very good people within these groups who were certainly authentic Cherokee descendants, and I still value them as friends!

Yet when I saw such troubling things as undeserved government grants being applied for against my advice because I knew, if granted, they would certainly take away from the bona fide Cherokee communities they were intended for; their acceptance of numerous members with inadequate or questionable proof of heritage; and their misleading adoption of so many Plains Indian customs, beliefs, and attire, I soon realized that it was no wonder the word "wannabe" has become so commonly used. This just wasn't somewhere that I belonged.

Now, to further clarify the "final rolls," an act of Congress dated March 3, 1893, (27 Stat. 645) provided for a commission to negotiate with the Cherokees (and also the Choctaw, Creek, Chickasaw, and Seminole Nations of Oklahoma) to dissolve their tribal governments and to allot their land to individual citizens. This commission became known as the Dawes Commission after Senator Henry Dawes, the commission chairman. The work of this commission went very slowly until finally Congress passed the Curtis Act of 1898, which provided that a new roll be created that would supersede all others. The Dawes rolls were taken in the years 1898 to 1907. And to restrict the enrollment even more, all applicants had to actually reside within the area then occupied by the tribe, which would eventually become a part of the state of Oklahoma!

To those who do not understand the applicable history, today two of the three federally recognized Cherokee tribes—the Cherokee Nation of Oklahoma and the United Keetoowah Band of Oklahoma—continue to use the Dawes rolls of 1898 as the *only* basis for determining their tribal membership. More than 250,000 people applied to this commission for enrollment and land. Just over 100,000 were approved! The rolls do not include the applications that were rejected, stricken, or judged to be doubtful.

The federally recognized Eastern Band of Cherokees in North Carolina use *only* the 1924 Baker roll, which is likewise also considered their "final roll." All three of these Cherokee tribes require applicants to provide proof of descent from a person who is listed on these rolls only. And courts have upheld this rule to exactness—even when it has been proven that a brother or sister of an ancestor was listed on the rolls, but not the direct ancestor himself or herself. Also, no other historical Cherokee rolls can even be considered.

In retrospect, there are many other earlier official Cherokee rolls (before Dawes) in our nation's archives. In his popular book *Cherokee Roots*, Volume 1, *Eastern Cherokee Rolls*, noted author, genealogist, and respected longtime leader in the Eastern Band of Cherokees Bob Blankenship lists nine rolls dating from 1817 through 1908. His other book, *Cherokee Roots*, Volume 1, *Western Cherokee Rolls*, lists two additional rolls dated 1851 and 1852.

The U.S. Department of the Interior, Bureau of Indian Affairs, lists four categories of Cherokee people in its "Guide to Tracing Your American Indian Ancestry." Categories 1 through 3 outline the membership of the three federally recognized tribes. Category 4 includes "All *other* persons of Cherokee Indian ancestry." The fact that this category even exists indicates that these "other" people are definitely not considered "wannabes" by the U.S. government.

Now, let me be quick to insist that I would be first in line to defend the undeniable and exclusive right of each of the above tribes to determine who is eligible for membership in their tribes. Back in the day, it was by mutual agreement of tribal leaders and the U.S. government that descent from a Dawes enrollee would be the sole basis for determining all future members. A new Cherokee constitution adopted and confirmed by the Cherokee tribal members in 1975 reaffirmed this. Like many Cherokee descendants, I've never fully understood the seemingly extreme exclusivity of that rule, but some of it does make a lot of sense. For example, why should the many Cherokees who voluntarily never moved to Oklahoma from the East, or those who didn't suffer the infamous Trail of Tears through forced removal, be entitled to share in the monies or final individual land allotments in the West?

So to avoid any misunderstandings, allow me to repeat—I fully respect the rights of all Cherokee tribes to make their own rules and to govern however they choose. Like many Cherokee descendants, however, I am disappointed that the final Dawes rolls left no provisions whatsoever for the future membership of bona fide Cherokee descendants of older historical enrollees. This is all the more reason that they should never be viewed or referred to as "wannabes!"

The first page of names on the old 1817 Cherokee Reservation roll includes the name of my seventh-generation mixed-blood great-grandmother, Lucy Briant, who was already a widow at the time of her enrollment. One of the prerequisites to accepting her 640-acre reservation in lieu of going west to Arkansas was that she relinquish her citizenship in the Cherokee Nation to become a U.S. citizen! Apparently, she decided it was in her best interest to do that, and I salute her decision. At the same time, however, I find it quite disconcerting to think that this action would result in all of her descendants possibly being looked upon as "wannabes" in the future. Why? Because she died in 1848, several years before the final Dawes rolls were taken, and her only direct descendant never migrated west to Oklahoma. Consequently, he did not meet the residency requirement of the Dawes Commission.

Tony Mack McClure standing in front of a dedication that reads "Chunannee Falls Land Lot 91: The 640 acre Reservation formerly known as Chunannee, was originally the home of Lucy Bryant/Briant. She was a Cherokee Indian widow, as shown on the Reservation Roll of 1817, who was granted this land under the provision of article 8 in the Treaty of July 8, 1817. It was here on Duke's Creek that gold was first discovered in 1828." (Photo Courtesy of Tony Mack McClure and Robin McClure.)

Today, Grandmother Lucy's old Chunannee reservation property on Dukes Creek in northern Georgia is a designated historical site in the impressive Smithgall Woods Nature Conservancy. And I'm also very proud to report that all of her many descendants who often visit there are looked upon by the conservators not as "wannabes" but as respected bona fide Cherokees!

In the forward to one of Bob Blankenship's books on Cherokee genealogy, he states, "*Intermarriages were frequent and as a consequence, Cherokee blood flows in the veins of millions of Americans living today*" (emphasis added). Since a recent U.S. census put the combined total membership of the three federally recognized tribes at only about 350,000, is it culturally appropriate, or even remotely reasonable, for anyone, especially federal Cherokee tribal members, to consider all those "millions" of other people with Cherokee blood referred to by Blankenship as "wannabes"?

Many years ago as a much younger man I had the good fortune to become acquainted with W. W. "Bill" Keeler, who was Principal Chief of the Cherokee Nation of Oklahoma from 1949 to 1975. In the interest of promoting tourism for lakes within the Cherokee Nation, Chief Keeler had invited 1973 National Bassmaster Classic Champion Rayo Breckenridge to film a television show there. Rayo was a Native farmer from nearby Arkansas whose sudden notoriety was parlayed into a long and successful TV career in which his popular fishing program, *Rayo Breckenridge Outdoors*, aired regionally from 1974 to 1985. I was the producer of that show.

During several conversations on that trip, Chief Keeler and I discussed my own documented ancestry and extreme pride in being a Cherokee descendant. We also talked some about this "wannabe" subject and how the rules of the Dawes rolls often made some of us feel somewhat excluded even though I personally accepted why most of those rules were necessary. I'll always remember Chief Keeler's response to me about this discussion:

> To be sure, the term "wannabe" isn't a very nice word, and unfortunately, its use is something that's often decided by tribal members who don't personally know a person or their family history at all. If it were up to me, I'd probably ban its use entirely, but at the same time you and I both know there actually are some real "wannabes" around who deserve to be looked upon as such and treated accordingly. This will probably never change.

I've also never forgotten, and often passed on in the Cherokee genealogical works and teachings that I've been honored to do over the years, the Chief's final words of advice on this subject:

> To be or not to be a "wannabe." It's up to each individual to decide! And those who make the right decision shouldn't ever be seen as "wannabes" by tribal members!

I felt especially proud when Chief Keeling ended our talk with a smile and said, "I don't think you'll ever have to worry about being called a 'wannabe,' Tony. Your extensive knowledge and obvious respect for our shared heritage definitely qualifies you as my Cherokee brother!"

Tony Mack McClure is a native Tennessean and mixed-blood Cherokee descendant. Before semiretirement, he was a certified member of the Native American Journalists Association, Woodcraft Circle of Native Writers and Storytellers, committeeman for the Tennessee Chapter of the National Trail of Tears Association, and frequent speaker before social, civic, and student groups. He has been the producer of Bill Dance Outdoors, *the nation's oldest and highest-rated television fishing program for over thirty-five years. The show airs several times weekly on NBC Sports, the Outdoor Channel, and the Discovery Channel's Destination America TV network. Tony's work has also appeared in numerous magazines and newspapers and on other television networks and major cable systems.*

Jim Crowfeather in Indian Country

Walking down to Dennis Pharmacy each morning from our small trailer, the smell of *picadillo, ropa vieja, palomillo,* plantains, and black beans and yellow rice would fill the air. A unique Spanish dialect would accompany this same space. Here everyone was known by "cuz," and mornings began with *café con leche* or *buchis,* with a side of Cuban bread drowned in butter. A few blocks east and we found ourselves regularly seated at La Lechonera or El Siboney. A quick bike ride north and my mom and I would find our prized guava pastries at La Bodega. A block south and one could hear the celebrations of an elder's passing enunciated by steel drums, fervent and melodic Negro spirituals, and the annual Goombay celebrations, or, better yet, remembrances of living culture, which typified the Bahamian identity of our island home. Cayo Hueso (Island of Bones), better known as Key West, was a place far from Americana—one without mention of "Mom and apple pie," the Pledge of Allegiance, or the trappings of white, mainstream conservatism or historical narrative. There were no powwows or fry bread here, only the misappropriated images of Plains Indians beloved by the local Cuban population that adorned their jewelry, eateries, and homes. The island, whose original Indigenous inhabitants' bones and memories are part of the very foundation of the land's soil, was as divorced from contemporary Indian Country as any place straddling the North American continent ever could be. Discussions of American Indian ancestry among the local population were nonexistent. Republican and Democratic mainstream political viewpoints were a thing of myth. While technically a part of the United States and Florida, this small land mass rests closer to the island of Cuba than to the U.S. mainland. It was much more Bahamas than Georgia. If ever a place existed in a vacuum removed from mainstream white culture and American Indian identity, this was the place.

My hometown of Key West was not the dream of tourist brochures and beach-strewn resorts (as is marketed now) during the days of my upbringing. An old friend of my parents provides his take on the island during this era in *Florida Travel & Life* magazine's March/April 2012 issue: "It was like the wild, wild West back then . . . smugglers and hush-hush barroom deals of the late '70s and early '80s." More well known and reputable magazines such as *National Geographic* showed Key West as a primary part of what they dubbed "The Cocaine Empire" (January 1989), and the December 1999 issue stated, "It is not disputed that back in the 1970s . . . the lower Keys were kept alive by drug traffic. It was cash-and-carry. Everybody winked."

This is the town where one of my high school coaches was relieved from his duties not for a losing season, but because of a crack cocaine conviction.

Sadly, this was part of my personal reality because of my own father's involvement in the drug industry, which ultimately led to his demise. Back in the day, many newspapers and even *People* magazine dedicated tons of print to his disappearance. They found his lifeless body, some money, and drugs months later beneath the wreckage of his plane. In some ways this is where the story ends and also begins for me.

I was not raised "Indian" or "white." I don't descend from a chief, council member, tribal judge, or anyone of particular interest or concern to history. I was not raised by white southerners who later "found themselves" as Indians. My mother abandoned all cultural aspects of her upbringing by moving from her native Canada to Alabama and then to Florida after eloping with my father, who is of mixed MOWA Choctaw descent, as a teenager and following his migration. I am highly cognizant of the privilege my white phenotype (making me one of only a few in my father's tribe) provides me and of the responsibility my tribal enrollment places on me in terms of assisting my tribe in maintaining historical legacy, continuity, and health. The reality that I was raised removed from Indian Country and white mainstream America during my childhood and the majority of my teen years is what makes me uniquely suited to take on these issues of identity.

Despite my direct engagement in Indian Country the past twenty-four years, my father's family members' tribal enrollments, my tribal community residence and cultural involvement, my marriage to a Kiowa tribal member, as well as the Indian identities of our four children, my identity was and is primarily that of a Conch—the name and cultural grouping given the white Bahamian, black Bahamian, and racially plural Cuban groups that settled and mixed with one another on the island of Key West in the 1800s. There, this group established an isolated enclave of culture and story known no other place in the world. My cultural foundations are connected to a people from whom I have no racial, historical, or cultural ties and were formed through the first eighteen continuous primary years of my life. I gained and have maintained complete and absolute acceptance from this cultural anomaly. I had no idea during my upbringing that people existed outside of this bubble who contested identity based on genealogical and tribal enrollment lines. Identity was a social and cultural experience for me, not one based on political manifestations tied to old census or Indian rolls. Not one based in perceived notions of blood. And no, my surname "Sunray" is not "Indian," but rather one of European origin. The reader may be familiar with its kin family of names, such as Ray, Wray, or McRae—the Mac or Mc in Scottish/Irish Gaelic standing for "son of," with the "Sun" in Sunray being another spelling of "son" (that is, "Son of Ray").

If I could change my life, I would not be naive or pretentious enough to say "I would change nothing," for I would. I would long for knowing. This is what I missed most as a child and teen. There was no sense of history and tradition or the foundation that such a knowing creates in relation to my biological or family lines. I understand now it washes over you and submerges you in its grasp, for better and for worse. I was lost on its value, yet crippled by its absence. Our children will never have such concerns.

Unlike my own, the identity of my father's people was never buried, misplaced, or in need or want of finding. In fact, Jim Crowfeather (aka Jim Crow) held a special place in "his" twisted ideologies for them—an ideology that sorely has not vanished even to this day. The MOWA Choctaw inhabit the third (bottom) level of the tripartite caste system of the region. This is an uncommon occurrence for most Indian communities that exist in areas predominated collectively by white, black, and Indian people. This has been born out throughout the region's history in a variety of ways to include a lack of access to employment and schooling opportunities (that is, while whites and blacks could work in the area's industrial plants and attend the segregated school systems, the MOWA Choctaw were disallowed employment and were sent hundreds of miles from home to attend Indian boarding schools).

My grandfather was an original enrollee of this tribal community who were beaten down by Jim Crowfeather and located in Alabama an hour or so drive north of Mobile. The tribe was known by various names during its long history to include misnomers or not readily identifiable Indian names such as "Cajan." At first glance this term closely resembles the more well known spelling of "Cajun," which of course is representative of some of the inhabitants of Louisiana. The "Cajan" term was a mix of both the Louisiana "*Caj*un" moniker along with "Indi*an*" and was concocted by a visiting Louisiana politician who believed the local Indian population in some ways favored his Cajun constituency back home. Alabama politicians embraced the name out of fear for land claims and settlement legislation, which had become prominent at the time for Indian tribes remaining in the eastern and southern regions of the United States. The contemporary term for the community became the MOWA Band of Choctaw Indians (though predominantly Choctaw, we are an amalgamation of various tribes, with some minor non-Indian ancestry), with the "MO" being representative of Mobile County and the "WA" being representative of Washington County, which are the principal counties of residence of our tribe's 3,600 members. Despite our deep history within Alabama, however, the MOWA are not recognized by the federal government.

The question of federal recognition is one of the most debated subjects in Indian Country and one that has been applied without equity for generations. Countless academics, historians, and Indian leaders have published works in literary journals, tribal magazines, newspapers, and books for years on the corrupt nature of the process and those who implement it. Today, there exist nearly 570 federally recognized tribes and over 60 state-recognized tribes, as well as other tribal communities that have no political recognition via federal or state designation. With over 300 other groups petitioning for "official" federal recognition, the issue has become almost irretrievable in its contestations.

The MOWA Band of Choctaw Indians resides on one of only nine state-recognized Indian reservations in the United States. Of the nine oldest Indian reservations in the country, eight are occupied by historic "nonfederally" recognized tribes. The concept that only federally recognized tribes reside on Indian reservations (though many do not) is not only a misnomer but is also one that portrays a fictitious historical account.

Another misconception that is often perpetuated involves the Indian boarding school system, which began in the latter part of the 1800s and continued until the modern era, and was run by both the federal Indian service (now known as the Bureau of Indian Affairs) and closely related missions. Thirteen historic "nonfederal" tribes in the East and South attended these schools alongside their federally recognized counterparts. The Euchee (Yuchi) of Oklahoma was the only "nonfederal" tribe that had more attendees than the MOWA Band of Choctaw Indians. Indian boarding school attendance began in the 1920s for MOWA Choctaw tribal members who, over the years, have been sent to Bacone (Muskogee, Oklahoma), Haskell (Lawrence, Kansas), Choctaw Central (Mississippi Choctaw Indian Reservation, Mississippi), and three other similar institutions with "Indian programs" across the country, as they were denied admittance to local white and black educational institutions prior to desegregation. Local Indian schools run by the MOWA Choctaw were deemed unaccredited, and therefore attendance at the Indian boarding schools was their sole tool in order to receive an accredited education. Tribal members as young as thirteen were sent hundreds of miles from home in order to receive this form of tutelage. During the time of their attendance, many of these institutions required a minimum Indian blood degree of one-quarter for admittance.

CHIEF BRAVES SQUAWS

THE INDIANS
FRONT ROW, LEFT TO RIGHT: Arlene Verdin, Gloria Billiot, Montegut, La.; Irene Snow, McIntosh, Ala. BACK ROW: Bennett Weaver, Galanced Weaver, McIntosh, Ala.; Russell Molivere, Montegut, La.

Acadia Baptist Boarding School (Eunice, Louisiana) Indian program students circa 1950 in the school yearbook. Those pictured are members of the MOWA Band of Choctaw Indians (Alabama) and United Houma Nation (Louisiana). Members of the Tunica-Biloxi Tribe of Louisiana also attended with them. (Photo Courtesy of Haskell Endangered Legacy Project [H.E.L.P.] via Cedric Sunray.)

The last completely fluent speaker of the Choctaw language within the community did not pass on until 1984. Indian language instruction in the community began in the local Indian schools in the 1960s and continues to this day. The linguistic reality of this is a powerful testimony to the cultural retention of the tribe, especially in light of the reality that over 100 currently federally recognized tribes do not have any fluent speakers of their ancestral languages, with some having lost their linguistic capabilities as far back as the 1800s.

Over the years, more than twenty federally recognized tribes have intermarried with the MOWA Choctaw, and they and their descendants reside on both reservation and privately held Choctaw lands in the communities of, and surrounding, Mt. Vernon, Citronelle, and McIntosh, Alabama. These tribes include the Navajo, Cherokee Nation of Oklahoma, Kiowa, White Mountain Apache, and many others. Over 90 percent of enrolled MOWA Choctaw tribal members live within a 20-mile radius of the main tribal offices, while many of the others reside in the state of Oklahoma due to their intermarriage with members of tribes located there.

The tribe currently holds resolutions/letters of support for their federal recognition from the National Congress of American Indians (NCAI) (the largest Indian organization in the United States), the National Association for the Advancement of Colored People (NAACP), federal tribes like the Tunica-Biloxi of Louisiana, numerous individual federal Indian tribal council members, state politicians, historians, anthropologists, academics, and other Indian organizational and tribal leaders. This goes along with thousands of pages of documents attesting to the Indian heritage of the community to include census, military, church, and educational records. The Weaver School (the predecessor of today's tribal Calcedeaver Elementary School) appears in the Library of Congress as an "Indian school, built by Indian labor." The school was established with federal funds by the federal government for the MOWA Choctaw community in 1835, five years after the removal of the majority of the Choctaw to Indian Territory (now Oklahoma). The same surnames of attendees are present today within the contemporary MOWA Choctaw community.

In 1993, a supreme court of South Dakota case recognized the MOWA Choctaw as "a federal tribe for the purposes of the Indian Child Welfare Act," making the MOWA Choctaw the only tribe in the nation not on the federal register to exercise this right exclusive to federal tribes.

The Alabama House of Representatives and the Senate have also passed resolutions affirming the sovereignty of the MOWA Band of Choctaw Indians. One such resolution declares that "all federal and state Acts and Judicial decisions pertaining to Choctaw Indians are reaffirmed and declaring that all state and county agencies shall be bound by those federal and state Acts and Judicial decisions."

Given this evidence, it isn't surprising that Vine Deloria Jr. (Standing Rock Sioux), the most well known Indian author and academic in contemporary Indian history, stated that "the MOWA are and have always been a self-governing community following the ancestral traditions. . . . Give the MOWA Choctaws a hand and let's get this recognition problem solved once and for all."

Despite all of this support, however, the MOWA Choctaw petition for federal recognition was denied. In 2004, former assistant secretary of Indian Affairs Kevin Gover (Pawnee), who was involved in this decision after only two days on the job, apologized for his involvement and admitted the denial was a mistake in congressional testimony regarding the problems with the federal acknowledgment process and in which he offered suggestions for amendments. In fact, efforts to successfully petition for federal recognition were thwarted by neighboring federal tribes in the region, such as the Mississippi Choctaw and Poarch Creek, who feared a possible gaming competitor in their midst.

In June 2013, I was invited by Assistant Secretary of Indian Affairs Kevin Washburn to the Department of the Interior in Washington, D.C., to speak to these issues and others related to the few historic "nonfederal" tribes who attended the Indian boarding school system. This invitation provided an audience consisting of the heads of the assistant secretary's office, the Bureau of Indian Affairs, and the Bureau of Indian Education. Three weeks later, through the efforts of many people over countless years, a revised federal recognition process was announced that hopes to eliminate the political dealings of the current acknowledgment workings and which will enable the MOWA Choctaw another avenue for recognition. Strangely enough, in the original MOWA Choctaw petition, the BIA stated that the Indian boarding school records, language tapes, and intermarriage records were mysteriously "received out of time and not available for consideration in the petition." After twelve congressional bills, multiple appeals through the BIA process, and a federal lawsuit whose merits were never heard as it was politically buried through a "statute of limitations" decision, the MOWA Choctaw are getting closer to our desired goal of equity.

For the few who have continued to fight against our inevitable recognition (all of whom have gaming interests in our region), they are simply the proverbial caricature of former Alabama governor George Wallace standing before the schoolhouse doors knowing that an era is coming to an end, but still gasping for one last breath. Unfortunately, that "last breath" is a telling and powerful piece of political and economic positioning that also manifests as a form of racism.

Over the years I have visited and fellowshipped with a great number of historic "nonfederal" tribes situated in the eastern and southern regions of the United States who endure the "elephant in the room" scenario. Through this experience I have noticed this telling and almost insurmountable hurdle, which is often silently acknowledged but rarely publicly spoken about. On one exceptional occasion thirty-eight years ago, this silence was broken.

In 1978, Terry Anderson and Kirke Kickingbird (Kiowa Tribe of Oklahoma) were hired by the NCAI to research the federal recognition issue and present a paper on their findings to the National Conference on Federal Recognition, which was held in Nashville, Tennessee. Their paper, *An Historical Perspective on the Issue of Federal Recognition and Non-recognition,"* closed with the following statement:

> The reasons that are usually presented to withhold recognition from tribes are 1) that they are racially tainted with the blood of African tribes-men or 2) greed, for newly recognized tribes will share in the appropriations for services given to the Bureau of Indian Affairs. The names of justice, mercy, sanity, common sense, fiscal responsibility, and rationality can be presented just as easily on the side of those advocating recognition.[14]

Of fifty-five continuous, identifiable, cohesive Indian communities in the eastern and southern regions of the United States (of whom I have intimate knowledge of), it was found that of the twenty-nine federally recognized entities, all but six were found to have been listed in historical records as having mixed-white ancestry. In the remaining six (all of whom battled the BIA more so than the other twenty-three), as well as twenty-six more that were not federally recognized, it was found that all had some perceived or real association in historical accounts to have some measure of mixed-black ancestry. As the BIA is run by whites, mixed-white Indians, and a smaller number of racially identifiable Indians, with few black employees or employees of mixed-black and Indian descent, it is clear that recognition is not about one's racial proximity to Indian, but rather one's racial distance from black. This is entrenched racism and the most obvious double standard one can imagine rearing its head in the Indian political spectrum. While tribes that are perceived or do have some black ancestry, as well as significant Indian ancestry, are being denied, tribes with large amounts of white ancestry and less significant Indian heritage have been acknowledged.

This racial animosity in the federal recognition process continues. In 1995, Lee Fleming, director of the Office of Federal Acknowledgment, agreed with highly controversial statements at a genealogical conference in Alabama which was sponsored by Samford University a year prior to his appointment. A conference attendee, Don Rankin, later recounted:

> Someone brought up the MOWA Choctaw and their attempt at federal recognition. At this stage, several people had gathered around and were talking. [Sharon] Brown [a notable instructor who spoke at the conference] responded in an even professional tone of voice that she felt that "they would not be successful." When asked why, she responded that "they had black ancestors" and in her opinion "were not Indian." Mr. Lee Fleming, who was at the time the Tribal Registrar for the Western Band of Cherokee and one of the lecturers, agreed with her. I was shocked at their statements.[15]

As shocking as these statements might have been, they expose a larger issue of the other "elephant in the room"—the one where racially white individuals who enjoy white privileges but also happen to be members of federal tribes run Indian Country. They also control resources and tend to place a few brown tribal members on the fronts of brochures and websites to project an image of racial (and presumably cultural) legitimacy. The issue gets even more complex as some tribes are opting to dis-enroll and subjugate some of their members due to genealogical attacks, which have nothing to do with their long-term social and cultural standings within their respective communities.

Collectively, as a society, we should not support those who attempt to humiliate others as was done to the MOWA Choctaw and countless other tribes. It is one thing to disagree with someone, but it is completely another thing to attempt to humiliate, belittle, and make others' lives only worthy of jokes and criticisms. And it becomes even more ridiculous when the individuals making the negative and demeaning comments are the very personifications of what it is they are attempting to belittle. I learned early in life, as I was surrounded by hustlers, that "what one uses against you is what they most fear themselves." They are typically compensating for their own insecurities related to a lack of an Indian identity of their own through blood, culture, tribal community upbringing, or a combination of all three, by attempting to bury the identity of another.

It seems Jim Crowfeather is still alive and well in Indian Country.

Cedric Sunray is a husband, father of four, and enrolled member of the MOWA Band of Choctaw Indians who was raised on the island of Key West, Florida. As an educator, he has worked at the pre-K, elementary, middle school, high school, and university levels in public, private, group home, youth detention center, inner-city, and reservation settings. His writings appear frequently in various regional and national media outlets and include subject matter from federal recognition/identity politics to issues related to language revitalization and domestic violence in Indian Country.

Cultural Grounding

At the core of Indian identity is culture. It shapes worldviews, defines values, and transmits knowledge and language across generations. Even in the face of great challenges, southern Native people have demonstrated an incredible resilience through their active engagement in cultural maintenance, revitalization, and redefinition. While some communities have been fortunate enough to remain culturally grounded over the past few centuries, others have sought to reclaim their cultural identities and histories—at the individual and community levels. This process is both formal and informal. In some cases it is led by families, groups of elders, or individuals who have a vision. In others, tribal governments have led the charge by establishing and funding specific departments to take on the responsibilities of cultural preservation, language restoration, graves protection, and public education endeavors. While so much has been lost in the way of culture and language across the South—and the nation, for that matter—it is important to celebrate what remains, or is being reclaimed, and the contributors to this chapter offer a good basis from which we can better appreciate this.

Culture bearers hold an important role within their communities as the keepers of knowledge and in the perseverance of cultural practices and lifeways. For example, Cherokee basketweavers from the Eastern Band of Cherokees in North Carolina—like many other tribal communities throughout the region—have successfully maintained the traditional art form by transmitting the knowledge of gathering, processing materials, and weaving to the current generation.[1] Maintaining material culture is not an easy endeavor. It hinges on the level of interest within communities, as well as having access to the natural resources necessary. Brooke Bauer, in her touching tribute piece to her mother entitled "In My Mother's Hands," discusses the potting tradition among the Catawba of South Carolina. She explains how potters like her mother have received tribal support to maintain the tradition in the face of challenges of waning interest and dwindling access to clay holes by launching a recent initiative to increase the number of community potters through classes and apprenticeships. These efforts not only expanded the interest and knowledge base, they also helped to further support an enduring collectors' market that prizes Catawba pottery. Unlike many aspects of material culture, other forms of Indigenous knowledge cannot be collected, held, or even widely shared with outsiders. The Pierite family of the Tunica-Biloxi of Louisiana, for example, are recognized as bearers of language and culture. In their collaborative piece "Nerataya: Spirit of the Deer and Passing the Gifts of the Tunica-Biloxi," we learn how Donna Pierite became a language and culture preservationist for her community and how different members of her family have emulated this responsibility in various ways through their own artistry, storytelling, and singing.

While some traditions have seamlessly endured over time, others have recently been revived. The Seminole of Florida, for example, had lost their flute-playing tradition until it was reintroduced in 1998 at Big Cypress reservation through a seminar led by a Comanche flutist.[2] Similarly, the Choctaw warrior tradition had been eroded as a result of the work of missionaries and the Bureau of Indian Affairs in Mississippi. As Harold Comby explains in "Reawakening Our Warrior Tradition," a whole series of practices surrounding the honoring of Choctaw warriors—or veterans—have been reintroduced into his

Mississippi Choctaw community. A veterans' memorial was also constructed as a way of acknowledging and reinforcing their great respect for the warrior tradition. Across the region, other memorials have also been constructed by Native communities and individuals to honor traditions or mark historically significant moments or places. Just over the border in the neighboring state of Alabama, for example, Yuchi descendant Tom Hendrix constructed a memorial as a way of honoring his great-great-grandmother Te-lah-nay, who was forced from her home in Alabama during the 1830s and moved to Indian Territory (Oklahoma). In an act of bravery and defiance, she then made a five-year-long trek back home to Alabama. Hendrix, as a gesture to commemorate her journey, spent over a quarter century constructing a monument in the form of eight million pounds of stones that range in height from four feet to almost six feet in some spots, making it the largest unmortared wall in the United States. The Wichahpi Commemorative Stone Wall—as it is called—is situated right off of the Natchez Trace Parkway in northern Alabama. Approximately 1.25 miles long, it has been written about in the *New York Times*, is recorded by the Library of Congress, and is visited by several hundred people a week. Hendrix spends his days greeting guests to the memorial wall and sharing stories told to him by his grandmother.[3]

As the first few contributions to this chapter attest, culture can be identified by traditions—whether they manifest in the material form or through practices. However, culture also plays a role in shaping one's identity and worldview through context and connections. Michael "T. Mayheart" Dardar demonstrates this beautifully in his piece, "In the Eye of Isaac," where he addresses the relationship that the Houma of Louisiana have with the land and water, which is the basis of their identity. Through the many natural disasters that they have endured, including devastating hurricanes, that forced them to rebuild time and time again, Dardar explains that the Houma have come to accept it as part of their life-cycle that serves to further ground them in their family and culture. The impact of industrialism and human-generated disasters has really left the "deep scars" that challenge the Houma worldview and way of life.

While Dardar discusses the important connection between culture and land, many of this collection's contributors also discuss the importance of language to culture and identity. For example, Maskoke (Creek) language revitalization advocate Marcus Briggs-Cloud, in "Being the Indians We Were Made to Be," stresses the important role that language plays in "decolonizing lifestyles" in the wake of the "institutionalized oppressive policies," such as removal and segregation, enacted against his ancestors. While he draws upon the knowledge passed down to him through elders, he is also pursuing an academic education to help further define his framework and understanding of how he can contribute to Indigenous language revitalization efforts. In the essay that follows, Marvin "Marty" Richardson describes how his journey has taken a different shape in "Generations within the Circle." Richardson did not grow up speaking his Native language, yet his process of (re)discovering it has been a source of deep connection with his ancestors—a connection that he now shares through powwow songs. Although powwows have only recently emerged among southeastern Native communities, Richardson reveals how they serve an important function in bringing people together, instilling Native pride among groups whose identities were previously oppressed, and offering a way to communicate with the public.[4]

Cultural revitalization and maintenance are most successful when they are community-wide efforts. As a result, many tribal governments throughout the South support and fund specific initiatives, departments, or museums dedicated to culture. Dana Chapman Masters, in "Putting the 'Community' Back into My Jena Choctaw Community," details her role as the Cultural Director and Tribal Historic Preservation Officer for her Louisiana community. In her efforts to "bring the community back together," she oversees programs that reach out to different generations that involve—among other things—language classes, storytelling, and the teaching of traditional art forms. Her office also oversees community events that promote economic stability for Native artisans, helps the Jena Choctaw build strong relationships with the other two federally recognized Choctaw Nations (in Mississippi and Oklahoma), and—like the Haliwa-Saponi described in the previous contribution—promote pride in Indian identity through events that are open to the surrounding non-Indian community. Like Masters, who dedicated her talents and education to work within her own community, Robert Jumper, author of "Finding My Sense of Place in My Ancestral Homeland," has also devoted his professional career to promoting his tribal culture as a member of the Eastern Band of Cherokee Indians Destination Marketing team. "The connection between a person and his sense of place is very strong," Jumper writes, and this comes through clearly in his description of the Cherokee Indian Fair. As a partially tourism-based economy, the Eastern Band of Cherokee reservation is consistently inundated by non-Indians who come to learn more about them. Jumper addresses the balance that must be achieved between sustaining this economic driver through tourism and public education, and the integrity of his culture. Cultural preservation is also an integral part of sovereignty, argues Robert Caldwell in "Native People Should Tell Their Own Stories." As an advocate and Choctaw-Apache tribal leader, Caldwell argues for a sustainable economic and political environment that promotes healthy living and repairs social divisions—both essential to the cultural survival of Native communities.

The final contributions offer two very distinct examples of how southern Native people internalize and negotiate the role of culture and identity on a personal level and within a modern context. Megan Young, in "*Vpuecetv* (To Dream): My Journey to Becoming Tribal Royalty," offers a poignant essay that takes us through her journey as an ambassador for the Poarch Band of Creek Indians of Alabama as the first southern Native person to be crowned Miss Indian World. This experience allowed her to bring more widespread awareness to the existence of southeastern Indian people; yet it also taught her a great deal about herself as she learned to distinguish between the need to "prove" herself as an authentic Native person versus simply "being" the Mvskoke (Creek) person she is. With such a large loss of culture and language across Native communities—on a national scale—many Indian people can relate to Young's experience in choosing to seek a better understanding of their culture and language through research and instruction. But what about the communities and individuals who have been immersed in their Indigenous cultures since birth? As some of the previous contributions demonstrate, there are many efforts to maintain, preserve, and pass down language and tradition. However, as Seminole artist Jessica Osceola demonstrates in "At War with Herself: Artistic Reflections of Culture and Identity," others are engaged in trying to reconcile what she deems a "hybrid culture," which is partly influenced by her Seminole culture and partly by American culture. Osceola demonstrates how culture and identity are fluid as she transforms traditional aesthetics and processes into contemporary artistic forms that make powerful statements about Indigenous stereotypes and cultural appropriation.

The cultural maintenance, revitalization, and redefinition efforts that southern Indian people have engaged in over the past several decades are a testament of strength and resilience. Although much has been lost, the fact that many Native communities still have cultural bearers to help guide and teach the next generation, as well as many others who have devoted their professional lives to their community's cultural health, is nothing short of amazing. Admittedly, it is impossible to adequately capture all of the nuances associated with how culture connects to identity, worldviews, and sovereignty; however, the selections within this chapter offer us a good vantage point from which to gain a deeper appreciation for these issues.

In My Mother's Hands

When invited to contribute a Catawba perspective on the preservation of traditional art forms, I thought immediately of my mother, JoAnn George

Bauer. She is in her seventies and lives on the Catawba Indian Reservation in South Carolina, where she was born and raised. She is a skilled potter, quilter, and basket maker. I would like to focus on the first of her many skills—making and maintaining Catawba Indian pottery. Before I share her story, one must understand Catawbas use specific terminology when talking about pottery.

Catawbas use certain words to express how they collect, make, and describe pottery. They always describe their creation as a "pot" or "pottery," not as a "vessel" or "ceramic." I learned this quickly when I used the term "ceramic" while talking with a group of older Catawba women. One of the women corrected me, saying emphatically, "It's not ceramic, it's pottery." The former label sounds cold and clinical, while the latter term sounds like an object loved and treasured. Indeed, each piece is beloved. The artists put not only hours and days into making a pot; they put their essence or spirit into each piece with their hands and knowledge passed down through generations. In addition, Catawbas refer to the creation of a pot as "making"

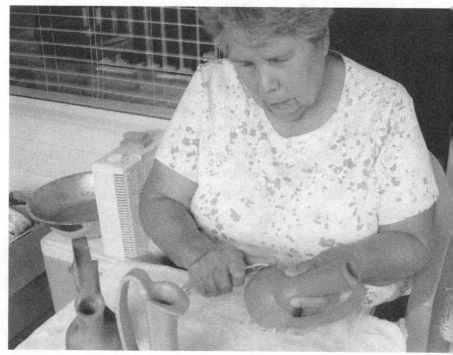

Catawba potter JoAnn George Bauer. (Photo Courtesy of Brooke Bauer.)

or "building" because of the many steps involved in making each piece. Catawbas make pots with their hands using one of two techniques, the pinch or coil method. They never use a wheel. They "burn" pots in an outdoor fire, not a kiln. However, before they begin making pottery, the process begins in the earth with Catawbas collecting clay from local ancestral clay holes, known as clay deposits by scholars.

JoAnn described the lengthy method of collecting and processing clay, a technique her ancestors practiced. When she was a child, she recalled that older Catawba women typically collected clay from clay holes located on the reservation. Walking from their houses to local creeks, they collected small batches of clay in their aprons. Later, men began digging clay from a source located on Catawbas' ancestral land but away from the reservation, which is how JoAnn receives her clay. When she receives clay, she usually gives her male relative a piece of her finished pottery in return for the gift of unprocessed clay.

Catawbas' method of processing clay has changed little over the years. The main exception is they now have manufactured tools to help prepare the clay. After collecting large, hard lumps of clay, potters follow several steps that prepare the clay for use. The clay must soak in water for a number of days until it becomes a watery-like substance. Using another container, potters strain or screen the clay to remove grit, sand, and roots. They allow the strained clay to dry for about a week until it reaches a pliable form similar to Play-Doh. Catawbas have followed these steps for hundreds of years. In the past, JoAnn's ancestors used a wooden mallet to break up the clay, their hands to remove trash from the clay, and tempered pots to soak and dry the clay. Today, they use hammers and plastic containers when processing clay.

As with clay preparation, the firing method that JoAnn practices has changed little over the centuries. Her ancestors burned pots using a fire pit, heating pots gradually over a period of hours. JoAnn burns her pots in a similar fashion, but modernity has influenced how Catawbas start the heating process. In the late twentieth and early twenty-first centuries, Catawbas began the burn process using the modern oven to heat pots slowly. Once pots reach a desired temperature, potters carefully transfer pots to an outdoor fire. JoAnn emphasizes that contemporary Catawbas rarely use a fire pit. Instead, to make their work less demanding, they reuse items like charcoal grills when burning pots.

Every Catawba Indian who makes pottery has her or his own bag or box of shaping, scraping, and smoothing tools. Some Catawbas are fortunate enough to receive heirloom tools previously owned by a close family member, tools that symbolize the continuity of the Catawba pottery tradition. Many years ago, JoAnn's mother gave her a knife and rubbing stone used by her maternal grandfather, Early George. Although Early rarely made pottery, most Catawbas recognized his extraordinary skills in scraping and rubbing pots. With the knife, he carefully scraped his wife's pots so thin they rang like crystal. Using the rubbing stone, he burnished her pots until they gleamed like polished wood. In addition to an array of other implements, JoAnn uses the two tools each time she builds a piece of pottery, a skill learned from her mother.

JoAnn began making pottery twenty-five years ago under the tutelage of her mother, Evelyn Brown George, who was a noted Catawba potter herself. Like JoAnn, Evelyn learned how to make pots from her mother, Edith Harris Brown, who learned from her mother and grandmother. Like these women, most Catawbas learn to make or build pottery from an older female relative.

Apprenticing under her mother in a class held at the Catawba Cultural Preservation Project, the tribe's cultural center, JoAnn learned to make turtles—the first and easiest clay effigy to make. Her memory of working in the clay her first time sounded much like my own experience. Her mother was "strict" she recalled. "If you didn't do it right, she made you tear it up. If it didn't suit her, she'd tear it up and make you start all over." Her mother, who taught many Catawbas how to make pottery, used such occasions as teaching moments for the next generation. Each Catawba who works with clay learns that clay was and is a valued resource, and the pots are symbols of Catawba culture. The lesson that JoAnn and other Catawbas learn is that one works diligently and carefully on their pots to make them "right," avoiding any wasted clay and poorly constructed pots because once burned, there is no going back.

When asked about her fondest memory related to Catawba pottery, JoAnn told a story of how her family used to travel to Ohio every summer and lived in a cabin at the Schoenbrunn Village. In the 1930s and 1940s, a group of Catawbas stayed at the historic village during the summer months making and selling pottery to tourists. Catawbas were familiar with making such trips to sell their pottery. As itinerant potters, they traveled throughout South Carolina bartering pottery. In fact, as a young girl, JoAnn remembered Catawba women making such trips to the town of Rock Hill. With sacks full of pots slung over their backs, they walked the 20-mile roundtrip from the Catawba Reservation to Winthrop College, the present-day Winthrop University, selling and bartering their wares. Today, Catawbas continue traveling to sell pottery, often to powwows, conferences, art shows, and craft fairs.

JoAnn maintains the tradition of pottery not only through making the art form but also in passing her knowledge about pottery down to other Catawbas. At the Catawba Senior Center, she explained, Catawba seniors work in the clay teaching one another unfamiliar potting techniques. Older Catawba women and men spend hours together making pots but also socializing, telling stories about their lives, and discussing genealogy. JoAnn has also taught her daughter, grandchildren, nephews, and nieces how to make pots. She believes that every Catawba has the opportunity to learn how to make pottery, but the main challenge for contemporary Catawba potters is the limited number of clay holes. She thinks the situation might be resolved if someone conducted further research in locating formerly visited reservation clay holes. However, she cautioned, "probably nobody remembers at this date" where the clay holes are located. Finally, she emphasized that even as things and people change, Catawba pottery is still a traditional art form.

Brooke Bauer is a citizen of the Catawba Indian Nation and a Ph.D. candidate in the Department of History at the University of North Carolina, Chapel Hill. Her research analyzes the day-to-day lives of Catawba women while concentrating on one woman—Sally New River. She focuses on how Catawba women of the eighteenth century adapted, promoted, and preserved their society's culture through kinship, land ownership, and material culture.

Nerataya: Spirit of the Deer and Passing the Gifts of the Tunica-Biloxi

The Pierite family sits in the den of their Marksville, Louisiana, home. Once displaced by Hurricane Katrina, they settled just outside the Tunica-

Biloxi tribal lands. The newest member of the family, Leilani Mora, plays with various toys and chatters while running. Each family member takes turns cheering on Leilani in English, Spanish, and Tunica. Leilani's mom, Elisabeth Pierite-Mora, is busy at work with her studies to complete a degree at Northwestern State University in Natchitoches, Louisiana. Visiting home from New England is Leilani's uncle, or "*tio*," Jean-Luc Pierite. Leilani's grandfather, Michael Pierite, laughs as he watches the young girl run around the coffee table and chase the indoor cats. Donna Pierite leads all the applause and launches into a recently Tunica-translated version of "Head, Shoulders, Knees, and Toes."

"It wasn't until my grandmother took me on the bus to Jena that I re-met my husband." Donna begins the story of her journey as a "language and culture bearer for the family." The retired French and Spanish teacher has a continuing second career as a language and culture preservationist for the Tunica-Biloxi Tribe. "We took a trip on the bus to go to the Choctaw Indian Days. I remember a conversation between my grandmother and my soon to be father-in-law. They both sat down and she told him, 'Joe, we're the same. You and I.'"

Two figures feature prominently in the passing down of the oral history to this generation of Pierites. Michael's father, Joseph Pierite Jr., was the first Tribal Chairman of the Tunica-Biloxi Tribe, as well as an accomplished artisan. Donna's grandmother, Julia Descant Normand, was a woman of Biloxi ancestry. Both individuals left the central Louisiana tribal lands to pursue job opportunities and a better life in the greater New Orleans metropolitan area. Joseph earned a living through construction, which he learned in Orange, Texas. Julia worked in the hospitals of New Orleans.

"My grandmother would carry a parasol to protect herself from the sun. She used bleaching cream to keep a fair complexion. One day during the times of integration, she called me into her room. 'Give me your hand,' she said." Donna holds out her left hand and begins to massage the top of it with her right fingers. As she voices her grandmother, she changes into a French patois. "We not white. We not black. We're beige. My daddy was Indian." Donna keeps a record of similar episodes from her life in a collection she calls "Tales from the Spirits at Work."

It is through Julia that Donna credits the family's maintenance of the clan tradition. Donna recounts an episode from the Marksville State Historic Site, or "Old Indian Park." A demonstrator at the park, Charlie Hunger, displayed several remains of a deer, including skin and bones. The skin was tattered from years of educational use. The demonstrator picked up the deer's femur and cracked it. Instantly, Donna felt a connection between the deer remains and her grandmother. Julia was a beautiful woman, and at that point she was bedridden due to various complications with her legs. Donna's brother, Steven Madere, who was also present, also felt the connection. Donna felt a shortness of breath, and she needed to tell the deer story as passed to her by Julia.

> We are Deer Clan. My grandmother once shared this story with me. There were two women in the house and one man. The older woman was cooking. The man became hungry, and he set out to go hunting deer. The older woman said, "Oh no. You don't have to go out hunting because in a little while there will be deer just outside." Sure enough, a little later on there was a deer just outside. The man went to go shoot the deer, but the younger woman told him, "Stop!" You see, it was the older woman. She had turned into a deer. For that reason, we don't kill or eat the deer.

Joseph Pierite Jr. is fondly remembered by the family as passing on gifts of stories, songs, and tribal art. Donna's sister, Stephanie Madere Escude, and their brother are regular exhibitors and vendors at the tribe's "Education Days," which are held prior to the Annual Tunica-Biloxi Powwow in Marksville at the Chief Joseph Alcide Pierite Sr. dance grounds. Two days each year are set aside by the Powwow Committee and its chairman, John Barbry, to educate local schoolchildren about Native culture, dances, and art. During this time, the schoolchildren, Native and non-Native, from the outer community come and participate in the celebration free of charge. Stephanie's art is designed to be affordable for all the kids gathered. Often, a child will come to her table with little or no pocket money. Stephanie sets aside trinkets and necklaces for these children. As she says, "That way, no one leaves empty handed." All of her materials are recycled from friends or thrift stores. When she comes up with an original design, Stephanie always remembers to thank "Papa Joe." The family further contributes to the education of the outer community by fulfilling requests from local schools, elementary through the university-level, throughout the year. Each presentation includes story, song, and dance. Through teaching vocables in songs, as well as social dances, all audiences are invited to learn and participate.

Elisabeth is likewise inspired by her grandfather. Her beadwork includes ornate medallions that were once on display at the state capitol in Baton Rouge for a "First Louisianans" exhibit. She maintains close relations with family friend Hiram "Pete" Gregory, who is a professor of anthropology and archaeology at Northwestern State University, as he advises her on her studies. Elisabeth frequently contacts museums, libraries, and universities to search for family and tribal artifacts.

Jean-Luc continues on in the footsteps of Joseph (Papa Joe) by maintaining the storytelling tradition. "We would take trips to the reservations, each summer. We would visit the Mississippi Choctaw and Marksville." This was partly because Fannie Lou Ben Pierite, Michael's mother and Jean-Luc and Elisabeth's grandmother, is a member of the Mississippi Band of Choctaws from the Standing Pine community.

> I remember that he [Papa Joe] was so proud of his truck. It was a Dodge Ram with a really detailed ram hood ornament. Each time he would pass a car on the highway, he would joke with me saying, "Watch, Doo. That old ram is going to eat them up." One time, Papa Joe turned down the radio and began to tell me a story, "Sometimes, early in the morning, if you have a little boy in the house, you gonna get a knock at the door. I can even remember sometimes you'd hear him scratch on the screen. It's this half-man. He's got one arm, one leg, and he lives up in the trees. And if there's a little boy in the house, that half-man will come take him away. But you don't have to be scared, because he's gonna teach you how to wrestle. And if you can take him, and throw him down, you gonna be the best doctor in the world."

Donna remembers Joseph as a mentor. "At his house in Kenner, my father-in-law had his workshop in the shed in the backyard. One day, I went to go talk to him and he was busy making necklaces. He looked up from his work, and said, 'It's gonna be you. One day, all of this will be yours.' I looked around at all the leather straps and beads. Is that what he meant? He said, 'You're the one, Donna, and I want you to teach the kids.'"

Later on, Joseph would call on her to demonstrate the tribe's corn ceremony. "He woke me up early in the morning during the Fête du Blé. He told me to come with him. When we got to the place, I noticed it was the men who gathered, including Chairman Earl Barbry Sr. 'Y'all know this is

Community activists Donna Pierite, Elisabeth Pierite-Mora, and Jean-Luc Pierite. (Photo Courtesy of Jean-Luc Pierite.)

my daughter-in-law. She's gonna be here and watch us as we do it.' Since then, it has been our family to carry on the ceremony each July 4th." A parishioner of St. Joseph's Catholic Church in Marksville, Donna continues the integration of the historic French missionaries' role within the community. In addition to tribal songs, she says the Lord's Prayer in French.

She is also a cantor at church and sings in tribal regalia during the annual powwow. She includes Choctaw translations of "Amazing Grace" and "How Great Thou Art" in her hymns in honor of the family's Mississippi Choctaw and Biloxi-Choctaw roots. Michael's paternal grandmother, Rose Jackson Pierite, was Biloxi-Choctaw from the Indian Creek tribal community near Alexandria, Louisiana.

Presently, the family continues weekly story and song demonstrations at the Tunica-Biloxi-owned resort, Paragon Casino. They also work with the owner of Alligator Park, Terry Rogers, to entertain and educate through feeding shows that feature animals that live in the atrium pond near the hotel's lobby. Leilani often chimes in during these shows by chattering along with the singing. In the den, Leilani stops her running and points to a hand drum displayed on a book shelf. The family fetches the drum for her and cheers her on as she starts beating a rhythm. "This is what is most important to me." Donna looks around the den. "A roof over our head, food on our table, and family."

The Pierite family currently collaborates with Tulane University in New Orleans, along with Brenda Lintinger and John Barbry, as part of the Tunica Language Project in an effort to revitalize the Tunica language. With over thirty years as a language teacher (French, Spanish, ESL), Donna continues her mission as the culture bearer of the family. Elisabeth's daughter, Leilani, is the newest addition and marks a shift in roles as the children now become teachers of the next generation.

Reawakening our Warrior Tradition

We come from a long line of veterans or *"Chata tuska"* (Choctaw Warriors). Stories of uncles, Grandpa, and Dad serving in wars from World War I to the Korean War were instilled in our family stories. One of my brothers later served in Vietnam, and I saw firsthand what war will do to a person and his family. He spent one year in Vietnam, but spent the next thirty years trying to recover from it. One uncle was drafted during World War II but failed the physical. He volunteered and was killed in action. Our paternal grandpa served in World War I without being a citizen of the United

States. A federal law eventually gave citizenship to our people in 1924. These stories influenced me to be the person I became as an adult.

One day in 1968 I came home and found a vehicle with a U.S. government tag in our driveway with two sharply dressed individuals. My brother, who had just finished his school finals, was carrying a small handbag and being escorted to the car. They left, and I asked Mom what was going on. With a concerned look on her face, she said, "David is going to *bina*." I knew that *bina* stands for "camp" in our language, but didn't know that it also meant "boot camp." My brother was going to be a U.S. Marine. The common saying that "he went to Vietnam on his senior trip" really happened to my brother. Two of my other brothers later became Marines also, one sister retired from the Air Force, and another sister served more than ten years in the regular army and National Guard.

As I got older, the chance to help out with our Veteran's Day powwow arose, and I became part of the powwow committee. I recall one time when the committee made a decision not to feed the dancers since food vendors were going to set up, and some committee members thought, "they can buy food themselves." I went to my mother's home and asked her if this was right, and she said it was not the "Choctaw way." She said dancers and singers come a long way to dance for us so "we are supposed to feed them." That year we had the biggest feast we have ever had. My mother was our "spoon keeper" for the powwow and continued teaching us traditional ways until she died a few years ago. I remember she told us that when a solider is going away, as well as coming home from boot camp or war, you are supposed to have a feast in his or her honor. She was truly a "war mother." Sadly, back in 1968, my brother David did not have a going away feast because he did not tell us he was going into the service.

Through stories, traditional teachings, and research, I later learned that our tribe had many traditions for *Tuska* (warriors/veterans). Our adult men got their traditional names based on the deeds done in battle, and only the bravest and most honest men wore eagle feathers. A victory song and over ten war dance songs were recorded by Francis Densmore, ethnographer from the Smithsonian Institution. Red was the color of war, and our stickball game was a way of preparing, as well as a substitution, for war. We were taught in Bureau of Indian Affairs (BIA) schools that Choctaws rarely went to war, but in actuality our tribe had deep war traditions. Due to missionaries and BIA policies of assimilation, most of these customs were against the law,

The Mississippi Choctaw honor their veterans with a procession. (Photo Courtesy of Harold Comby via Tammy Greer and Choctaw Communications.)

frowned upon, and discouraged. As traditional people who refused to walk on the Trail of Tears, we kept our ways private within family settings.

Our warrior tradition is being reawakened on our reservation with the powwow, a veterans' parade, the reestablishment of the eagle staff and song, and the building of a veterans' memorial. Our young men and women are properly being welcomed home after proudly serving our country.

Harold Comby is a member of the Mississippi Band of Choctaw Indians and lives on the Choctaw Reservation near Philadelphia, Mississippi. He received a degree in social work from Jackson State University and has worked in law enforcement for over thirty years. He is currently the Deputy Director of Choctaw Public Safety and spends much of his free time serving as a powwow emcee in Mississippi and across other southern states.

Te-lah-nay's Wall

"We honor our people with stones."

These words were spoken to me by an elderly Yuchi woman at a gathering nearly thirty years ago. And these were the words that inspired me to build a wall memorializing my great-great-grandmother's long, solitary walk from the Indian Nations in Oklahoma back to her home in north Alabama.

My great-great-grandmother's name was Te-lah-nay. Her people were the Yuchi, who lived along the banks of the Tennessee River. Along with other Indian tribes they called it *nun nuh sae*, the Singing River, because they believed a young woman who lived in the river sang songs to them and protected them. When Te-lah-nay listened to the rivers and streams in the Indian Nations she heard no songs, so over a period of roughly five years she traveled back to the Singing River.

When I was a little boy, my grandmother would wrap me up in an old quilt and tell me wonderful stories of "How Brother Rabbit Lost His Tail," "How Sister Hummingbird Came to Be," and, my favorite, "The Woman in the River." I asked my grandmother where the stories came from, and she said from my great-great-grandmother.

My grandmother was very good with herbal medicines. As I got older, she told me that this knowledge also came from my great-great-grandmother.

My grandmother waited until I was old enough to understand, and then she told me Te-lah-nay's story.

In 1839, as part of the Indian Removal, Te-lah-nay and her sister were in a group of Native people forcibly taken from Lauderdale County, Alabama, to the Indian Nations. The soldiers in charge hung metal tags around their necks. My great-great-grandmother was No. 59; her sister was No. 60. In Oklahoma, the two young girls and an elderly Yuchi man were placed with the Creek people at Muscogee.

Te-lah-nay spent a winter there; then one spring morning she slipped away and started on a journey home that would take her roughly five years. She returned with her knowledge of the medicines, her stories, and the No. 59 tag. She said, "We all thought that the Shiny Buttons had changed our names, and I thought I might need my new name when I got home."

In about 1844, Te-lah-nay met my great-great-grandfather, Jonathan Levi Hipp. They couldn't marry legally, but accepted one another as man and wife and settled in a remote place called Chigger Ridge on the Alabama/Tennessee state line. People began to come to her for her medicines. Among them was Wiley B. Edwards, a Methodist minister and teacher whom she cured of "a bad case of yellow toes and a disorder of the middle." In return, he wrote a 168-page journal about her journey, her stories, and her knowledge of medicines.

In the early 1930s, my grandmother's sister went to Oklahoma to try and gather some information about my great-great-grandmother. She first went to Tahlequah, then to Muscogee, then to Sapulpa, where she found that the Yuchi were the tribe to which Te-lah-nay belonged.

Almost seventy years later I began having a recurring dream of an old woman at the river's edge, beckoning me with her arm raised. My wife suggested that the woman could be my great-great-grandmother, wanting me to tell her story. In 2000, we published *If the Legends Fade*, based on family history from my grandmother and my recollections from Wiley B. Edwards's journal. At The Wall and from our website, the book has sold almost 11,000 copies and has carried Te-lah-nay's story all over the world.

"We honor our people with stones."

About twenty-three years ago, on our property at Threets Crossroads in northwest Alabama, I began to build a memorial to Te-lah-nay, one stone at a time, perhaps one for each step she made on her long walk. Weighing my truck at a nearby cotton gin, I found that a load of stones weighed 900 pounds. As of today, Te-lah-nay's Wall is approximately 1.25 miles long and contains more than 8 million pounds of stones.

The Wall symbolizes both Te-lah-nay's journey to Oklahoma and her return home. It draws visitors almost daily, sometimes dozens and other times only a few. Most find it to be a spiritual place, a place of peace, renewal, and inspiration. My hope is that it honors and commemorates for all time the life of a courageous woman, my great-great-grandmother.

Tom Hendrix by the side of "The Wall." (Photo Courtesy of Tom and Doreen Hendrix.)

Tom Hendrix is a lifelong resident of northwest Alabama and a retired autoworker. Husband, father, grandfather, and great-grandfather, at heart he still is the little boy who, in a game of cowboys and Indians, never chose to be a cowboy.

In the Eye of Isaac

It seems so long ago, those days on the water with my dad trawling for shrimp in the lakes, bays, and bayous of our beloved homeland. The two seasons—one in May and the other in August—were the most important and productive times in the seasonal cycle of the Houma People during my adolescent years in the late 1960s and early 1970s. Second to these was the winter trapping season when we roamed the marshlands in search of nutria, muskrat, and otter.

Through the teachings and example of my father I learned how the land and water provided for untold generations of our people. Though we lived in a modern world, I would still be taught the traditional medicine plants, how to construct a blowgun from the elderberry stalk, and how to build a home from the leaves of the palmetto. These skills continue to keep me grounded years after my father has walked on to the other side.

All this served to make real to me the basis of the Houmas' relationship to land and water, the very basis of my identity as Houma. It is the connection we have as a people to one another and to this homeland that feeds us, cares for us, and has given birth to us that make us the people we are.

As children of the land and water we have known hurricanes and their effects better than most. They are a part of our life cycle, ingrained in our storied past and alive in our dynamic present.

In my own life story, Katrina was the third hurricane in which I would lose my home and most of my belongings. The first two, Betsy in 1965 and Camille in 1969, I would experience as a youth, but the lessons were well learned. My

Damage inflicted on Dardar's home from Hurricane Katrina. (Photo Courtesy of Michael T. Mayheart Dardar.)

dad would admonish me, "You can't take it with you when you die," emphasizing that material possessions could easily come and go with the storms and that I needed to be grounded in family and loved ones. I saw firsthand, as a young man, how to start over and rebuild; for my people, the land and water were always there to provide a foundation to rebuild on.

I would learn a much different lesson as an adult, a lesson made real by my experience with Katrina. My eyes were open and I saw clearly how a century of unchecked economic development had devastated my homeland long before Katrina made landfall a few miles from my home. Levees, jetties, oil fields, and pipeline canals had left deep scars and substantially reduced the capacity of the land and water to protect, provide, and heal. By 2005, the foundation upon which we had rebuilt ourselves time and time again was almost completely gone. Now every storm that comes takes away more than can be restored; the ground beneath our feet is literally washing away.

So with the memory of Katrina still fresh in my mind, I sit in the eye of Hurricane Isaac and I tremble. I don't fear the power of the wind and rain; I've known them my whole life. Rather, I fear the insatiable appetite of colonial capitalism that continues to devour the homeland that I love. When the skies clear tomorrow Isaac will be a memory, but the realities of industrial avarice and the coastal land loss it brings will still be here with us.

They call Louisiana the "Sportsman's Paradise," which, for me, always brings to mind the lyrics of one of my favorite Eagles songs: "You call some place paradise, kiss it good-bye."

Editor's Note: This essay first appeared in *Indian Country Today Media Network*, August 30, 2012.

Michael "T. Mayheart" Dardar was born in the Houma Indian settlement below Golden Meadow, Louisiana. He served for sixteen years on the United Houma Nation Tribal Council (retired in October 2009). Currently he works with Bayou Healers, a community-based group advocating for the needs of coastal Indigenous communities in south Louisiana.

Being the Indians We Were Made to Be

One of the most vivid and meaningful memories I have among elders in my family is a moment with my great-grandfather's sister, Aunt Belle Cloud, a Maskoke woman who died several years ago at the age of ninety-six. We visited her on many occasions, but I recall one special visit when I was thirteen years old. Following my granddaddy Colbert's funeral services, my father and I decided to join Aunt Belle for a lunch meal since she was unable to attend the funeral. In her older age, Aunt Belle could not hear well, so she often shouted in conversation in order to hear her own voice. Eager to pose a multitude of culturally related inquires about her childhood, I proceeded to ask about some particular Maskoke traditions using both Maskoke and English vocabulary. She quickly placed her hand over her mouth as though no one would hear her loud words echo throughout the dining space, interjecting, "Boy, don't you know you don't talk like that in public . . . they'll send us to Oklahoma!" I started to chuckle, thereupon finding my father's elbow in my side, subtly commanding I cease the increasing laughter. When we returned to the car, he explained that after Aunt Belle's mother passed away at a young age, she was raised by her father and maternal grandparents, who lived during the latter part of Indian Removal and thus continually embraced a legitimate fear of being removed to Indian Territory, just as many of her grandparents' and great-grandparents' siblings had been.

Moreover, my father explained that during segregation, Aunt Belle and my great-grandparents were made to use "colored" bathrooms and drink from "colored" fountains, and were prohibited from attending white or black schools. Considering the ambivalence white people had about Indigenous Peoples in the South, Aunt Belle lived her entire life with a genuine anxiety of potential displacement. Interestingly, I often hear rhetoric spouted in the mainstream like "that was so long ago . . . when are you Indians going to just get over it?" I maintain, however, that I am only a young man, and in my own lifetime I witnessed the psychological damage of my own kin, wounds that are discursively traced to institutionalized oppressive policies enacted against my ancestors through mechanisms like Indian Removal and segregation.

From firsthand encounters with overwhelming injustice, my family has long embraced resentment toward the world around them, often turning to substances and finding themselves in abusive relationships with their spouses and children alike. These unhealthy character types, molded by oppressive environments, have unquestionably been transmitted to my generation, for which I persevere to break the cycle. The theme in Aunt Belle's story is not an uncommon one among Indigenous families in the South.

But it is a story that belongs to me and my family. More important, though, the story does not end with Aunt Belle's testimony of devastation.

Regularly hearing accounts of discrimination among my people in the South, I become a bit discouraged; many have allowed their identity as an Indigenous person to be defined solely by the oppressor, the racist, the colonizer. In conversation, I try to gently posit that African Americans, women, and those from the LGBTQ communities are also discriminated against. Like them, we have experienced discrimination because we are different, not because we are Indigenous. Indeed, discrimination is unarguably a legitimate contributor to our identity today, but it is only one facet of our postcolonial narrative. That is to say that what makes us Maskoke is not our victimization, but rather that we have our own unique language, cosmology, ontology, and set of cultural traditions that we have inherited from our ancestors and that evolved in accordance with the sacred. These elements of Maskoke life are separate and distinct from all other People's, revealed to us and made for communal participation and interaction with such elements so that we might employ them to acquire and maintain wellness within our communities. Perhaps it is an immense challenge, but we must be confronted with the question of whether we are merely descendants of Maskoke People from a distant historical past or, conversely, if we are the embodiment of a living Maskoke identity.

I remain dedicated to the communal cause, and thus I am uncomfortable writing about the self. Therefore, as I unfold a piece of my life journey here in written form, I hope it is conveyed in a humble way. Growing up, it never crossed my mind that I would be involved in Indigenous rights work, let alone that I would become a language revitalization advocate. Like most children who perceive much of the world around them as a flawless reality, I thought the Maskoke world was perfectly functional and semipristine, and I naively conceived that everyone spoke Maskoke and practiced Maskoke traditions. Since my father's Maskoke People are a matrilineal society and my mother is white, I do not have a clan. Provoked by a somewhat reasonable prejudice from my peers on account of my not having a clan, I cannot remember a time that I have not been self-conscious of my inherent cultural shortcomings. Moreover, these insecurities have long postured notions that I am perhaps too inadequate to ever make a significant contribution to a society long exemplary of tenacity and one that had seemingly managed to preserve long-standing cultural traditions and language for millennia before my existence. To my disappointment, the picture I imagined as a child has been altered in my adulthood. I now acknowledge that the cultural and linguistic continuity of Maskoke People is unequivocally threatened.

Over a decade ago, I entered into what I believe to be my life's vocation in the realm of Indigenous language revitalization work. When I was eighteen years old, a scholar of Southeast Indigenous languages, Jack Martin, offered to take me to a linguistics conference at the University of Alabama with the hope of encouraging me to become interested in language revitalization. There, I found myself intimidated by non-Indigenous scholars who knew more about my own language than I did. Jack also introduced me to the late Maskoke language preservationist Margaret McKane Mauldin, who invited me to come to the University of Oklahoma to study, where she expressed that she could teach me how to teach the language. Having lived in a context where language was used daily, but not considering myself a speaker proficient enough to impact the survival of a dying language, I was naturally apprehensive. Nevertheless, the following year I entered the University of Oklahoma and found myself among a minority community of Indigenous language advocates. I became more cognizant of just how dependent on language our traditional ceremonies are—whereas in my youth, I took for granted the gift of language that elders possessed and executed in order to ensure ceremonial efficacy. I also came to understand that elders would not live forever, nor would the Maskoke language.

At the age of twenty-four, having a more comprehensive articulation of the intricacies of intentional language work and experience in the struggle to save my own language, I was invited to address the United Nations on the importance of Indigenous language revitalization following increasing attention to global language preservation in light of the United Nations Educational, Scientific and Cultural Organization's (UNESCO) report that 90 percent of the world's languages are expected to disappear by the end of the twenty-first century. Subsequently, I was afforded the privilege of visiting some of the most efficacious language revitalization endeavors worldwide to witness firsthand pedagogy and curriculum at work in Aotearoa (New Zealand), Hawaii, Alaska, Peru, Brazil, Greenland, Senegal, Philippines, and many other places all over this Turtle Island. Some programs have proven successful in producing fluent speakers more so than others. In my travels, I found a common thread among the most effective language projects—that is, the inextricable link between language work and other cultural revitalization efforts. More specifically, this includes a resurgence of agriculture, aquaculture, ecological sustainability, traditional diet, sovereignty assertion, ceremonial revival, and cosmological reconstruction. While observing these contexts, I regularly maintained both written and mental notes with the intention of one day materializing a similar holistic vision for my own People.

In the Maskoke case, we are not afforded the time to await unborn generations to assume the responsibility and task of language and cultural revitalization work. On the contrary, considering that there exists no current model of language instruction producing fluent speakers in the world, the Maskoke language is ascending on an irrevocable route to extinction, projected to perish within the next two to three decades; therefore, this reality inevitably debilitates any opportunity for language acquisition among the emerging generation.

With mentoring support from a few individuals, namely the Rev. Dr. Rosemary McCombs Maxey, my relative and Maskoke language advocate, I pursued further Western education. Completing a master's degree in theology at Harvard Divinity School and currently working on a Ph.D. in ecology at the University of Florida, such intellectual and educational environments have revealed the tools I need to construct a larger holistic paradigm in which language could flourish in conjunction with other areas of concern, such as proliferating domestic violence, food sovereignty issues, ceremonial fragmentation, and poor housing for the elderly. I sought to assemble a small intentional community of Maskoke individuals interested in reviving village life among our People. Now, we are in the process of materializing this community situated in the central region of what is commonly and colonially known as Alabama. The village community has been named *Ekvn-Yefolecv*, which implicitly embodies a double entendre: returning to the earth, and returning to our homelands. *Ekvn-Yefolecv* is committed to exemplifying the nexus of Maskoke traditional lifeways and widespread contemporary ecological sustainability techniques. This includes, but is not limited to: Maskoke language revitalization, traditional worldview and cosmology, organic agriculture and aquaculture, renewable energy sources, ethnobotanical conservation and knowledge preservation, resurgence of endangered native animal species, and the rehabilitation of at-risk Indigenous youth.

Language is the gateway to embodying and embracing any given worldview in its most authentic form. Considering the endangerment of the language, its revitalization has appropriately become the focal point of the village, thereby strategically securing the sustainability of the language by inherently equipping the rising generation with concepts they need in order to carry this vision forward to the unborn generations. More specifically, this is achieved by establishing a language immersion model where children are schooled in diverse academic disciplines exclusively in the Maskoke language. Therein, the vision and practices of the village get transmitted as second nature through conceptualizing Maskoke worldview *instinctually* by having command of the language. This is, of course, the antithesis of the most commonly found attempt to conceive of our ancestors' lifeways solely through historical anecdotes rendered from a foreign written text instructed by a non-Maskoke teacher. While the majority of Maskoke People today only hear of, in ceremonial contexts and other storytelling spaces, Maskoke philosophies once subscribed to by our ancestors, *Ekvn-Yefolecv's* targeted concepts regarding ecological sustainability are actually embedded deep within the language. Therefore, one's worldview is molded by inheriting these concepts via transmission of them to first-language learners— that is, children—who grow up in a *lived* firsthand experience, thereby awakening the symbiotic correspondence between language, traditional concepts, and tangible lived-experiences. Here, gaps in traditional Indigenous logic, created by colonial fragmentation apparatuses, can finally be bridged.

Since becoming an Indigenous language advocate, I visited Aunt Belle again with the intention of extending a spirit of empathy toward her alarming trauma caused by experiences of oppression. Having been made to feel inferior in a variety of social contexts, Aunt Belle shared that as a child she was ashamed to be a Maskoke person. But as she entered her adult life, Aunt Belle developed sentiments of guilt for ever having adopted shame for her identity. I will never forget her assertion to me: "I'm so proud of you for keeping this language and culture alive in our family. . . . We were not allowed to be the Indians we were made to be. . . . Indians are getting stronger today and that's good." Through absorbing Aunt Belle's personalized anecdotal journey of identity being shaped in relationship to the world around her, I was inadvertently introduced to critical analysis of colonialism in a systematic and generational light. I have come to understand that I am shaped by my ancestors' experiences, as well as by their spiritual presence in my sociocultural consciousness today. I am now partnered to a Maskoke Kvlice woman, Tawna Little, and together we have a son, Nokos-Afvnoke Mekkaneko Cloud, and a daughter, Hemokke Soweke Cloud. Reflection on our families' struggles has elicited a social justice agenda in our lives. We wholeheartedly subscribe to a decolonization framework in guiding us to healthy ways of living as Indigenous persons: Maskoke is the primary language spoken at home. Wearing traditional clothes daily is important to us as an outward way of asserting our identity in the midst of a mainstream culture that upholds ideologies of homogeneity. All other responsibilities take a backseat to ceremonial obligations. Engagement with traditional Maskoke gender constructs, kinship structures, cosmological worldview, and medicinal practices are all nonnegotiable components of home life. We perpetually seek ways to decolonize our lifestyles, for which we turn to language as the key to accessing our traditional worldviews. Today, we do not have to drink from fountains designated by race, nor are we made to use bathrooms apart from anyone else. Fixating our goals on linguistic and cultural liberation, we take advantage of the chance to be the Indians we were made to be. It's just what we have to do.

Marcus Briggs-Cloud, a Maskoke person, is an activist who works to protect the rights of Indigenous Peoples globally. As a musician, Marcus has received two nominations at the Native American Music Awards and in 2012 served as the choir conductor and composer in Rome for the Vatican Canonization Liturgy of the first Native American Catholic Saint, Kateri Tekakwitha. As a scholar, his work intersects ecology, linguistics, liberation theology, postcoloniality, and gender theory.

Generations within the Circle

For the Indigenous Peoples of America, the circle is an enduring symbol of vitality, connectedness, change, and continuity. In a variety of ways I see myself as part of a circle and connected to several generations within the circle, which has guided my journey through life and helped me make decisions about who I want to be as a person and a scholar. I did not always realize these associations, but as I have gotten older, the relationships between my ancestors and myself have become clearer. My twin sister,

Stacey, and I were born in Rocky Mount, Nash County, North Carolina, in 1976, approximately 30 miles from the small unincorporated towns of Hollister and Essex on the border of Halifax and Warren Counties. My tribal name, Haliwa-Saponi, is partly derived from these counties and Saponi, one of the aboriginal groups from which our people descended. Our area was traditionally called the Meadows, and this name is still used by some today.

With few job opportunities and two young mouths to feed, my parents, Barry Richardson and Brenda Lynch, packed up and moved north to Baltimore when we were just three years old. By migrating to Baltimore, our family joined other Native families in the area, but also followed the pattern of generations of Haliwa-Saponis and other Native peoples who have migrated from their tribal territories to find work and better opportunities. As early as the 1930s, Haliwa-Saponis moved to Philadelphia, Maryland, Richmond, Washington, D.C., Detroit, and as far away as California. While migration was a tremendous benefit for our families, it also placed a strain on those families who wished to maintain an Indian identity and a connection to our aboriginal roots. Depending on the era and the family, some Haliwa-Saponi families moved away and seldom came back, while others worked hard to keep strong ties to home, tribe, and culture. My family represented the latter, by frequently coming home to Hollister, as well as participating in intertribal functions with other migrant Native families in Baltimore and the wider area.

As a Haliwa-Saponi Indian, I realize that one meaning of the phrase "generations within the circle" refers to the powwow circle. When I could barely walk, my parents pushed me out into the arena with a ribbon shirt, beaded headband, blue jeans, and moccasins. As I grew older, my regalia became more sophisticated, until I had a full-fledged fancy dance outfit. Powwow dancing was fun and helped reinforce my Indian identity. It made me "feel Indian" and also made me feel different from others. I took pride in dancing at our powwow in Baltimore, my home Haliwa-Saponi Powwow, and others. My daddy served as the Director of the Baltimore American Indian Center (BAIC) and pushed hard to provide cultural activities for us urban Indians, which consisted mostly of transplanted Lumbee Indians from Robeson County, North Carolina, and a few Haliwa-Saponis, Lakotas, Coharies, Cherokees, and other Natives from all over. Members of my tribe—such as Arnold Richardson, Senora Lynch, Archie Lynch, Anthony

Harris, Jody Richardson, Wayahsti Richardson, and many others—regularly came to Baltimore and acted as childhood mentors. Some even stayed at our house for a time. We never saw Baltimore as our permanent home, and the interactions with Native folks from Hollister and other places made Baltimore a home away from home.

As I got older, I came to appreciate why my father and mother were so dedicated to our dancing and being proud of who we are. Both of my parents danced Indian dances and participated as members of the Haliwa Indian Dance Group. Back then, the group not only danced at the Haliwa Powwow but also traveled with Chief W. R. Richardson to perform at festivals, in parades, and at the powwows hosted by other tribes. The Haliwa-Saponis were the first to have powwows in North Carolina, starting in 1965, and shared that knowledge with other tribes. Our tribe learned eastern woodland–style dances from the Chickahominy Indians of Virginia, who were the featured dancers at our first celebration in honor of our state recognition. From the beginning, powwow dancing served a dual purpose that helped instill pride in our Native people and communicated our Native identity to outsiders as well.

In middle and high school, I developed a deeper connection to the circle through singing, history, and language. Around the age of ten, I became interested in the powwow drum by singing songs while I danced in intertribals. At that time, the most influential drum groups were Shallow Water (Haliwa-Saponi) of Hollister, North Carolina, and Running Water (Lumbee) of Fayetteville, North Carolina. In the early 1980s, Arnold Richardson founded Shallow Water, named after *Moni-Seep*, a Saponi word meaning "Shallow Water" as recorded by William Byrd in 1728. Richardson was the nephew of Chief W. R. Richardson and born in Philadelphia, Pennsylvania, to a migrant Haliwa-Saponi and Tuscarora mother. Around 1979, Richardson brought the drum and both plains-style and Iroquoian-style dances to the Haliwa-Saponi community. Richardson also did research on the Saponi and Powhatan languages, and was the first to use and teach those languages to tribal members. After Shallow Water disbanded in the late 1980s, Richardson's son Wayahsti helped form the White Tail Singers. White Tail, like its predecessor, traveled extensively up and down the East Coast singing songs of well-known powwow groups such Red Bull, Black Lodge, Sioux-Assiniboine, and Porcupine Singers. Later, they pushed the envelope by composing their own songs in Saponi, Powhatan, and Lakota.

Marty Richardson, Fancy Dancer. (Photo Courtesy of Marty Richardson and Brenda Lynch.)

I got my start by "sitting in" with White Tail and developing an extensive repertoire of songs through powwow recordings.

While I traveled on the weekends to powwows from North Carolina to New Jersey, my classmates at school constantly challenged me about my heritage. At the same time, I wondered why my tribe was never mentioned in those lousy sections about Native Americans in social studies or history. My classmates asked me if I was "mixed," and I would respond, "No, I'm Indian," and they would act like they didn't believe me or ask me questions about my people that I could sometimes answer and other times not. I got in a fight one time when an African American student called me black and I told him that I wasn't black, that I was Indian. He insisted, "No you're not, you're black." Proclaiming and maintaining our identity and having "others/ outsiders" recognize that identity has been an enduring struggle for our people for decades, perhaps centuries. Members of my grandparents' generation were used to being called "colored," "yellow issues," or "free issues," while whites and African Americans denied their Indian identity. Starting in the late 1940s, and after several attempts at organizing themselves and seeking recognition, my people finally came together in 1953. They established the Haliwa Indian Club, which grew to be the modern tribal government. Our people did research, formulated strategies, and sought advice from the elders and allies. Through my own struggles, I responded to non-Indian ignorance in a similar way by pushing myself to absorb as much as I could about my tribe and other southeastern Native peoples, including our languages and histories.

Around the age of fifteen, I began seeking out information about the history and languages of my people and others. My research led me to books such as *Siouan Tribes of the East* by James Mooney, *The Indians of the Southeastern United States* by John Swanton, and other classic works. Eventually, I exhausted the resources at the local library and moved on to the local university to find more. Though I knew about the handful of Saponi words recorded by explorers in the seventeenth and eighteenth centuries, finding out that a significant portion of the Tutelo language, a language mutually intelligible with Saponi, was documented and published changed my life. I found and copied all of the published works of the language I could find. When I learned that unpublished Tutelo materials were held at the National Anthropological Archives, I had my parents drive me to Washington, D.C., in order to hand copy the words. Since rediscovering the Tutelo language for our people, I have felt a deep connection to my ancestors by teaching the language to young people and using the language in powwow songs. The language allows us to express ourselves and communicate the history and values so important to our people.

My family's move from the Baltimore area back home to the Meadows during my senior year of high school was another life-changing event. Because I lived in the community, I began to understand the enduring struggle our people have faced to maintain our identity. I learned that while a lot of people in my community were proud of their Native heritage, not everyone was. Through observation and talks with my grandparents and others, I discovered that our people suffered and still suffer historical trauma because many whites and blacks wanted to enforce a southern racial binary, which includes a category for whites and then one for all other nonwhites. Some of our people went along with this classification, while others did not. The elders of my grandparents' generation and those before them sacrificed their lives and livelihood to ensure that our people were recognized and could have a tribal organization of their own to push for the goals and agenda of Haliwa-Saponis. My experiences were mostly positive, though, and I immersed myself in the tribal community at the Red Earth cultural class and in church, and by engaging in a rich social life. In 1993, Otara Mills, Jesse Richardson, John Oxendine, Terry White, Bobby Farley, Derek Deese, Paul Walters, myself, and a few others started Stoney Creek Singers and went to work teaching others how to sing. The Tutelo-Saponi language remained a constant presence, and we used the language more and more to make songs. For the first time in my life, I felt like I lived in a place I could be comfortable and have friends I could truly relate to.

When it came time to pursue my college career, I decided to follow my passions about American Indian history and followed in the footsteps of my father by entering the University of North Carolina at Pembroke (UNCP). UNCP was founded by the Lumbee Indians and offers a bachelor's degree in American Indian studies. College life provided me the freedom to express myself and the resources and education to expand my knowledge. At Pembroke, I learned from Stanley Knick about archaeology and engaged in contemporary issues of our Native people. I was very active in the Native American Student Organization and other activities on and off campus. UNCP had an active Greek life, but no Greek organizations for Native people. On February 13, 1996, we founded Phi Sigma Nu American Indian Fraternity with a mission to engage in academic, social, cultural, and physical realms to make a difference in Native communities. Today, Phi Sigma Nu is the largest American Indian fraternity with over 300 brothers and eleven chapters. I practiced the motto of hard work and hard play by attending all of the local powwows, as well as others on the East Coast. Weekend visits home kept me rooted there and engaged. Whenever I had a class project to do, I tried to somehow document my tribe or take an opportunity to learn more about my ancestors.

My academic journey continued at Indiana University in the fall of 2000 as I pursued my master's in anthropology. At Indiana, I learned about ethnic identity, participant observation, ethnography, and the history of Native peoples all across North America. Most significant, Indiana offered a course in Lakota, a Siouan language very similar to Tutelo-Saponi, and anthropological linguistics classes, which provided me a linguistic basis to study, relearn, and teach my language. Being in Indiana was challenging, though, because I was far from my comfortable network of North Carolina Native people, my tribe, and my family. Though other Natives did attend Indiana, I got a firsthand lesson on the diversity of Native people; we are all different and share varying cultural values and experiences. After I finished course work, I came back home to work on my master's thesis, which focused on the importance of the powwow to Haliwa-Saponi Indian identity. My plan was to finish my thesis in the summer and then go back to Indiana and pursue my Ph.D. Instead, I got married to Melissa Silver and became a permanent resident of Hollister and settled down, at least for a while. Though my thesis topic was exciting and I was obviously knowledgeable on the topic, like other Native scholars, I found it difficult to write about my experiences and analyze a subject and a people I felt so close to. I finally finished my thesis in 2007.

After a brief stint with the North Carolina Commission of Indian Affairs as an academic counselor for the Talent Search Program, I accepted a position at the Haliwa-Saponi Indian Tribe as the tribal planner in 2001. My official duty was to write grants for tribal programs such as housing, day care, health care, and economic development, but the job also provided the flexibility to pursue my interests in tribal history, language, and culture. Long before I was the tribal planner, my interest in our tribe's federal acknowledgment efforts grew, and I took up the cause myself. When I was not writing grants, I visited local archives to do research, interviewed tribal elders, and worked on the tribe's genealogy. Although I took on a job and other causes, I never let go of my other pursuits. I still went to powwows regularly with Stoney Creek. We traveled all over the United States and Canada. I continue to study, teach, and use the language. Wanting to complete my academic journey, in 2011 I decided to pursue my Ph.D. in history full time and enrolled at the University of North Carolina, Chapel Hill.

My experiences in the tribal community, my talks with tribal elders, and my research reinforced my belief that our people are closely connected to our ancestors and part of a generation within a circle. I found that our tribe's struggle to become federally acknowledged did not begin in 1978 when the Bureau of Indian Affairs (BIA) regulations were adopted, but goes back as far as 1896 when 300 of our people sought recognition as an Indian people. I feel connected to those people because three of my great-great-grandfathers—Cofield Richardson, Alfred Richardson Jr., and Dudley Lynch—led the group. My relatives and I carry on that legacy and the burden of achieving full recognition of our people. Though 1953 is touted as the date of Haliwa-Saponi organization, the efforts and roots of that organization sprouted much earlier. Our tribe has yet to achieve full federal acknowledgment; however, we have, for a long time, enjoyed special benefits as Indians from the U.S. government.

The concept of tribal sovereignty has been much debated in our community and other communities in North Carolina, especially among the non-BIA-serviced tribes. In my opinion, tribal sovereignty is a fundamental, inherent belief that is not bestowed by anyone. Either you are sovereign or you are not. Federal acknowledgment of an Indian group does not give sovereignty to your tribal nation. My belief in tribal sovereignty stems from my knowledge of my tribal history and our contemporary situation. Our tribe has documented our people in the Meadows since at least the 1750s. We are the descendants of the Saponis, Nansemonds, Tuscaroras, and other Indian peoples who came together to live in the Meadows. Our people have always regulated our own affairs and associations. The same is true today, since one of the fundamental rights of our tribe and others is to determine our own membership. Only sovereign nations can decide who is a citizen or not. In 1957, our people got tired of non-Indians denying their Indian identity and forcing us into a "colored"-white racial dichotomy, so they started the Haliwa Indian School. Only a sovereign people would make a decision to do what is right for their people. The founders of the Haliwa Indian School and the reorganized tribal government are my heroes because they had the courage to stand up for who they are. Their actions of selflessness, courage, volunteerism, and sacrifice guide my journey. Though the strategies and methods have changed over generations, the Indian circle endures.

Marvin "Marty" Richardson is a citizen of the Haliwa-Saponi Indian Tribe and a Ph.D. candidate in history at the University of North Carolina, Chapel Hill. His research focuses on Haliwa-Saponi social

organization and how Haliwa-Saponis navigated and reacted to the
South's black-white binary to maintain their Indian identity between
the years 1835 to 1971.

Putting the "Community" Back into My Jena Choctaw Community

I have been a Tribal Council member for the Jena Band of Choctaw Indians, a federally recognized Indian tribe located in Louisiana, for four years. I am also the Cultural Director and Tribal Historic Preservation Officer (THPO) for the tribe. I work with anything that is culturally relevant to the tribe. This includes, but is not limited to, the archiving of photos and documents and consulting with federal agencies pursuant to the various historic preservation laws and other federal regulations, mandates, and executive orders for projects on federal lands across the entire Gulf area. I also facilitate and participate in repatriation ceremonies as provided by the Native American Graves Protection and Repatriation Act (NAGPRA) and investigate crime scenes associated with violations of the Archaeological Resource Protection Act (ARPA). In addition to protecting our human and natural resources, I work with all of our elders and youth.

This past year, my office created an Elders Program that provides a weekly lunch and activity. The activity may be to play bingo for commodities and prizes or possibly have a guest speaker attend to discuss important issues such as Medicare and Social Security. We are able to provide benefits to our elders through creative avenues that will not affect their tax obligations or their federal benefits. We hope to build a senior citizens center in the very near future. Our youth program, or Young Leaders Program, consists of monthly events focused around cultural practices and language. We host fun, energetic, monthly events to bring our youth together for lessons on our history, our traditional cultural practices, our language, and leadership skills. Along with our monthly events, we host several large events throughout the year to capture more of the membership, such as a living history exhibit with the Chalmette National Battlefield; a field trip to Philadelphia, Mississippi, for the Annual Choctaw Fair; site visits to other significant historical sites; and a Culture Camp that includes canoeing, archery, stickball, history lessons, language workshops, and more. The funding for these two programs is generated by my office through our consultation efforts with federal agencies.

We also provide online and face-to-face Choctaw language classes. We have contracted an instructor from the Choctaw Nation in Oklahoma to teach these classes. I, myself, am self-taught for the most part, but attend these classes to become more fluent. These classes have been very successful in that we have more adult students than ever before.

For me, it is a great accomplishment to have adult students. Since the early 1950s, the Jena Choctaw were taught to not speak the Choctaw language. The elders today remember being told by their parents that they could no longer speak Choctaw and were forced to learn English. The teachers had visited the parents to tell them their children would not be successful if they continued speaking in their Native language. They would fail out of school and not be able to provide for their families or themselves if they continued. The language is not the only thing that is not practiced as it once was. All of the material cultural practices were put to the side as well. People continued to make some items and practiced the skills as a hobby, but they were no longer practiced as a way of life. There are many things that our tribe had almost lost before we began working toward our current initiative of bringing our community back together. So, to have adult students attend these classes, it really brings the whole picture together.

Our office also hosts three other community events. The first of these events is a tribal expo. We invite our tribal members and others who practice these skills to participate in the expo. Our office provides historical and cultural exhibits to view, while those skilled in the various crafts demonstrate their skill to the public. This is free to visitors and is designed to create a market for our craftsmen to sell their merchandise. The number one reason why tribal people cannot focus on perfecting their craft is that they must have an outside job to survive. If we could build a large enough market or demand for the skilled craft, or items our members build and create, then they could potentially quit their outside jobs and work to maintain our traditional culture. Although this type of large-scale market is likely improbable, we are trying to build a market base that will at least foster the continuance of traditional skills.

The second event is a new event. It is the United Choctaw Nations Conference. We hope this conference grows into something really special. We not only invite our tribal members, but we invite all Choctaw people to attend. All three federally recognized Choctaw tribes come together, along with various presenters from all over who either have Choctaw lineage themselves or who in their professional careers impacted various Choctaw communities, both state and federally recognized. Our motto is to build a stronger united Choctaw Nation through our shared culture. This year (2014) we will host the second of these conferences.

Finally, our third community-building event is our annual powwow, "Pow Wow in the Pines," which was started in 2008. This powwow is a celebration for our tribal community to commemorate our federal recognition. Before, we planned small events and hardly anyone attended. We began this event to encourage more people to participate in the celebration. We still have many adults who do not quite understand why or what a powwow is all about, but we are working on that. This year's powwow will be very special as we will induct nine of our youth into the arena. They are the first of our people to participate in the powwow.

I am very proud of the work this office does within our tribal community. It is a lot of effort, but we are seeing progress. My mission when I first stepped into this role was to create a community that gave back to the community and not just everyone separately living our lives. When I first started developing this department I presented my idea to the Tribal Council of "bringing the community back to being a community." Being a small tribe of 323 members here in the South, most of our tribal members were raised to be mainstream Americans. We have less than five fluent Choctaw speakers, and currently have seven who are participating in the language class. We have about forty-five kids who in the past five years have learned a vocabulary of 100–200 words and know how to use them pretty well. Over the past sixty years, through the effects of assimilation and in simply just trying to survive in our local communities, it has caused us to have less contact with one another and use our traditional practices less.

My vision is to bring the community back together, and the way to do this is to start with our kids and then bring in the elders. My thought is if we capture the youth and revive our elders, then those who fall in between will have no choice but to come back to the tribe. Through the efforts discussed earlier we have been able to see this positive trend.

We have a lot of participation in all of our events. We have tripled the number of events that we host since I was a kid. Then, there was not any type of history classes and few language classes. Granted, we were taught to count from one to ten and the names of a couple of animals; however, that was the gist of it. We were not taught about our creation legends or our traditional stories. Our tribal government was working so hard to become federally recognized that they were leaving out what made us who we are. Once federal recognition was acquired in 1995, our tribal government set their focus on the development of a casino and left the cultural stuff to grandma and grandpa at home. If kids weren't getting this information at home, they just weren't getting it.

My main initiative now is to have a good base of people who have an interest in carrying on the traditions. We need to have at least one or two of these people become expert craftsmen to ensure that we don't lose this piece of who we are. Being an anthropology student, I often wondered why cultural preservation was not more important or higher on the list of things to do. Why it wasn't more important for the Tribal Council to push and fund cultural events to make sure that this part of who we are did not die. Now, as a Tribal Council member myself, I sit at that table and see and hear why. I am able to understand why because I am afforded the opportunity to hear the comments such as, "Now, these are the real issues that actually affect the immediate livelihoods of our tribal members."

I understand, as an example, why we aren't going to fund the language program right now. We may have four elders who need access to health care that will prolong their lives. I have actually had my eyes opened in the last four years in my understanding of the governmental side of things, whereas working on the cultural side of things alone, I was left wondering "why doesn't the government support us more." I realize now that it is because they have bigger issues to deal with.

We do a lot of work, but it is a lot of fun. My office staff will cringe when I walk in the office saying, "Hey guys, I had this awesome idea this morning," as I do so often. My work is my passion. The events we host, the classes we teach, the camps we run, and the programs we initiate are all founded from one central idea—"Community Involvement." How do you stop the effects of assimilation? You don't. All we can do is protect our culture and keep what makes us Choctaw strong by being together—as a family, as a tribe, as the Jena Choctaw community.

Dana Chapman Masters is the youngest member of the Jena Band of Choctaw Indians' Tribal Council and youngest of all department directors in the tribe. She has studied anthropology and ethnoarchaeology under Hiram F. Gregory at Northwestern State University and has written, managed, and facilitated applied anthropology research projects through federal grant funds. Masters has helped in developing and negotiating agreements leading to the successful construction of five economic development projects, including Jena Choctaw Pines Casino, for her tribe during her tenure as a Tribal Council member. Masters has presented on numerous occasions to the Culture and Heritage Committee of the United Southern and Eastern Tribes (USET). She also presented at the "To Bridge a Gap" conference on repatriation ceremonies, and participated in several consultations on national issues leading to the development of federal regulations and executive orders.

Finding My Sense of Place in My Ancestral Homeland

I was born in 1960 to a Cherokee father, Azure Jumper, and a Caucasian mother, Mildred Conner. Like many in Appalachia, and particularly in western North Carolina, my parents were quite poor. Like many impoverished couples, my father was both verbally and physically abusive to my mother. When I was born, he began a pattern of abuse with me that prompted my mother to separate from him, but not before having two more children. Later, she would reconcile briefly with him and have another son.

My Cherokee lineage goes back into the foundations of the continent. My father was the son of Stancil Jumper and grandson of Ute Jumper, who both lived their lives on the Qualla Boundary (also known as the Cherokee Indian Reservation of North Carolina). Each is recorded on the Baker roll of those Cherokees who remained in the western North Carolina mountains after the 1838 removal. The land of the Cherokee people straddles two counties, Jackson and Swain, and carves out a slice of Graham County. I was born and raised in many different homes in Jackson County. Sometimes we would only be in a home for a few weeks before having to move to another location, mostly due to not being able to keep up with the rent.

Growing up in poverty, I learned the value of a good education. And because of federal Indian grants, I was afforded the opportunity to attend college and earn a bachelor's degree (I later worked toward and earned an MBA). After graduation in 1983, I went into the management program with a large drug store chain. Five years later, I accepted a position with the largest retail goods company in the world, Philip Morris International.

It was in 1986 that I made a couple of life-changing decisions. I married my wife, Vickie, and firmed my soft relationship God. Becoming a Christian solidified my ethical viewpoint. Marrying Vickie reinforced my commitment to family and provided the support I needed to make difficult decisions and face the challenges that were ahead in my life.

Working for large corporate firms allowed me to build a family and live comfortably. Yet I had always wanted to work with and for the people in my ancestral homeland. The connection between a person and his or her sense of place is very strong, and once a person has an understanding of his or her people and place, there is always a longing to be in physical contact with it. When I entered the workforce in 1983, the tribe had very little money and very few employment opportunities. So, I settled for being able to live near my Cherokee homeland while pursuing opportunities elsewhere.

That wasn't enough for me. My work passion was always to be a communicator and provide people with a release or distraction from the everyday. That desire probably came from my own longing to do what I loved instead of doing what was necessary for survival. And while I was very successful in the sales organizations, I always wanted to share my knowledge and talent with my Cherokee people. During the twenty years I spent in management and sales, I believe the Creator was preparing me for the opportunity to come back to the Cherokee reservation and work among my people. As the years progressed, the tribe opened a casino, and the economy on the Cherokee reservation supported more jobs. The Tourism Office, which had previously been a welcome center, was expanded to include a marketing framework that more closely represented the incredibly diverse and vibrant economy of the tribe. A friend made me aware of this expansion and the need for someone to assist in the tribe's marketing efforts. I applied and quickly became a part of the tribe's new marketing team.

Since coming to work for the tribe, I have had a role in each of the hundreds of special events that Cherokees have either hosted or entertained over the past decade. The event that brings the most satisfaction and sense of accomplishment to me is the Cherokee Indian Fair. This event evolved from a small community festival into the largest single annual event on

Cherokee Indian Fair, October 2009. The event is the Corn Shucking Contest where participants competed for prizes in a race to see who can shuck the most ears of corn during a set time limit. Many of the games on "Community Day" of the fair reflect the everyday tasks of tribal farm life dating back hundreds of years. (Photo Courtesy of Robert Jumper.)

the Cherokee reservation. Over 100 years old, the Cherokee Indian Fair is the showcase and celebration of the Eastern Band of Cherokee Indians of yesteryears and today. It is the outpouring of Cherokee culture and the joy of our accomplishment. From agriculture to craftsmanship, the Cherokee Indian Fair highlights the ingenuity and unmatched talent of the Principal People. Year after year, enhancements have been made to this event to provide a vehicle for presenting the finest in arts, crafts, and gardening.

We also show the community livestock and have Indian or stickball games in the finest of Cherokee traditions. We celebrate each community on the Qualla Boundary (communities are basically voting precincts that constitute our Tribal Council) with friendly, family competitions in display creation and parade float design. Each community creates a display that remains in the Exhibit Hall of the fairgrounds for the duration of the fair.

These displays are judged for creativity and relevance to the fair theme. Likewise, there is a contest for parade float design based on similar criteria. We also sprinkle in some internationally renowned entertainment, hold Miss Cherokee pageants for our beautiful and talented young ladies, and organize spirited local competitions like Cherokee Idol, Pretty Legs, and Kiss-A-Pig. There is nothing like the Cherokee Indian Fair to experience the traditions, culture, and modern-day lifestyle of the Eastern Band of Cherokee people.

The Eastern Band of Cherokee Indians places a high value on tourism in its economic future. Prior to the 1950s, the Cherokee people in this area had logging as their primary industry. That industry, along with federal supplements, was the foundation of the Cherokee economy. In the mid-1950s, economic conditions and consumer demand changed the focus of the tribe to a tourism-based economy, but again with a heavy dependence on government assistance. This was the revenue picture until the mid-1990s, when the tribe won the right to establish gaming on the Qualla Boundary.

Since then, the Cherokee economy has shown rapid growth. There are multiple areas where the benefit of this growth is evident as more things have been developed that draw outsiders to the Cherokee reservation, including cultural presentations and exhibits, outdoor activities, sporting events, and adult gaming. There are approximately forty people directly employed by the tribe to support tourism efforts. There are hundreds of others who are front-line staff to provide services for the tourists. We also employ outside agencies to execute elements of the marketing strategy, such as media planning and execution to audio and video production.

The Cherokee people are very sensitive to the way others perceive their ancestors and traditions. In advertising and presentations at the many functions that the tribe participates in, great care is taken to keep from dishonoring those who have gone before us. Tourism is a great economic driver, but it takes a backseat to the honor of the people.

The type of people who are drawn to the Qualla Boundary range from outdoor fun seekers to cultural hobbyists to those interested in adult gaming. Visitors to our homeland are national and international in origin. International travelers are particularly interested in Native American culture and history. Many people who are not familiar with the very different subcultures within the North American tribes assume that all Indigenous peoples are alike. They, for example, presume that all Native Americans lived in tepees and wear elaborate feathered headpieces. It is of high importance that, in our service to our Cherokee community and to the traveling public, we educate those with misconceptions about the Cherokee people's cultural history. Many visitors come to Cherokee, North Carolina, with a desire to immerse themselves in the Cherokee culture in a quest for their own sense of place. Several make claims to being blood relation to the tribe.

Most of the marketing for the Qualla Boundary is governed by the tribal leadership. While there is a healthy private merchant presence in Cherokee, they have been a loose coalition and could not advertise on the world stage in the same fashion as the tribal government. So, it is up to the tribe to collaborate with the business community and cultural attraction entities and plan, develop, and execute the marketing for the destination of Cherokee, North Carolina. As part of the Eastern Band of Cherokee Indians Destination Marketing team, it is an honor to work for my people in using state-of-the-art technology and modern strategies to tell an age-old story about our modern-day Native culture.

Robert Jumper is an enrolled member of the Eastern Band of Cherokee Indians who shares his life with his wife, Vickie, in North Carolina just outside of the Qualla Boundary. In 2014, he was appointed to serve as the editor of the tribal newspaper, the Cherokee One Feather. His great loves are serving his God, his family, and the Cherokee people.

Native People Should Tell Their Own Stories

I have long been committed to activist scholarship and community engagement. I believe that any use of knowledge has social, economic, and political ramifications because history is not unbiased. As the old adage goes, history is told from the perspective of the victors, so my mission is to make sure the lies and half-truths that are told about my Choctaw-Apache community are challenged. History is a battlefield, and our cultural heritage is the redoubt from which we are able to carry out this fight. My experiences in life have led me to not turn away from this battle but to face this challenge head on.

I grew up in Shreveport and Bossier, Louisiana, about 70 miles north—

Robert Caldwell served on the Choctaw-Apache Tribal Council from 2011 to 2014. (Photo Courtesy of Robert Caldwell.)

but a world apart—from our Indian community. I spent most of my youth in a multiracial setting, which was not typical for that part of the South. We lived near an air force base where kids came from everywhere. I spent most of my time around my (white) father's family, especially my paternal grandmother and great-aunt. They grew up poor as children of sharecroppers and timer workers and were proudly influenced by Huey P. Long's populist administration in Louisiana. They instilled in me the interest for the past and the importance of social struggle that would later shape my decisions.

My maternal great-grandparents, George and Susan Remedies, also had a huge impact on my way of thinking. They lived in a small home just outside of Many, the seat of Sabine Parish, just southeast of Ebarb and Zwolle where most Choctaw-Apache citizens reside. I remember going there often as a kid, especially in the summer. My mother spent years of her childhood there and was very close to them, so we visited often. Growing up in the 1980s, I remember outsiders coming to interview my great-grandfather George. They asked him questions about being Indian, about his life experiences, farming, working in the woods, and food traditions. Once they left, these academics went on to write about the community. Although some of their writing was accurate, they also misunderstood many things about the community.

After my maternal grandparents passed away, my mother acquired their land from older family members and moved there. Today she gardens and gathers and is connected to the land through her grandparents, as I am through her.

After graduating from high school I stayed in Shreveport-Bossier and worked full time for five years and obtained my associate's degree from a local community college. Then, I moved away to attend the University of New Orleans full time. It was there that I met Donna Pierite, who was working hard to preserve Tunica-Biloxi heritage, and she was a great inspiration to me. During the same period of time, I also became increasingly involved in environmental and economic justice issues on campus.

I later went to graduate school to pursue a master's degree in labor studies at the University of Massachusetts in Amherst. During that period, I sent periodic and small donations to my tribe and kept in touch through word of mouth and newsletters. After I returned to New Orleans, I became more interested in tribal affairs, but found it hard to be involved from a distance since New Orleans is about 300 miles away from Ebarb.

About three years after Hurricane Katrina, I decided to move closer to my parents in northern Louisiana. During the immediate aftermath of the hurricane, I had thrown everything into fighting for the right of displaced residents to return to their homes and for justice in the reconstruction efforts, but I had neglected myself and my own relationships as a result. The change of pace that I found in moving closer to my tribe was well worth it. Yet I still had a strong need to help people and put my energies to use.

In 2009, I enrolled in a master's of heritage resources program at Northwestern State University in Natchitoches. The program allowed me to use my academic talents in a way that benefited my tribe. I did oral history interviews and undertook a thesis project focused on Choctaw-Apache foodways, which resulted in interpretive panels and an outline for a book on our traditional foods.

Cultural survival now drives my work. Although not every aspect of culture will continue forever, it is important that each tribal nation decides which aspects of their culture are most important and worth preserving. That is an integral part of sovereignty, of self-determination. Not only do

I want future generations to be able to live in a healthy environment and enjoy the water, air, and land, I also want them to have access to formal education as well as to be knowledgeable about our traditions. It is a balance. For example, I think it is important for them to have health care but also to know that traditional knowledge sometimes works in ways that confounds Western medicine. All of this is based on inspiration from my great-grandparents George and Susan Remedies.

Recently, I was a member of the Choctaw-Apache Tribal Council, and I was forced to confront a number of issues related to poverty and economic development. The local logging industry has faced a slow, but persistent, decline, and fewer tribal members are engaged in farming and other traditional vocations. The scarcity of living-wage jobs in the tribal area leaves younger people with a tough challenge: either move away to find work or face very long commutes. Men often work in the oil and gas industry offshore or faraway hydraulic fracturing. Women often commute an hour or more each way for nursing jobs. Those jobs mean good wages, but pull our young people away from their elders and, increasingly, from their own children. This makes continuing our traditions that much harder. I want my people to have access to local employment so that they can have the opportunity to shape the future of the tribe, but sustainable economic development requires meaningful work that supports healthy communities. I don't have a silver bullet to fix the problem in the short term, but we must move toward sustainable local economic development.

At the same time, our tribal foodways are under assault. Long commutes mean less time to work the gardens and less time in the kitchen. It often means more fast food and sugary drinks. One solution to jump-start healthier eating and revitalize our food traditions was to establish a tribal garden. Under the supervision of our past chairman, John W. Procell, and working with Johnny Lee Rivers and a number of volunteers, I completed a tribal garden pilot project and distributed fresh vegetables and over 150 packets of heirloom seeds to local families. Following that success, the tribe now has a greenhouse, and plans are under way for a farmers market.

The public knows far too little about the Choctaw-Apache community of Ebarb, and to the extent that people outside of Louisiana have heard of us, misperceptions abound. My goal is to produce a book that explains the complex 300-year history of our people that weaves together archival materials, previously documented oral history and ethnographic materials, and the rich oral traditions we still have today. To that end, I am also currently enrolled in a Ph.D. program. Thus far, I have written numerous papers documenting the history of my community, from early colonial times until the present.

I try to leverage my academic relationships to build infrastructure for the tribe and to heal divisions. Together with Jason Rivers, Amelia Bison, and Tom Rivers, I have founded a committee to map our traditional cultural places. That committee has hosted mapping workshops where tribal members can learn the basics of GIS (Geographic Information Systems) from an expert. The work of that committee is ongoing. Over time, political factions inside the tribe have contributed to the fracturing of institutional memory. Given this reality, one of my current side-projects is an institutional history of the tribe from the 1970s to the present that seeks to fairly portray all elected administrations in that period.

It is essential that Native peoples tell their own stories. At the same time, every Native community has a variety of perspectives on their collective past. My hope is to help collect and synthesize those perspectives from my community in a way that lifts up the entire community, rather than one family, clan, or political faction.

Robert Caldwell is a student in the Transatlantic History Doctoral Program at the University of Texas at Arlington. He served on the Tribal Council of the Choctaw-Apache Community of Ebarb from 2011 to 2014.

Vpuecetv (To Dream): My Journey to Becoming Tribal Royalty

Dreams and aspirations are what we make of them. They fill our hearts and lives with hope and motivation. However, sometimes they cause our world to be shadowed with disappointment. Nevertheless, where would we be without them?

Imagine living a life where you never set goals or have visions of what the future might hold. Just contemplate a world without dreamers. What would we miss out on if it were not for those visionaries? Would we have electricity? Cars? Cellular phones? Furthermore, imagine the experiences you would have missed out on if you hadn't made a plan and followed through with it. I am convinced that life would be a bland, uneventful experience without following our dreams.

I am a Native American woman and a member of the Poarch Band of Creek Indians. I did not grow up on the Poarch Creek Indian Reservation, but my mother did, and she always identified herself as a Creek Indian. Thus, regardless of where my family was physically located during my early years, I was always reared with the knowledge that I was a Poarch Creek Indian. This knowledge fueled a sense of pride and a thirst within me to learn more about my Native American roots.

As soon as I was old enough to visit the school library, I remember searching through the card catalog for all of the "Indian" books I could find. My school librarian was quite patient and helpful in assisting me with my quest as well. Ironically, most of the Native American books found in the little South Alabama school library were about tribes living on the plains and in the Southwest. Publications about Alabama's Indigenous southeastern tribes seemed to be nearly nonexistent (not to mention way above my elementary level reading skills). But this lack of available information did not deter my mission to learn what it really means to be a Creek Indian.

Each year we visited my mom's family at Thanksgiving and Christmas. Thanksgiving in Poarch, Alabama, did not consist of the traditional turkey-day fanfare. Instead, we always attended the "Annual Thanksgiving Day Powwow" hosted, of course, by the Poarch Creek Indians. The powwow features all of the usual things that one might expect to see at a Native American event: elaborate and colorful regalia, powwow drumming, Native American dancing, and arts and crafts vendors. This is also the event at which three young women are crowned the Poarch Creek Indian Princess (Elementary, Junior, and Senior) and embark upon a yearlong ambassadorship.

The princess competition is a source of family pride for many of our tribal members. For my family, it has been somewhat of a legacy. I can recall seeing the trophies, pictures, and sashes that my mom kept from her "princess" days. Both of my aunts served in this capacity as well. Naturally, at around nine years old, I decided that it was time for me to carry on this legacy and compete for the title of Poarch Creek Indian Elementary Princess.

I was scared to death. Three judges were staring back at me during the interview portion as I frantically tried to recall the answers to their questions. It is a wonder I didn't leave the room crying (I've always been a bit emotional). Needless to say, I did not do very well my first year. But I eventually regained my courage and decided to compete for the Junior Princess title. Thankfully, my parents agreed to transport me ninety minutes (one way) every Sunday so I could once again be at the required practices.

At these group practices, we learned how to powwow dance, bead earrings, and fringe our shawl. We were also given a couple of printed pages that explained our tribal history to us. During the course of these practices, not only did I acquire some new skills, but I also had an opportunity to spend some valuable time getting to know my extended family.

I won the Poarch Creek Indian Junior Princess title that year, and a few years later won the Senior Princess title as well. I was so happy to know that I was following in my mother's and aunts' footsteps. Nevertheless, as my reigning year as Senior Princess dwindled closer to its end, I began to wonder if there were other similar competitions elsewhere.

My search of other Native American "princess" contests revealed that there were several across the United States. One in particular continued to stand out above the rest: the Miss Indian World pageant. I was in awe as I read the information about the women who had served in the capacity of Miss Indian World. I knew that I wanted the opportunity to compete in this prestigious event. However, the rules required, among many other things, that you must be eighteen years of age before you could compete. This was slightly discouraging considering I was only sixteen years old at the time.

The truth is that I felt a sense of accomplishment knowing that I made my parents and family proud. I also sincerely enjoyed representing my tribe and learning more about my Creek heritage. The more I learned, the more I realized just how little I knew. I truly wanted to immerse myself in Creek culture.

Before I knew it, life happened. I graduated from high school, started college, and got a job. Needless to say, my dream of competing in the Miss Indian World pageant was pushed to the back of my mind and nearly forgotten.

It just so happened that I found out about the Alabama Indian Affairs Commission hosting the first Miss Indian Alabama competition. I was intrigued and decided that I wanted to be a contestant. I had competed in beauty pageants and talent competitions in the past, but this was an opportunity for me to represent not only myself but also my tribe on a state level.

The Miss Indian Alabama contest required that each of the five contestants submit an essay, demonstrate a talent, and answer an on-stage question. For my talent, I decided to give a creative sign language interpretation of "Amazing Grace" as I sang the song in English and Creek. Singing is a facet of my life in which I am truly confident. But please realize that confidence has been attained through years of practice and perfecting my craft. I can't ever recall a time when I haven't sung. Some of my most precious memories are of me following my granny Mildred around her house and mimicking her as she sang; I was only two or three years old at the time.

The most difficult obstacle of my talent presentation is the fact that I am not a fluent Creek speaker, nor am I a frequent user of sign language. My brain was on coordination overload! Thank God for good friends. My dear friend Kayla coached me on the sign language portion, while I received Creek tutoring from longtime comrade Marcus. My talent presentation would have been sorely lacking without the help I received from those two. I had to keep practicing, but I was prepared for the talent portion of the Miss Indian Alabama competition.

My mom has always told me that she can never tell if I'm nervous when I'm on stage. Despite any calm exterior I might manage to bolster, I am nervous and frantic on the inside. After the judging was completed, I'm honored and humbled to say that I was chosen to serve as the first Miss Indian Alabama. At the time I was crowned, I could not have imagined that my reign would only last a short five months.

Shortly after I was crowned Miss Indian Alabama, my mentor and now uncle Alex approached me with a proposition. Apparently, he had received a flyer through the mail soliciting contestants for the Miss Indian World pageant and thought that I should enter the contest. I told him he was crazy. The mere mention of the Miss Indian World contest made me feel intimidated and overwhelmed.

In my mind's eye, I could see the list of requirements for the contestants; I saw the pictures of all the previous Miss Indian Worlds that reminded me of Native American Barbie dolls. But I realized that, in all of the pictures of these beautiful Native women, I never saw a Miss Indian World that represented southeastern Indians. Even through my trepidation, I knew I wanted to help bring recognition and representation to my southeastern tribe in a way that had not yet been done.

Still, I remember saying, "Alex, have you actually researched this pageant? I've looked into this before. You have to sell a bazillion raffle tickets. There's an essay portion, traditional talent, on-stage question, and an interview. The girls that I would compete against are probably fluent in their Native language and can probably hunt with a bow and arrow and skin their own deer!" Undeterred, he replied, "I can get you ready for it." I said, "Alright then. But if I go down, you're going down with me"—famous last words.

The next several months were spent driving back and forth from my hometown of Andalusia, Alabama, to the tiny Poarch Reservation to meet Alex for my coaching sessions. I was inundated with Creek history, culture, and language. Through this endeavor, I realized that I had a thirst that could only be quenched with knowledge of all things Mvskoke.

It's important to understand that the Poarch Creek Indians are the descendants of several Creek families that were allowed to remain in Alabama after the enforcement of the Indian Removal Act. As a result, these families assimilated into the surrounding communities as a means of survival. Unfortunately, much of the Mvskoke language, culture, and history was forgotten and lost. However, the Poarch Creek Indian community has always remained cognizant of one thing: they've never forgotten that they are Creek people.

Through my preparation I learned that it is one thing to see your "pedigree chart" on a piece of paper and prove that you are Creek. However, it is another thing entirely to *be* a Mvskoke person. I am truly thankful that I was given the opportunity to understand the distinction between "proving" and "being." Once I understood the difference, I resolved that I would be what God had intended me to be: Mvskoke.

So, session after session, I learned and became more confident in the knowledge of who I am and the people from which I come. Before I knew it, the months had flown by, and it was time for me to put all of that knowledge into action.

We *drove* all the way to Albuquerque, New Mexico, from Atmore, Alabama. That was the longest road trip I had ever taken. It felt as if we would never get there, but we finally made it (after twenty-two hours). My whole experience in Albuquerque was unlike any other I had ever had. All of the twenty-one young women I met were unique and intelligent, beautiful and strong. Each was immensely proud to represent her people, as was I.

I knew that my winning was a long shot; but winning the pageant was never the driving force behind my decision to compete. I just wanted people to know that there are still Mvskoke people in Alabama. The Gathering of Nations powwow draws about 80,000 spectators each year, and I wanted them all to hear my tribe's name announced from the loudspeakers.

To summarize my competition experiences, my interview went better than I could have expected. My traditional talent, which incorporated storytelling, a traditional Creek lullaby, and Creek stomp dancing, went smoothly. The dance portion of the contest was interesting to say the least. We were instructed to dance a traditional style that represented our tribe, but to powwow music. I remember feeling silly, but I was so happy to be out in that arena shaking my aunt Rosalind's turtle shells; I just couldn't stop smiling. My on-stage question did not go very well at all, and I kicked myself for not thinking of a more intelligent answer.

The truly spectacular part of the entire competition is the grand entry. I've never seen so many dancers under one roof. They line up on the upper deck of the arena and then dance down the stairs until all you can see is a vision of moving colors like you can't imagine. It gave me chills, and I had to suppress the urge to cry. The thought occurred to me that it was a miracle so many Native Americans were still alive to dance, sing, and showcase their culture given the multiple attempts to annihilate and suppress them. And I was blessed to be able to take part in this moving sea of thriving, vibrant Indigenous life.

Saturday night arrived, and with it, the moment of truth. Which young Native woman would become the next Miss Indian World? They announced the essay winner: "From the Poarch Creek Indians, Megan Young." They had called my name. I was thrilled! Then they announced the winner of the public speaking portion. It wasn't me. Next they announced the interview winner: "From the Poarch Creek Indians, Megan Young." I was shocked! The announcers proceeded to name the winner of the dance portion and talent portion, congeniality, second alternate, first alternate, and then "The moment you've all been waiting for. Your 2007 Miss Indian World is, drum roll please, from the Poarch Creek Indians, Megan Young!"

I thought I was going to melt into the floor! My knees buckled beneath me, and the tears started flowing, and of course, the pictures from that

Megan Young was crowned Miss Indian World in 2007. (Photo Courtesy of Clayton Lisenby of The L House Photography.)

moment captured my "ugly cry" face. I was in utter disbelief. I still have to pinch myself sometimes to make sure that it wasn't all just a dream. But, then again, it was. It began as a dream, a vision of a sixteen-year-old girl who wondered if more opportunities were available for her. By the grace of God, and the support of family and friends, that dream became my reality.

That year passed by so quickly, and it was filled with fond memories, learning opportunities, and challenges. During my reign, I traveled across the United States and Canada. One experience that stands out in my mind occurred while I was visiting Canada. I had the opportunity to meet with a group of young girls. While there, I learned how to make one of their traditional foods, they took me on a tour of their school, and we sat around in a circle and talked. In that moment, looking at those young, impressionable faces, I realized more than ever that I had to be someone worth looking up to. I didn't want to let them down or disappoint any expectations that they might have of what Miss Indian World should be.

Throughout my reign, I struggled with balancing people's expectations and being who I really am. I learned that I couldn't make myself taller or darker, and I sure couldn't change my southern accent. But I learned that those aren't the things that really matter. What truly matters is the genuine way in which you approach people and listen to them. No one likes a fake. You have to be who you are because there's no one else like you in the world.

I can't say with certainty how impactful my reign as Miss Indian World actually was in raising awareness of my tribe. However, I can say that there are so many friends I made and lives that crossed paths with mine. My life was certainly changed as soon as my name was announced. It was truly the experience of a lifetime, and I am humbled to say that I was the 2007 Miss Indian World from the Poarch Band of Creek Indians.

Megan Young is a member of the Poarch Band of Creek Indians and is an active participant in both her community and Mvskoke culture. She enjoys singing, working in her yard, practicing traditional Creek artistry, and researching her tribe's history, customs, and culture. Young is a passionate supporter of education, Mvskoke culture, and tribal sovereignty.

At War with Herself: Artistic Reflections of Culture and Identity

We are all adorned with labels. Some we put on ourselves, but many we are given whether we accept them or not. My journey begins with the earliest label I can remember: "ADOPTED." No, I am not in fact adopted, but several of my peers confronted me with this question at the ripe age of five. You ask yourself why they would even ask that. Then you find out that my mother is Caucasian with blonde hair and blue eyes and is of Irish and Romanian ancestry. I look like my father who has black hair, brown eyes, and a dark red/brown skin tone. He is full-blooded American Indian, Seminole to be specific. The confusion with identity that others see would soon become a relevant question in my life.

The question of who I was haunted me. I did not see my identity as any different as my mother's until that very moment. For the next twenty-five years I would continue to search for who I was, first in the eyes of others, and more recently through my own.

I will only briefly tell you that I was raised in a Seminole village with my parents, grandmothers, and uncles and that I attend traditional ceremonies. What I will elaborate on is how my whole life has been an amalgamation of traditional Seminole culture and rules with that of an American lifestyle. My once-called "struggle" with identity, place, and society is not the same thing it used to be. For a long time, I let others define my being and impact my self-esteem. This finally took a toll on my emotions, which inadvertently trickled into negative actions like drinking and missing classes. Years of misunderstanding myself and other people finally surfaced in the form of depression and anxiety. I filed it away as a part of my journey and use it as an instrument for art in today's conversation. I could not have gotten where I am today if I had not gone through all of these character-defining moments. I came out stronger and more confident.

Art is a medium through which I can best communicate. For my entire twenty-nine years of living, public speaking has been my number one adversary. Naturally, I grasp for another language to speak with an audience, and that would be through sculpture. Molding clay, sculpting wax, and casting metal have become prominent ingredients in my self-expression. The other half of the recipe, of course, is a unique hybrid culture from which a contemporary artistic perspective is born.

My perspective is really a product of my upbringing and environment. At a young age I lived in the Seminole village off Tamiami Trail in Naples, Florida, with more than one family unit. The Seminole side of my family did not believe in living on a reservation, so they settled into a campsite in Collier County. My mother, who was born and raised in Ohio, met my father shortly after moving to Florida. The union was an uncommon relationship from the start. Together they had three daughters, and my mother insisted that a traditional culture was best for her children over mainstream American culture.

It was not until college that I would reflect on these dramatic differences in lifestyle. Growing up in a traditional setting inherently made me the odd one out in the classroom. How many children do you think went home to cook and eat dinner under a thatched-roof structure called a chickee? How many kids' fathers fished in the waterway running along the village or went to pick up a whole cow for butchering? I could not help but respond to my upbringing and feelings of being marginalized by adopting an interest in all things opposite from what I was accustomed: an opposite skin color, an opposite lifestyle, and opposite appearance. . . . opposite, opposite, opposite! I knew that I certainly couldn't be the only one fighting this battle.

My whole university undergraduate work became about finding the voice for those like me, who come from a multiracial home with a distinct culture that is vastly different from the mainstream. I titled the body of artwork that I created during 2008 "Exploitation of the Unidentified." It was made up of forty-eight cast masks from my own face, and each embodied a different identity. I found the ability to understand and then purge the negativity that secretively comes with being not-quite–Native American and not-quite–American. That space in-between where people are lost. This sculptural work was a foundation for the art that would follow.

After graduating from Florida Gulf Coast University in 2008, I moved to Santa Fe, New Mexico. There, I worked, lived, and was a student among other contemporary Native artists on the forefront of a new movement in art. I studied for a year at the Institute of American Indian Arts and worked in the ceramics studio for Karita Coffey. The move to the desert was a drastic change from the swamps of Florida, but for once I was able to relate to my peers. Many, like me, faced adversity in the home, struggled with societal norms, and questioned their place in their own traditional cultures as modern Natives, or those from a biracial background.

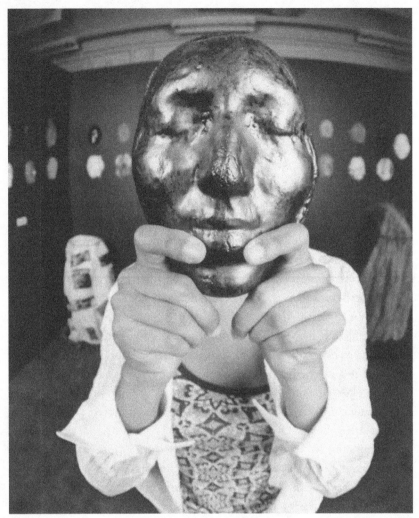

Seminole artist Jessica Osceola displays one of her mask sculptures. (Photo Courtesy of David Alpert and Jessica Osceola.)

My art began to develop a new flavor during this time, as I grew more confident and passionate. Working in Santa Fe helped me grow because I was constantly challenged and inspired by my peers. I worked with clay, cast iron, and bronze during this time and created sculptures that reflect on the toxicity of language: body, verbal, or otherwise.

In 2009, I moved back to my home in Florida and took on a job as a traditional arts specialist for the Seminole Tribe.

In this new role, I stepped back from contemporary art for about three years and focused solely on traditional crafts like basketry, sewing, doll making, and more. At the time I had no idea how important this was, but years later it proved to have a huge impact on my art. In the fall of 2012, I was confronted with a major fork in the road. I was either going to graduate school or going to take a higher position within the tribal politics. Luckily, I chose to become a full-time artist and student again when I began an MFA program at the Academy of Art, University of San Francisco, rather than do a job I was less passionate about.

My involvement in tribal arts led to a blending of traditional and contemporary concepts, materials, and techniques in my sculptures. I was really affected by the appropriation of tribal arts by leaders in fashion such as DKNY, Urban Outfitters, and Anthropologie, to name a few. I produced a body of ceramic sculptures that confronted the theft and mass production of specific Seminole/Miccosukee/Independent patchwork designs. To me, this was a theft of identity, and it became personal. From clay, I sculpted a large trompe l'oeil–style DKNY shopping bag and two brightly painted red legs that jutted out. The basic concept was the "ignorant red man" being shoved into the bag as if owned. This was another landmark in my career because I began to take on an activist art style.

As an older version of myself, I can see how my perspective has changed from being confused about my identity to having a more concise voice in the world. The balancing act relating old and new, traditional and modern, and Seminole and American has shaped my cultural identity and artistic perspective. I realize that I still have a long way to go and a lot of learning to do, but as a student of the arts, and, more important, of the world, my culture and lifestyle continue to evolve, and the artwork that depicts this journey is no different.

Jessica Osceola was born in Naples, Florida, and was raised in her great-grandparents' village of Tamiami Trail. She currently works and lives in Naples and recently had her first child. Jessica is in school full time getting her MFA at the Academy of Art, University of San Francisco. When she is not in classes, she works with the Seminole Tribe's Health and Fitness program to promote healthy lifestyles that combat diabetes and obesity.

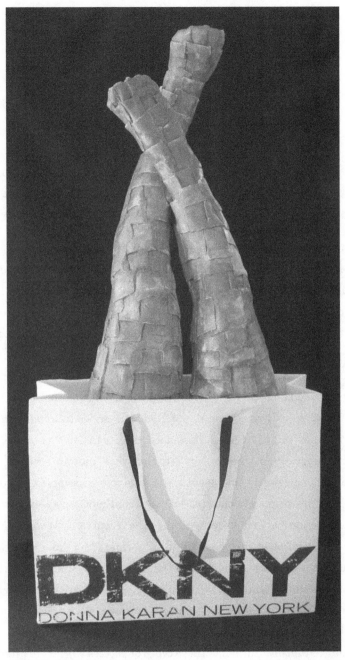

A sculpture by Jessica Osceola addressing the commercial theft of Indian identity. (Photo Courtesy of Scott Snyder and Jessica Osceola.)

Moving Forward

This final chapter offers powerful contributions that share the experiences, visions, and hopes of tribal leaders as they move deeper into the twenty-first century. In the decades following World War II, the context and circumstances in which southern Native people live shifted while some communities gained increased access to resources and political leverage and others began to initiate efforts to follow suit. As a result, many southern tribal nations have become significant economic and political players at both the local and national levels. The Mississippi Choctaw, for example, were described by Congressman Mike Parker in 1998 as going from "deep poverty to being a notable success story." In fact, he goes on to explain that "they are now among the ten largest employers in the state of Mississippi."[1] The role that the Mississippi Choctaw played—and continue to play—in the state's economy is further recognized in the recent book *Mississippi Entrepreneurs*, which includes a profile of former Chief Phillip Martin right alongside some of the area's other influential businessmen and businesswomen.[2] Similarly, the Seminole of Florida have received a great deal of attention for positioning themselves globally within the cattle ranching industry and for helping to pave the way for Indian gaming nationally.[3] Although these types of success stories are often portrayed as a "rags-to-riches" narrative, the emphasis should be on the way they reflect how tribes are exercising their sovereign rights through the development of an economic base to support their political and social infrastructures. The level of development across the region varies, however, among both federally and nonfederally recognized communities. Many have experienced dramatic shifts in their political, educational, and economic situations, while others have seen more subtle changes in the past few decades and are presently laying the foundation for future endeavors. This chapter offers examples from both sides of the spectrum as it represents the work of Indian leaders in not only the political and economic realms but in education, housing, and health and wellness as well.

This final chapter begins with a contribution from Ernest Sickey, who was Louisiana's first Deputy Commissioner for Indian Affairs and Director of the Office of Indian Affairs. In his piece, "A Reflection on a Lifetime of Leadership," he offers a rare glimpse into the strategic thought-process of someone who not only led his own Coushatta community toward developing a political and economic base but also led the charge for the larger Southern Indian Movement within the state of Louisiana, which gained momentum in the 1970s. Setting the Indian movement apart from civil rights–based advocacy efforts, Sickey argues that "Indian people have a legal issue, while non-Indian people have a social issue." As a result of this distinction that places Indian people into a unique position nationally, he modeled a particular type of leadership that involved "learning the system," meeting with key political and economic figures, and finding opportunities to develop partnerships. These partnerships led to the development of Louisiana's first state Indian agency, and then an Inter-Tribal Council, both of which generated new opportunities to leverage resources to assist tribal communities across the state. There were many growing pains, however, as described by Indian advocate Jeanette Alcon in "Initiating Intertribal Efforts in Louisiana." A newcomer to Louisiana, Alcon first came to work with Sickey in 1975 as part of the Louisiana Office of Indian Affairs, and then later as the founding Executive Director for the Inter-Tribal Council. Her contribution offers a glimpse into some of the challenges associated with working among a group of diverse tribal communities—all within a single state—and how their needs, expectations, and level of trust varied, making it difficult—although not impossible—to develop consensus among tribal leadership.

The biggest challenge to intertribal efforts across the region is—by and large—defined by the varying political statuses that tribes hold. As seen in other contributions throughout this collection, obtaining federal recognition is one of the primary concerns of tribes who are presently unacknowledged. Resources and certain levels of economic development capabilities are connected to federal recognition. State recognition, although it does have its benefits, comparatively offers very little in the way of resources and opportunities. As a result, it is not surprising that there are challenges associated with aligning the interests of tribal leaders who are in different developmental stages of tribal nation-building. Charles "Chuckie" Verdin, Chairman of the Louisiana state-recognized Pointe-Au-Chien Indian community, offers a clear illustration of the barriers his tribe faces in "The Oil Companies Stole Our Lands." In addition to the struggles associated with the rapid diminishment of their homeland, they face the dilemma that many southern Indian communities face in their efforts to petition for federal recognition—a lack of historical records. The series of circumstances and practices that coalesced to result in many southeastern Indian people being left off of historical records is not the only challenge that nonfederally recognized tribes face, however. As Framon Weaver, Chairman of the MOWA Band of Choctaw Indians, reveals in "Finishing What I Started," intertribal politics and resource competition also have an impact on the federal acknowledgment process. Although Weaver describes some of the struggles his Alabama community encountered as a result of the parallel efforts to gain federal recognition by the Creek Nation East of the Mississippi (later the Poarch Band of Creek Indians), he also describes his efforts behind creating the MOWA Choctaw Housing Authority.

Despite not having federal recognition, the MOWA Choctaw—under Weaver's leadership—were still able to access federal funds in order to develop tribal facilities and housing for community members. This massive undertaking demonstrates not only the perseverance of this community, who are still engaged in working toward federal recognition, but also their unwillingness to let their present political status dictate the trajectory of their development. Michael "T. Mayheart" Dardar, in "Looking South," argues that many Indian leaders have a tendency to adopt tunnel vision when it comes to federal recognition. "To look 'north' toward the marble edifices of Washington, D.C., for direction," Dardar states, is not genuinely moving toward a sovereign future. The perspective offered here helps to shed light on the persistent tensions that many tribal communities face as they seek to find a balance between their cultural and sovereign integrity and the pressures to conform to an external and imposing system.

Today's leadership across southeastern tribal nations has emerged to build upon the infrastructures that their predecessors have laid. With them, they bring new ideas and perspectives on the futures of their communities' development. This is certainly clear in the inauguration speech of Mississippi Choctaw Chief Phyliss J. Anderson, who emphasizes her vision of improved education, health, language preservation, and economic growth in her community. As the first woman to hold this position, the speech is a historically significant document in its own right; however, it also reflects her understanding of the role she plays in carrying on the legacy of other great leaders who came before her. Like the Mississippi Choctaw who are major economic players within their home state, the Coushatta have also come to play a prominent role within Louisiana's economy. In his speech delivered to the National Indian and Native American Employment Training Banquet, entitled "Building an Entrepreneurial Spirit within Tribal Nations," David Sickey shares how the Coushatta have become an "important economic engine" as a result of their casino and other businesses. The tribe's practice of taking the profits from their business endeavors and reinvesting in their own community's education and job-training initiatives is one of the many ways they are building for their future and exercising their status as a sovereign nation. The Poarch Band of Creek Indians in Alabama have developed a similar model, as shared by Chairwoman Stephanie Bryan in "Seeking Prosperity and Self-Determination." Just like Chief Anderson of the Mississippi Choctaw, Chairwoman Bryan was the first woman elected to this office—in itself demonstrating a new era in tribal leadership. Like others who rise to the ranks of this position, Bryan already held a great deal of leadership experience in helping her community build an economic base through gaming. Recognizing the controversy that gaming generates, she details several examples of how the revenue has positively impacted the Poarch Creek by funding cultural and social programs. The tribe also shares their success by giving millions of dollars to other organizations outside of their own community. The experiences of the Mississippi Choctaw, Coushatta, and Poarch Creek may not necessarily represent other Indian communities across the South—particularly since they comprise three of the eleven federally recognized tribes; however, the examples provided in this chapter help to further define the economic drivers of tribal nation-building and how the line between business and politics often becomes intimately entwined.

Despite the diversity of tribal nations across the region—and nation, for that matter—it is not difficult to find similar patterns in the values that their leaders articulate and in the areas of tribal development and support where they place their resources, no matter how robust or meager. The final contributions offer insight into three of the many important issues tribes are concerned with: higher education, health, and building leadership skills among the youth. First, Lumbee professor Malinda Maynor Lowery offers a keynote address that she delivered to a group of incoming students at the University of North Carolina at Chapel Hill. In this address, called "Defining Moments," she makes a powerful statement, one that embodies a similar message seen in various forms throughout this collection: "[take] responsibility

for your own education and for assuming control over your destiny."
While tribal governments have focused a great deal of energy in
building educational infrastructures and supporting the pursuit of
higher education, ultimately individuals must take the responsibility to
overcome their fears, be resilient, and move forward. While Lowery's
message is particularly aimed at a general audience of students, she
encourages them to seek what they can learn from Native people in
their persistent demonstration of overcoming obstacles that are both
internal and external. This message can be applied to a variety of
situations, but it particularly resonates with Indians in higher education.
On a national scale, the number of Native people pursuing college
degrees is increasing; however, recent literature reveals that there is
still much work to be done to further increase this upward trajectory of
enrollment, as well as in the area of retention. As a result, efforts have
been made within many colleges and universities across the country to
better understand and serve the unique and multifaceted issues and
needs of Indian students.[4] Whether this is being done successfully or
not varies from campus to campus; yet what we do know is that college
graduates are well represented across southern tribes. Many of them
even steer their professional paths toward working directly within
their own communities. Ahli-sha Stephens, for example, is an exercise
physiologist who chose to share her knowledge with her community
of the Eastern Band of Cherokee by promoting health and wellness
at the Cherokee Life Fitness Center. In her piece, "Working Toward a
Healthy Future for the Cherokee Nation," she discusses some of the
challenges faced on her reservation in combating chronic diseases, as
well as maintaining healthy lifestyles. She points out that, as with other
gaming tribes, casino revenue has been instrumental in supporting
the community's health initiatives. The "health-focused" mindset
that Stephens and her colleagues at the Cherokee Life Fitness Center
promote is also successfully being integrated into their tribal educational
system to help the community's youth make positive lifestyle choices.

This forward-looking perspective that is reflected in initiatives and programs aimed at the youth is also evident in the pride that many tribal nations demonstrate in their emerging young leaders. Flip through any tribal newspaper produced in the region and you will find examples that range anywhere from congratulatory announcements of scholarship recipients to profiles on young community volunteers. Since Native youth are a crucial component in the ability of tribal nations to "move forward," this chapter concludes with a contribution from one such leader—who also happens to be this collection's youngest contributor. Elliott Nichols, an eighteen-year-old Coushatta tribal member and aspiring veterinarian, was selected as the only Louisiana student to attend the first annual Native American Youth Agriculture Summit. In his essay, "Native Youth in Agriculture," Nichols shares what he learned during the summit and how it relates to his perspectives and experiences as part of the next generation of caregivers of the land. This is, indeed, encouraging and brings us full circle within this chapter that begins with the contribution of fellow Coushatta member and seasoned leader Ernest Sickey. In addition to reflecting upon his own vast career, Sickey also expresses his hopes that while Native youth "are walking in that world of change, . . . that they will still remain who they are and stay true to what their people want." Nichols represents an emerging generation who will face this challenge, and time will tell *how* and *if* they will maintain this balance.

For southern Indian people, moving forward is about building on the past and planning for the future. Historical, political, and economic circumstances often dictate or influence the resources communities have or the challenges they face; however, the savvy decision making and dedication exhibited throughout this chapter illustrate several ways that tribal leadership identify opportunities and blaze their own paths. Just as no two communities are identical in circumstance or trajectory, neither are their leaders. They each bring their own experiences, ideas, and visions to their positions, which they have to carefully align with the needs and values of their communities as a whole. This is a tall order—particularly given the challenges posed by intergenerational gaps in experiences and values, internal community politics, and new external pressures that seem to frequently present themselves. These barriers pale in comparison to what southern Indian people have endured in previous eras as they consistently defied predictions that they would sink further into obscurity. Instead, they have emerged into the modern era as thriving communities, poised to reach new heights in their development as tribal nations.

A Reflection on a Lifetime of Leadership

Indians of the Southeast have so much to offer. We have always survived. We fought battles, formed treaties, created legislation, and settled many cases in the first supreme courts of this country. The message is very clear, that Southeast Indian people laid the foundation for modern Indians. Those of us who were fortunate enough to join that battle, and extend the message of what our ancestors started through treaties, organizations, and confederacies, have been given a gift that is just incredible. I give all the credit to my ancestry to be able to stand where I do today, and I hope the next generation will share that same journey with the same drive and determination that we had. It must be carried on even with a different way of messaging, even with a different way of looking at things.

The Southern Indian Movement of the 1960s and 1970s was the outcome of a modern battle in which Indian people fought for the survival of their culture, their history, and the preservation of what they had left. The movement itself was not on the front page of every newspaper in the South; it was primarily underground. It is also distinguished from other groups' movements in that as Indian people, we have signed treaties, which gives us a legal right to speak up because, along the way, the federal government didn't come up with their end of the deal. This means that we have an argument and a process over a condition that we have to resolve. When people ask me "why do we have to treat Indian people different from any other ethnic group in the country?" my argument is that Indian people have a legal issue, while non-Indian people have a social issue. That is the difference. It is not to downplay others' plights. It isn't something that we invented; it is something that white people invented. We signed treaties, so we have a legal understanding of what should be done in partnership. This is an im-

Ernest Sickey served as Tribal Chairman of the Coushatta Tribe for twenty-six years and continues to mentor the next generation of tribal leaders. (Official Coushatta Tribe of Louisiana Photo by Sara Sawyer.)

portant distinction and part of what people need to be educated about in order to better understand Indian people.

This journey in working for the betterment of the Coushatta and other southeastern Indian people has been a beautiful one for me. I hope it has made me a better person. It has offered me an opportunity to give back to my people, just as my ancestors did centuries ago. I know that I probably speak for other leaders who were involved in the early years of the struggle for their communities when I say that we gave all that we had to give.

The only way that I was able to accomplish anything was that I had to learn the system. The Coushatta didn't have any money, so I decided to learn how the political system works. I was very fortunate to be able to gain the support and trust of a lot of people who were influential in the system and who came to my side to make a difference, and to make a change. First, I had to learn to message my needs and create an atmosphere that was going to create a partnership and understanding as I worked with the state, federal, and local governments. In 1973, two decades after the federal government walked away from the Coushatta, we were officially recognized as an Indian tribe by the state of Louisiana. Then, a few months later, we reclaimed our federal status. Yet the Department of the Interior told us that we weren't officially Indians until we had land. They really didn't care about Indians; they were more worried about the land. Well, we didn't have reservation land anymore since it was taken out of trust status and divided between two families in the 1950s, and none of the families wanted to give up land because they didn't trust the federal government. A lot of the older Coushatta people had no love or trust for the federal government because all they heard were these horror stories about the government taking land away from them. So, I had to educate them that this would be separate land that we can use, and it wouldn't impact our private homes and land. I had to go through an education process within the tribe. Since no one was willing to donate land and we didn't have any money to purchase any, I worked with a nonprofit organization out of New York who helped us buy 10 acres from a finance company that repossessed some land in our area. Those 10 acres were the beginning of our reservation and our being an Indian tribe officially. Now, the reservation lands are checkerboarded with Coushatta private landholdings. Where the tribal office sits today is on 20 acres of reservation land. Then, there are 40 acres across the street from the tribal office, and an additional 80 acres where the cultural center is located. Only two or three families actually live on reservation lands.

After federal recognition, we had many community meetings where I explained what it meant and what services we might get. I kept telling them, "It's not going to be easy working with the government. Nothing is going to happen fast, so we are just going to have to be patient and work the system." At that time, I also began working with a congressional delegation in both the House and Senate to see what could be done to create a revenue base for the tribe. I met with senators and congressmen and talked about our needs in terms of housing, education, and health care. I also met with different agencies to discuss our needs, such as the water and sanitation departments. It was my job to go out and create this relationship with the congressional delegation of Louisiana. The hard work began after we got recognition. The old people said, "I thought the government was going to send all kinds of money to help us." It was also my job to explain to them that it doesn't work that way. It really was an educational process.

We had to wait two or three years to get into the federal budget cycle to get whatever few programs we were able to get at the time. Indian Health Service did come in and started offering services, but we shared a budget of $50,000 with the Chitimacha Tribe. That is the only money we got from Indian Health Services to provide health care.

Despite the challenges with getting federal services in place, the Coushatta were fortunate in that we had a good relationship with the non-Indian community in Elton. I don't know if it is because the tribe was very small, and I think a lot of the community was multiethnic anyway. The community of Elton was settled by people from the Midwest, so the Coushatta people were very fortunate to be in a community that was not just one ethnic community, but it was made up of Germans, Italians, English, and some blacks, and later some French came in. It was mostly a midwestern community, and Indian people were accepted right away into the community, so it has always been a good relationship. Indian children were admitted into white schools during the segregation period, and during the hard economic times, everybody seemed to develop an attitude of "well, let's help each other." When farming became a major industry, many of the tribal people were offered employment. Even though it was seasonal, that is what they had to work with, so they went to work.

We also have a long history with the other tribes in Louisiana. I was fortunate to work in the state system to help other tribes get what they needed done legislatively, and to connect them with the right people to help them progress along. I had a good relationship with all the tribes in Louisiana back in the early days. It has been a good journey, and I hope whatever life I have to give, that I can continue to mentor and help to improve the lives of Southeast Indians. There is a lot of work to be done, and Indians should not be afraid or too prideful to ask for help when they need it. I wasn't shy about asking for help. Even as a young person, I would go meet with senators and other people who, supposedly, had some tremendous influence over me. I would think to myself, "How can you help me? How can we be partners?" That is the approach I took because they are no better than I am. I just come from a different culture. I didn't go in there scared half to death. I would go in there and sit down with different people and know that we were on an equal basis. I did not want to be threatened or to be told "You're just an Indian." I wanted to be treated as an equal, who just happens to be Indian. When I took that mental attitude, in some cases I came out successful. It is very important that Indian people today take that same approach because we are equal. We are not victims. Nobody gives you any attention until you speak up, so that is what Indian people need to do in the Southeast.

I really had to educate non-Indians about the Indian way of life. My job was to create a foundation for a greater and better understanding of what our future was going to be for the Coushatta in order to gain support and resources. So, it was very important to me that I express the wishes of the community. When I would go to the state legislature, I had to be very careful about what I wanted. I had to do a lot of homework before going in front of the legislature and congressional people so that I could carefully construct the message from the Coushatta people that I wanted to relay, and nothing else. This is because the first thing I would get from them is what suggestion they would have to offer, as opposed to what I wanted. That is not what I wanted from them. I wanted them to listen to me—one on one—and contribute to getting something done together, so that it could be a win-win situation for all of us.

There were many challenges that I faced due to stereotypes and misinformation about Indians. On several occasions, when I was introduced to someone they would say, "Oh, we could have a great tourism program. You guys can do war dances and paint your faces and tourists would come to Coushatta. You guys can make all kinds of money." Well, that isn't what I wanted. First of all, we aren't people who paint our faces and jump around in feathers. Just in that arena, I had to educate people on what Southeastern Indian cultures were as opposed to Natives of the Southwest and other tribal groups in the country. Often times they would say, "Oh, I didn't know that. I thought all Indians lived in tepees."

We have a much larger vision for our future. In the modern world, everyone talks about global outreach, and the Coushatta have participated in this by reaching out to different countries around the world to give the gift of what the Coushatta have to offer. The message we give is that we offer our hand in friendship as one nation to another, just as we did during the formation of the United States when we expressed our cooperation through the signing of treaties. We now have an opportunity to continue extending our hands in friendship to other nations as the global picture changes rapidly. In an effort to better understand treaty rights and their relevance in a modern context, Indians should be partners in the global strategic planning, communication development, and the formation of partnerships around ideas. I hope this is part of the future of tribes because we are hopeful that we are getting a new population of educated people who can walk in that world that we could not fifty or sixty years ago. I hope that while they are walking in that world of change, however, that they will still remain who they are and stay true to what their people want. That is important to me.

How we deliver is how we will be remembered. I hope that history will extend beyond treaties and that we keep the movement going. I hope young people will be inspired to step up and seek assistance from those of us who are left and would be happy to mentor future Indian leaders. I would be happy to do that and contribute what I can for the rest of my life. I can be there for them and show them that the way to get to where we need to be is to learn the system just as I did.

I have been very fortunate to have a life where I have been able to give back. I think that is the life of Indian people: to give what they can, as much as they can, and for as long as they can. I would like to propose that kind of message to the non-Indian world and to academia. We can all make a difference if we just understand where each other is coming from. It was fascinating to be part of the movement in the South, in helping the Coushatta, and then to be able to extend that friendship and partnership to different tribes in the Southeast as they sought to achieve their own dreams and visions.

Ernest Sickey (Turkey Clan) is a member of the Coushatta Tribe of Louisiana where he served as Tribal Chairman for twenty-six years and led the successful effort to have his tribe officially re-recognized by the U.S. Secretary of the Department of the Interior in 1973. During the 1970s, he served as Louisiana's first Deputy Commissioner for Indian Affairs and as first Director of the Office of Indian Affairs, and he established the Inter-Tribal Council of Louisiana. He has a half-century of experience in local and national Indian affairs.

Initiating Intertribal Efforts in Louisiana

I come from a family of advocates. My mother took on many issues for the downtrodden, and I watched her advocacy work as a child without really knowing what it was. It is in my blood, so it is no surprise that I followed in her footsteps.

I am originally from New Mexico. My mother was of Santa Clara and San Juan Pueblo descent and my father of Ute descent. I was raised in Roswell, New Mexico. I ended up in the South after my mother passed away when I was twenty-five, out of college, and kind of lost. My aunt was working in New Orleans, and she asked me to come and work with her. I started off as a community organizer in New Orleans, and eventually came to work with the Louisiana Office of Indian Affairs in 1975 after my aunt recommended me to Ernest Sickey, the Coushatta leader and Commissioner of Indian Affairs. I remember the day he interviewed me. When I walked in he was sitting at his desk in a dreary state office, and one of the first things I saw was this sign on his desk that said "Indian Affairs are the best!" We laughed about that over the years.

He hired me to run the program that was funded by the Department of Labor, and, at that time, it was called the Comprehensive Employment and Training Act (CETA) program. We had a substantial grant that provided for vocational training of tribal members across the state. I came on board as a state employee, but was never able to gain traction at the state level. It was also difficult to operate the CETA program because state civil service rules and regulations proved to be insurmountable roadblocks. Since becoming Commissioner of Indian Affairs, it had always been Ernest's dream to form an intertribal organization in the state, so the lack of being able to run the program effectively through the state provided the impetus to create Louisiana's Inter-Tribal Council. We started with only the CETA program, but over time we developed programs within many different arenas. I worked for the state Office of Indian Affairs for six to eight months. Then, I went to work for the Inter-Tribal Council, which was then formed as a nonprofit organization.

I was the founding Executive Director for the Inter-Tribal Council. This meant that I was involved in the development of the organization. I did a lot of the legwork to get the organization set up and made the transition of money from the state over to the Inter-Tribal Council. The Board of Directors was made up of the tribal chairmen of five tribes in the state of Louisiana and two other members from each tribe selected by the tribal leadership, so at that time I had three members of each tribe on the board. The five designated tribes had three of which were federally recognized and two of which had been state recognized before the Inter-Tribal Council came into existence. They included the Chitimacha, Coushatta, Tunica-Biloxi, Jena Band of Choctaws, and Houma. The Houma were an interesting group to work with because they were subdivided into two different leaderships, and only one of them affiliated with the Inter-Tribal Council. They did eventually come together, though, as the United Houma Nation under one government.

The first years were very challenging, and we had no sooner opened the doors to the Inter-Tribal Council and we were immediately under investigation by the state. For three months, our finances were scrutinized, and we had not even had any expenditures. I'm not sure why this all transpired, but there was certainly a lot of miscommunication and maybe something political happening behind the scenes.

Another challenge that we faced was that although tribes in this state had coexisted side-by-side—some of them not even but a few miles from one another—they had never come to the table together before. The Inter-Tribal Council really sparked the communication between the tribes, but it was difficult to build comradery between them. Initially, there was a lot of suspicion and distrust toward me and between the tribes. What I think worked in my favor was that I was not a member of any of the tribes in Louisiana. I was an outsider, and I brought a different perspective to the table. I had no vested interest in the process or outcome except to make this a cohesive and successful situation. Plus, it was my calling. I felt like I had been called to this since childhood. I had never had an experience like this, and I really wanted to be a part of this thing that was greater than me.

An example that comes to mind of how I was put into an advocacy position happened early on when I was still working in the Office of Indian Affairs. Ernest received a request from one of the Houma groups in Golden Meadow for a meeting with either him or one of his representatives, so he sent me. Here I was only about twenty-eight years old and new to my job, so I really didn't know what to expect. I drove all the way out there, and we met in the back of a bar. I walked in and introduced myself, and they immediately start talking to me in French, which is their primary language. I got very nervous and said, "I'm sorry, but I don't speak French." To which they replied, "I thought they were sending an Indian." I responded by pointing out that "not all Indians speak French." As the day wore on, I was able to connect with them and hear their plight and concerns, which I brought back to the office and was able to advocate on their behalf. Their main concern was one of recognition. They were just treated terribly in their area because the surrounding population was very prejudiced against them. Since they didn't fit into a black or white racial category and the neighboring communities didn't consider them Indian because of the mixed-blood nature of their background, there was prejudice leveled at them from all directions. The Houma had suffered a lot of pain and suffering, and they just needed someone to hear them. Although I knew zero about the French language, we were finally able to communicate. They just needed to be heard. Unfortunately, there was really nothing that the Office of Indian Affairs could do for them other than to acknowledge the problems that they faced. A lot of the early part of my work was just to hear what the needs and the problems were because no one had ever collected that information before. Every tribe had such a different perspective and a different need. Today, the United Houma Nation is still struggling for federal recognition.

Just to sit together and make decisions about the goals of the Inter-Tribal Council was incredible because the tribes had been so fragmented. I think Ernest envisioned that in speaking as a group they would make an impact at the state level. As a united group speaking within a single organization, there was a chance that we would be heard. While the political ramifications of bringing this together were tremendous, it became somewhat of a nightmare to pull off. It took a lot of years to build the communication between the groups and to get tribes to actually be able to start trusting one another. We had a lot of battles over the blood quantum issue, and who were the "real" Indians and who were not. In Indian Country, that is such a big "to do" regarding who is and who isn't a "real" Indian. This was made even more difficult because tribes have different criteria by which they determine their membership. For the Coushatta, you cannot be any less than a quarter, and you have to live within the area in order to get services. Then, you have the Chitimacha who recognize up to one-sixteenth blood quantum, yet they are the only ones that have a Bureau of Indian Affairs–funded school for Indian children. This goes to show the diversity of Indian communities in Louisiana alone.

Given these differences, it was a huge milestone that we were able to develop the criteria for the tribes who could belong to the Inter-Tribal Council of Louisiana. That was a very difficult and strenuous task. In the South, tribes were just in the formation stage during the late 1970s. They weren't established tribes like across the nation. So, we were really in a position to be in the developmental stages of tribal governments. There were a lot of questions that we grappled with, such as how do you define a tribe? How do you define who is Indian? Do you define it by culture? Is it really a linguistic question? Is it a political question? I guess you can say it was like exploring a new frontier. Of course, we looked to the Bureau of Indian Affairs guidelines for federal recognition as we developed our own process. To me, it was impressive to have a group of five tribal leaders be able to come to an agreement of what the membership was going to look like in the Inter-Tribal Council.

In addition to coming up with our own localized criteria, the Inter-Tribal Council was also able to support the efforts of tribes as they petitioned for federal recognition. For example, we were able to support the efforts of Earl Barbry when he became the new Chairman of the Tunica Biloxi Tribe. He was just elected and reached out for support to put his paperwork together for his tribe's efforts toward federal recognition. That was a huge breakthrough in the way of building trust. We were able to break down many of those tribal barriers.

Another major breakthrough that the Inter-Tribal Council was able to achieve was in program development. I hired people within the tribes to do the actual on-site fieldwork for the employment and training program, as well as other programs. We were able to get grants to address many needs within the tribes. It was exhausting, but it was a joy to do this kind of work at the same time. When you begin to see some of these pieces come together, it is amazing. I feel very fortunate to have been in the right place at the right time and to have been a part of this. To be able to advocate for people not of my blood, but of kindred blood, made my heart sing. This was a time when tribes were struggling financially. The resources were beyond limited, and it took a lot of creativity to bring the grants to the table. We used to write grants until the late hours of the night. My children, who are now thirty and thirty-four, recount stories of how they were raised under the conference room table of the Inter-Tribal Council. Since their dad worked out of town, I would pick them up, take them home, feed them, and give them their baths. Then, we would all go back to the Inter-Tribal

Council office where I set up little pallets under the conference room table because it was dark and that is where they would sleep while I finished writing grants.

The work and energy that it took to pull this together, and then convince others that this is what we needed to do, was huge. In 1980, we were able to take this assistance to the next level, creating the Institute for Indian Development, which was an offshoot of the Inter-Tribal Council. It was established primarily to offer technical assistance to the tribes in the way of planning and organization because many of them did not have the trained staff to help them develop their plans. We helped the Tunica Biloxi get their economic development plan in place because they had bought a pecan factory, and we put the business plan together for them. We were involved in a lot of areas that required technical assistance for individual tribes. Another example that comes to mind involved the Choctaw-Apache group in Ebarb who worked with anthropologists but sought additional assistance that we provided.

Besides the programming, we also did a lot of legislative activism. We were actually able to create a subcommittee on Indian affairs within our state legislature that would hear nothing but Indian affairs–related issues. It never really got off the ground, since politics change so quickly as new legislators and tribal leaders come into office, but it still represented the fact that we had made some major strides. As we were getting this subcommittee into place, Ernest left tribal government and my time at the Inter-Tribal Council was coming to an end as well. Honestly, I was burned out. I had reached a level of pure exhaustion in pushing multiple agendas through diverse processes. I was coming into my fifteenth year when a lot of elections took place among the tribes and new tribal leadership emerged who had not been a part of the start of the Inter-Tribal Council. As a result, suspicions were starting up all over again. I had to try and reconnect people who were brand new blood, but I found it hard to build strong relationships with them because they were suspicious of the old administrations, which they associated with me. Around 1987 is when I decided that it was time for me to back away from the Inter-Tribal Council.

In looking back to those years, I realize how enriching it was for me to work hand-in-hand with these diverse tribes. At the time, I didn't see what we were doing as "making a mark in Indian history." That wasn't in my head as I was so focused on the day-to-day tasks that needed to be done. I don't think it was in Ernest's mind either. His tribe had just been re-recognized by the federal government, so he was in the midst of trying to get their federal funding in order. At the same time, his efforts for his own tribe caused him to push for other tribes in the state to get together at the same table so that the state would be forced to acknowledge who they were.

It was an exciting time, and I'm thankful that I shared in part of it.

Jeanette Alcon resides in Broussard, Louisiana. She is pursuing entrepreneurial efforts and being a grandmother to her new—and only—granddaughter in Atlanta.

The Oil Companies Stole Our Land

Back in the time of my parents and grandparents, my tribe had a lot of land in Bayou Pointe-aux-Chien. The Europeans said it was uninhabitable and useless land, but we planted, trapped, and fished the land anyhow. That is how we survived.

When oil was found on some of this land beginning in the 1940s, the oil companies started claiming it as their own. They began cutting off sections, said that it was their land, and started paying the taxes on it. They sent people out there to talk to the Indians and collect money from them saying that they were going to pay their taxes for them. They did not pay their taxes because these people really worked for the oil companies. Once the Indian people realized what was going on it was too late because the oil companies had already taken over. They had lawyers and they were educated, and the Indian people weren't educated.

My grandfather and some elders hired attorneys in the early 1960s, and since they didn't have any money to pay the attorneys, the attorneys said that they would work for a percentage of what they got back. The attorneys turned out to be crooks too and made deals with the oil companies, giving more of our land away for a share of the oil money coming in. I have seen documents and maps where they made deals with the oil companies and divided up the land. They told our people that they would be receiving money from oil. Most never did. The few who did receive anything got checks for only a few dollars—and some even less than a dollar.

About 90 percent of our land was taken by the oil companies. What we have left out there to call our own is just a small fraction of what we had before. Even if we were able to get the land back, most of it is under water or just marsh, and you cannot really plant anything there anymore because of the salt water. So, if we would ever win the land back, the only thing that it would really be good for is fishing.

Since our community is so close to the Gulf, the erosion that has been accelerated by the oil companies has caused many of our people to move away. The areas where most of the people used to live in now mostly marshland, so we cannot build homes where we used to. This is taking away our community. Our historic community land and cemetery are also in jeopardy of being washed away. This is happening all along the south Louisiana coast, where it is affecting a lot of people.

Starting in the 1980s, I remember going to meetings where we just got together and talked about land issues, hurricanes, and other events happening in our community. Then, in the 1990s, we started to get more formal and brought in an attorney to consult on how to get our land back. He suggested getting federal recognition first, so after several other meetings, we incorporated the Pointe-Aux-Chien Indian Tribe in 1994. In 1996, Cleveland Verdin, Sidney Verdin, and I drove to Washington, D.C., to submit a petition for federal recognition. We have since been recognized by the state of Louisiana and by Lafourche and Terrebonne Parishes. I was elected Chairman of the Pointe-Aux-Chien Indian Tribe in 1999 and still hold that position today.

We have plans for the future, but until we get federally recognized, it is hard to do much. After submitting our petition in 1996, we received a preliminary report that stated that we met four of the seven criteria. Where we came up short is in the historical records. For our community, it is even harder than most petitioning tribes since we are located so far back in the marsh. The Europeans did not communicate with us, so there is hardly anything written on us. What is written is mostly in the old Spanish or old French. It is hard to hire people who can read these texts that were written 150–200 years ago. We are still hoping to one day become federally recognized and are fortunate to be working with some people from the local universities who are helping us to document our history. We may not be able to save our land, but we can preserve our history.

Charles "Chuckie" Verdin followed in the tradition of his grandfather, father, and uncles and became a commercial fisherman (shrimping) following high school. By 2000, he owned four offshore shrimp vessels working the Gulf of Mexico and along the East Coast. With the decline in shrimp prices in 2003 due to imports, he began shrimping part-time, and started also working on boats catering to the oil field. In 1999, he was elected as Tribal Chairman of the Pointe-Au-Chien Indian Tribe, which has since been recognized by the state of Louisiana and by Terrebonne and Lafourche Parishes. They are still hoping to one day meet the criteria for federal recognition.

Finishing What I Started

I have been honored to represent my people for a major portion of my adult life. I only hope I can see us achieve the recognition and status that the Choctaw people here in Alabama deserve.

The MOWA Band of Choctaw Indians was first recognized by the state of Alabama in 1832. However, over time our political status within the state became ignored and uncertain. In the early 1970s, the Nixon administration adopted policies of self-determination that encouraged tribal governments across the country to take on more responsibilities and provided grant money for those that were recognized by either their state government or the federal government. As a result, and outside of our awareness, the Alabama legislature passed legislation for tribal state recognition since at the time none of Alabama's tribal communities were federally recognized. Up until then, we received a few services from the Mississippi Choctaws until about 1978, but then the Creek Nation East of the Mississippi (CNEM) started receiving all the money for Indians in Alabama. Soon, the leadership of the CNEM also secretly applied for recognition for a part of its membership as the Poarch Band of Creek Indians. They received grant money to serve not only the MOWA Band of Choctaw Indians but also most of the Creeks in Alabama, southwest Georgia, and northwest Florida. They went across the country lobbying for the Poarch Creek and against the rest of the Indians who they were funded to serve, gaining the support of the Mississippi Choctaw and the United South and Eastern Tribes Inc. (USET).

MOWA Choctaw leaders Gallasneed Weaver and Bennett Weaver felt that CNEM leaders lied to them, asking them to hold off on trying for state

Framon Weaver is a longtime leader of the MOWA Band of Choctaw Indians. (Photo Courtesy of Framon Weaver.)

recognition and stating that they were going to get both the Creeks and the Choctaws state recognition. I guess CNEM leaders were very convincing because they both agreed to let them pass their bill, which resulted in the 1978 Mims Act, which established the Alabama Indian Affairs Commission that was comprised of the CNEM's Tribal Council.

In the summer of 1978, the MOWA Choctaw held a tribal meeting, and everyone was invited. We set up a temporary Tribal Council, and we formed a Constitution Committee. After about four months, we had a constitution. We selected a Tribal Council, but we had no money, no phone, no office, and few prospects. No one was very anxious to become the chairman. I was the only one who worked shift work with days off in the middle of the week three weeks a month. I had time to run errands, make meetings, and be available for telephone calls. Bennett Weaver nominated me for chairman, and with no one else accepting a nomination, I became the first Tribal Chairman (Chief) under the new tribal constitution.

I realized I had my work cut out for me. We started working to get our tribe state recognized as soon as the legislature convened in 1979. I had supported newly elected state representative J. E. Turner in his effort to defeat the incumbent. So, we explained what we needed, and he went to work on it. Although Representative Turner introduced our bid for state recognition as a local act, we still ran up against opposition from a few white legislators and several powerful black legislators. We found out their reasons for opposition and worked out an agreement that allowed the MOWA Choctaw bill to pass both houses.

The Creek Nation East of the Mississippi found out that our bill had passed and started lobbying Governor Fob James to veto it. They nearly had him convinced to do it. Gallasneed Weaver and I met with the chief of staff for the governor and convinced him that we were not taking anything from anyone, only seeking recognition for our tribe. The bill was signed into law by Governor James, and the MOWA Band of Choctaw Indians had its first victory over the Creek Nation East of the Mississippi.

Our next battle was to try to get an accurate count in the 1980 census, which previously underrepresented us. We contacted census officials and made sure we had enumerators in both Mobile and Washington Counties. They did an excellent job in getting our Choctaw people properly enumerated. With this new census data we had a great tool to work with. Though we still had an undercount, we were in much better shape than we were before. This new census data enabled us to get the Alabama Indian Affairs Commission restructured, with J. E Turner taking the lead and Senator Pat Lindsey lending support in the Alabama Senate. We now had a new Alabama Indian Affairs Commission that actually represented all Native Americans in the state of Alabama. Getting to this point was no easy accomplishment; we had to engage in political battles with the Poarch Band of Creek Indians all the way to the final signature of Governor George Wallace.

The MOWA Band of Choctaw Indians operated several federally funded programs by 1983. We were even invited by Senator Jeremiah Denton to go to Washington, D.C., and testify before the Senate Select Committee on Indian Affairs. While on the trip to Washington, Russell Baker, our new Executive Director, and I planned the entire week to visit government agencies. The most important visit we made was to the Department of Housing and Urban Development (HUD). We found out that state-recognized tribes were eligible for funding from HUD if the tribe had an approved Housing Authority. We immediately returned home and drafted a tribal resolution to create the MOWA Choctaw Housing Authority in April 1983. HUD took a year to tell us that we needed a state act in order to fund our Housing Authority. It was a long struggle, with the original act having to be amended four different times, but we broke ground in the fall of 1992 for our first development. This funding enabled us to build a new tribal office complex with a clinic, council chambers, and administrative offices; a football and baseball field; and a community center in McIntosh, Alabama. Also, twenty-six housing units were built in Washington County and twenty-six in Mobile County. In addition, we applied and received funding for twenty mutual help housing units in the following funding cycle.

Just as we were feeling good about our success with housing, the Department of the Interior sent Virginia De Marce to do an on-site visit with the MOWA Band of Choctaw Indians. I waited for her to visit our reservation, and after a while I called the Department of the Interior and was informed that De Marce had already conducted her visit to the city of Mobile and asked questions about the MOWA Choctaw to people on the street. She determined that she did not need to visit the place where the Choctaw people actually lived, go to church, attend school, buy groceries and gas, get married, and have children. The places where we go to court or the doctor, or any of the things all tribal people do in their daily activities. It was a deliberate decision to not visit and see where we live, how we live, or talk with our neighbors. She thought she could be better informed by strangers who did not know about the MOWA Band of Choctaw Indians. Most of them didn't even know the names of the counties that share a common border with Mobile County on the north, east, or west. Some may not know that the Gulf of Mexico is on the south end of Mobile County! I know this is true because when people say they have never heard of us, I ask some of the same questions, and many times those are the answers I get. Try it sometime yourself; most non-Indian people in the area don't know the difference between Choctaw, Creek, or Cherokee, and they certainly don't know which tribes are located in their county. Those are the people De Marce made inquiries to on her visit.

Despite all of the challenges we faced, the MOWA Band of Choctaw Indians have accomplished a great deal during my seventeen years in office. The following lists some of these accomplishments: We negotiated for funding for Community Services Block Grants and Low Income Home Energy Assistance with the state of Alabama, making it the very first tribe-state agreement between a state and a non-Bureau of Indian Affairs–listed tribe. We were also awarded $150,000 of the Pipeline Law Suit Settlement, and it was used to establish the MOWA Choctaw Culture Center. We purchased more than 300 acres of land and adopted a new constitution that included three branches of government. We established a Tribal Police Department, and the state formally recognized it a few years later under Chief Taylor. The state of Alabama recognized all MOWA Choctaw lands as our tribal reservation. We filed suit against the Poarch Band of Creek Indians and the Department of Labor to get the Work Force Training Program, which led to the creation of the Alabama Inter-Tribal Council to administer the program for all Indians in the state of Alabama. We received grants from the Administration for Native Americans to fund a petition for federal acknowledgment and establish a catfish farm, a flower nursery, a truck farm, and a peach and blueberry orchard. We also received funding for seventy-two housing units, a new tribal office, and a clinic. I left office in November 1995.

In September 2011, I was elected to serve my people once again. I hope to finish the project I started in December 1981 and have the federal government acknowledge the MOWA Band of Choctaw Indians.

We are once again working to achieve federal recognition. However, this time we have chosen to enlist a few allies in our quest. In early 2012, several tribal leaders started talking about forming an alliance of tribes with similar histories in the East. The Alliance of Colonial Era Tribes was formed and has already started to have an impact. A member tribe had representatives at three of the Department of the Interior public hearings on federal recognition across the country, and friends attended the other two.

The MOWA Band of Choctaw Indians have struggled for survival since the

1830s, and we have reached a point on several occasions when it looked like we were defeated and there was little hope. Each time, however, new leaders emerge with fresh ideas and new energy. This is why the fight continues.

Framon Weaver has been the Tribal Chairman of the MOWA Band of Choctaw Indians since 2011, a position he previously held from 1978 to 1984 and then from 1986 until 1995. He is a Vietnam veteran who also joined the Teamsters Union and drove trucks on construction jobs, worked for the Olin Corporation, and eventually operated his own trucking business. He is the father of seven and grandfather of four.

Looking South

> You have given him dominion over the works of your hands; you have put all things under his feet, all sheep and oxen, and also the beast of the field, the birds of the heavens, and the fish of the sea, whatever passes along the paths of the seas.
>
> Psalms 8:6–8 (English Standard Version)

> We must protect the forest for our children, grandchildren and children yet to be born. We must protect the forests for those who can't speak for themselves such as the birds, animals, fish and trees.
>
> Qwatsinas, Nuxalk Nation

Economic crashes, global climate change, resource wars, and political instability are just some of the complex challenges facing the world's peoples in these early years of the twenty-first century. As the governments of the world profess a desire to find solutions, we need to look beyond the rhetoric to the foundation philosophy to determine the sincerity of those professions.

The theology of dominion came to our shores with the Columbian landfall in 1492. Armed with the papal decrees that subjected the lands under his footfall to his Christian king, Columbus established the pattern for devouring the peoples and resources of the land. For Indigenous Peoples, the struggle, over the centuries, would be to reconcile these two opposing worldviews and to define their own position in an ever-changing world, a world that saw the ever-increasing ascension of the European man and the increased subjugation of the Native world.

For the original peoples of the Gulf Coast, the question is how we survive as Indigenous communities in the face of the decades of wholesale destruction brought about by the unchecked economic exploitation that European dominion has brought. As we still deal with the aftereffects of the BP oil spill and the ongoing challenge of coastal land loss, the question is on what will we build the foundation for our path to the future?

In the early years of the nineteenth century, this conflict of values and identity would surface in the Southeast among the Creek Nation. Inspired by the great Shawnee leader Tecumseh, the Red Sticks from the Upper Creek towns attempted to draw a line between themselves and the assimilated Lower Creek towns. The Red Sticks sought a return to traditional culture and values, while the Lower Creek towns pursued an alliance with the growing American empire. The conflict quickly escalated into a full-scale civil war. The Americans, using this as a pretext, sided with the assimilated Lower towns led by William McIntosh seeking to ensure the ascendancy of a compliant Creek government.

The following year the alliance of U.S. forces, Lower Creeks, and pro-American Choctaws defeated the Red Stick efforts at Horseshoe Bend, but the cultural, spiritual, and social conflict at the heart of the struggle continues to this very day here along the Gulf Coast.

The treaty that marked the Red Stick defeat and the land concessions granted to the United States (which was essentially a Creek civil war that produced an American, and not a Creek, victor) was signed at Fort Jackson adjacent to the Hickory Grounds, the capital of the Creek Nation. This was the social/sacred heart of the people and the resting place for the bones of their ancestors.

Today the site is owned by the Poarch Band of Creek Indians, the cultural, if not genealogical, heirs of William McIntosh. The Poarch have decided their path to the future is dependent on building a multimillion-dollar hotel/casino complex atop the graves of the old ones. The theology of domination has come full circle, now infesting the hearts of Indigenous societies that it had failed to totally destroy.

Much has been made of the meetings between tribal leaders and the recently reelected president of the United States. There was much pomp and circumstance surrounding what amounted to a half-hour of face time with the president for a handful of selected Native politicians. These were, for the most part, representatives of successful gaming tribes who had contributed handsomely to the cause of the Democratic Party. You can rest assured that the conversation was more about the security of tribal "economic development" than any human rights discourse. The tendency of tribal leadership is to look "north" toward the marble edifices of Washington, D.C., for direction, hoping to secure the crumbs that fall from the empire's table. It would seem that a nod or handshake from President Obama is of greater value than any substantial move toward genuine sovereignty.

For the Indigenous Peoples of the Gulf Coast recovering from oil spills and hurricanes and facing the rising tides and shrinking land base, the choice is clear. Do we commit our precious resources to the quest for recognition by a government that has marginalized and ignored us or do we look for another path toward the future?

If we listen we can hear the voices of our Indigenous brothers and sisters rising with the songs of the Red Sticks. From the mountains of southern Mexico to the tundra of northwest Canada, they are singing the same song. They are indeed "Idle No More," and they are determined to lay hold of the vision of sovereignty and self-determination that the words of Tecumseh have carried across the centuries.

If we are to resist assimilation and survive as the free, self-determined people we were destined to be then we have to seek out the embers that burned at Horseshoe Bend and relight the fires of our people. We must dedicate ourselves to our survival as a People; this is not the struggle of the individual.

Only in the mind of Western man do you prepare for the apocalypse by hoarding canned goods and weapons and pretending to be John Wayne. If we are to survive we must do so as a tribe, as a Nation. Our strength and tenacity have always been anchored in our collective ties to one another and to the land that has always sustained us.

If the Indigenous Peoples of the Gulf Coast are to survive, then we must look away from the path of assimilation and look "south" for a fresh vision and a firm foundation for ourselves and the generations that will follow us.

Tecumseh's goal was to clear space on the ground for the free and un-fettered existence of Onkwehonwe. His goal was not to live without white government, culture, and society, but to live *against them*. To do this today, Onkwehonwe warriors will need to engage the colonizer in a rebellion of truth, redefine the meaning of our renewed world in a mystic vision of struggle and justice, and force a reckoning with our regenerated and unified Onkwehonwe power through rites of resur-gence. This is the warrior's path of spiritual self-determination that has been laid before us by the ancestors and the brothers and sisters who share our values and vision. (Taiaiake Alfred Wasa'se)

Editor's Note: This essay first appeared in *Raging Pelican*, Écoulement no. 4. Permis-sion to reprint has been granted.

Michael "T. Mayheart" Dardar was born in the Houma Indian settlement below Golden Meadow, Louisiana. He served for sixteen years on the United Houma Nation Tribal Council (retired in October 2009). Currently he works with Bayou Healers, a community-based group advocating for the needs of coastal Indigenous communities in south Louisiana.

Inauguration Speech of Phyliss J. Anderson, First Woman Chief of the Mississippi Choctaw, Tuesday, October 4, 2011

Good morning. What an honor it is to stand here today before my Choctaw people. Many have told me I have won the hearts of the Choctaw people. Well you have won my heart, and I am so grateful to each of you!

Dear friends, fellow Choctaws, and fellow citizens of the great state of Mississippi and the United States of America, I stand before you amazed, filled with joy and humility on this unbelievable day as, hand-in-hand, we march to our shared destiny.

I want to thank each of you for being here and sharing this moment with me, my husband, my family, and the proud Mississippi Band of Choctaw Indians. This journey has been remarkable. To the Choctaw People, *okla ha-chi yakokili* . . . thank you for believing in me. Thank you for standing as ex-amples of strength and uniting in the spirit and hope to rebuild and prog-ress this tribe, *our tribe*, the Mississippi Band of Choctaw Indians, *forward together*.

Phyliss J. Anderson is the first female chief of the Mississippi Band of Choctaw. (Photo Courtesy of Candace McKay Images, Mississippi Band of Choctaw Indians.)

Our journey to this moment has at times been long and difficult. We faced challenges together arm-and-arm. We listened to many concerns, many issues, and after each community visit, we prayed for brighter tomorrows. We cooked, served, had great fellowship, marched together, and knocked on each and every tribal member's door campaigning for new leadership and opportunities for our children. . . . Long after I am done here, I will never forget that!

The campaign was marked by vigorous discussion of the issues and the passionate support for the various candidates as it should be in a democracy. Unfortunately, these passions can sometimes result in ill feelings, and I understand it may take time for those feelings to subside. But subside they must, for we shall come together as we meet the major challenges that face our tribe now and in the future.

As Chief of the people, I ask for your full support, whether you voted for me or not. I need your prayers as we go forward in these uncertain times. I stand before you today ready to take on this new journey and awesome responsibility as your Choctaw Tribal Chief. I am excited and humbled, but most of all I am blessed and grateful for this opportunity. I know there are many challenges ahead, and I am ready. I've been waiting . . . and with your faith and trust, our destiny has arrived. This moment, next to accepting God in my life and the birth of my children, is an unparalleled experience; there is no other like it.

My Choctaw people, our goals are the same. We want our children to graduate from tribal schools equipped with skills to pursue their dreams in the twenty-first century. We want our Choctaw Health Center to dispense the best care possible. We want to preserve our language and culture. We want to continue to expand the role the tribe has as an engine for economic growth in the state of Mississippi. These goals are within our grasp, but we *must* pursue them as one people.

While our journey to these shared goals has been progressive, it was interrupted, partly by factors beyond our control, such as the current economic downturn, but partly by problems of our own making, for we allowed disunity to deter us from our goal. Even though there are some things that are beyond our control, we must unite to change the course of events so that conditions will improve over time.

We must be patient; it takes time to regain our path. But there is one thing that is ours alone, that no outside force can control and no power on Earth can take from us. It is the most powerful weapon on our journey, and that is the spirit of optimism. It is part of our inheritance and is here for the taking! Abraham Lincoln was so right when he said, "A house divided against itself cannot stand."

Our ancestors courageously and optimistically overcame seemingly impossible obstacles to survive because they thought that one day their descendants would thrive and prosper. My own mother worked tirelessly every day at unskilled jobs because she believed that life would be better for her children. And you know, she was right, as this day clearly demonstrates.

Who would have thought that I, a woman raised without electricity or plumbing and who labored in a cotton patch under the blazing Mississippi sun to help support her family, would stand here before you, sharing the mantel of Pushmataha and Phillip Martin—great Chiefs and great guides on our epic journey?! Our ancestors, like my mother, believed in us. . . . They had that positive outlook for the future. Surely, now it is our duty to carry forward this optimistic attitude.

Let us pledge today to start our journey anew—let us put our differences aside, join hands, and freed from intimidation that has bound us during recent years, again seek the path forward. It is not so distant, and it is reachable.

We need help on our journey—partners who will share the load and, in turn, share our joys along the way. We need honest non-Indian partners who will hand-in-hand share the victory of hard-earned successes for our tribe.

Fellow tribal members, we occupy a unique position: an independent nation—Choctaws, yet proud Mississippians, and patriotic Americans who have stood alongside our fellow citizens from the Battle of New Orleans to Afghanistan to defend and protect the freedoms that, as Americans and Choctaws, are our birthright.

On this beautiful morning, the realization of today's event gripped my heart with pride and great, *great* determination. I am amazed, for because of you, the members of the Mississippi Band of Choctaw Indians, this very day marks the day that I, Phyliss J. Anderson, am the first woman Chief in Choctaw history! I thank you!

Thank you again for sharing this moment with me—this is *our* moment in Choctaw history.

Ha Chi Yakokali Chitto!

Phyliss J. Anderson, a native of the Red Water community in Leake County, Mississippi, serves as the first female Tribal Chief of the Mississippi Band of Choctaw Indians and was officially inaugurated on October 4, 2011. As Tribal Chief, she is committed to building tribal financial stability; operating an accountable, responsible, and transparent government; and building the quality of life on the reservation. Chief Anderson is married to Ricky Anderson Sr. and is the mother of three, stepmother of four, and grandmother of ten.

Building an Entrepreneurial Spirit within Tribal Nations

Speech delivered by David Sickey, Coushatta Tribe
of Louisiana Council Member, at the National Indian
and Native American Employment Training Banquet,
April 12, 2012, Marksville, Louisiana

It is my sincere privilege and honor to speak to you today. I greatly appreciate this opportunity, and I would like to thank the organizers for asking me to deliver the keynote address. I believe that this event comes at a critical time for Native peoples, and I take very seriously my duty to convey an appropriate message that addresses the challenges we face. More important, I feel that it's my duty to not only provide you with important information and ideas, but to deliver a rallying cry. . . . I believe that it is time that we stand up and loudly proclaim the value of work-training and employment programs, while also drawing attention to our achievements and successes. We must show each other, our communities, and our country that investment in training and education is an indispensable investment in the future.

Training, education, and employment are the keys to working our way past the obstacles established by our current economy and overcoming any new challenges that may arise. This is true for all people, not just Native Americans. Earlier this year, I began a speech with these words: "Together, starting today, let us build a future for our children." I was speaking to members of my tribe—the Coushatta Tribe of Louisiana—and I was addressing the importance of our ongoing economic development efforts and the important role that education plays in preparing our young people for jobs of the future. I believe that this theme is appropriate tonight as well. The current economic environment has been difficult for all job seekers, but it has been particularly harsh for Native Americans. The importance of job-training efforts and federal support for these efforts has never been greater. Unfortunately, the threats to federal funding for job training have also never been greater. In March, not one but two bills—HR 3610 and HR 3611—were introduced in the U.S. House of Representatives that threatened to eliminate all employment and training funding for Native American grantees receiving funding under the Workforce Investment Act, as well as Native Employment Works Program funding.

These programs date back to the early days of manpower programs, and they were authorized with the understanding that American Indian tribes are sovereign nations that have a unique trust relationship with the United States government. The Inter-Tribal Council of Louisiana, which has been with us since 1974, has used government funding to provide a program for job training and support services. Programs like this across the country have provided service and training to millions. We must not let cuts to programs such as these become law. We must reach out to our representatives and explain to them that funding for these programs provides support and services to individuals who otherwise would not access mainstream employment and training programs because of cultural reasons or the remoteness of their communities. Not only must we stand up for this funding but also we must stand up for our sovereign status. We must not let this or our unique trust relationship be ignored or, worse yet, eliminated entirely.

In order to ensure a brighter future, we cannot let history be forgotten. Nevertheless, while we must work hard to make sure that others uphold their end of the bargain and maintain their commitments, we have obligations as well. We must do a better job at showing the world what we have done—and are doing—to contribute to our communities, our local governments and local tax rolls, and our people. We must highlight our business achievements, and we must show how our training and education have led directly to new opportunities and new ideas. Many of us are building for the future with an entrepreneurial spirit, and it's time that we are recognized as the business and community leaders that we have become.

Like many Native American tribes around the country, the Coushatta Tribe of Louisiana has built a successful gaming business. Our Coushatta Casino Resort in Kinder is not only a critical source of revenue and jobs for our tribe but also it has become a critical business and job provider for our entire region. We employ more than 2,500 people, representing nine different Louisiana parishes, and we plan to increase the number of employees when construction of our new 401-room hotel and casino expansion is completed later this year. Further, the Coushatta Tribe of Louisiana has been ranked as one of the top five largest private employers in the state of Louisiana for a number of years.

In addition, our tribe has expanded its economic development into new and diverse areas that provide employment and on-the-job training for our people. For example, our tribe has received grants for the construction of a hydroponic facility that is now run by one of our tribal members and provides employment to local community members. Similarly, our tribe diversified its business portfolio internationally in 2011 when we became the sole U.S. distributor and importer of an innovative natural skin care product line produced overseas, in Israel. Members of our tribe are gaining indispensable experience as they integrate into operating our international skin care business. We have made it a point to draw attention to the fact that our casino and other businesses have become important economic engines for our community, our region, and our state. We did not want to be taken for granted or overlooked. Indeed, we wanted our voice to be heard at all levels, so we became active members of our local Chamber of Commerce and of business and economic development organizations around the state. Many of you are doing similar things, I'm sure . . . and you should be. This kind of involvement and outreach is a vital and necessary way to not only guarantee continued business success but also to show the value of the job and skills training programs that create knowledgeable, dedicated workers and nurture the entrepreneurial spirit. It shows that such training leads to real-world success.

There are other things we can do as well. During the past five years, my tribe has exercised its sovereign status through unprecedented outreach to foreign governments and businesses. In 2008, for instance, we created the Department of Commerce to coordinate all economic development and diversification efforts for the benefit of our people. That same year, we took a significant step by officially recognizing the state of Israel and welcoming official representatives from that country. This step led directly to mutually beneficial cultural, economic, and business opportunities between our two sovereign nations. I am both very proud and pleased that this unique relationship continues to flourish to this day. Through self-determination, we, as a sovereign nation, have found a new way to invest in our future and create job opportunities for tribal members, while contributing to our regional economic development.

I share this unique story of sovereignty and business development not because I want to boast about our achievements, but because I want to point out that any of you can do these things. Any of you can come up with new economic development ideas and approaches (and, in fact, I'm sure many of you are). And any of you can use the financial rewards to reinvest in your communities as we have. Any of you can, as we have, promote your

David Sickey presents Israel ambassador David Roet with a Coushatta basket. (Photo Courtesy of Permanent Mission of Israel to the United Nations.)

successes so that government representatives and the voting public know that federal programs are paying off in amazing ways.

And finally, any of you can, as we have, take the rewards of your business initiatives and reinvest in your own education and job-training initiatives. In this way, we will be prepared if all our best efforts fail and federal funding for job training is cut or eliminated. In the opening, I mentioned a rallying cry. I believe we have one, but I do not believe it is something like "Save our funding!" or "Let's succeed in business!" No, I think we must be inspired by the specific reasons we would want either of these things: Our children. Our future. "Together, starting today, let us build a future for our children." That's our cry.

I am the father of three beautiful children, and our latest was born only a few months ago. This has given me new perspective. It has helped me recognize that all of these big issues—job and skills training, education, economic development—all of it is about securing the future for our children, our next generation, and ensuring that they have more and greater opportunities than previous generations.

Let us go forth after this wonderful week of events and discussions and actively work to secure that future.

Thank you.

David Sickey (Deer Clan) was the youngest person ever elected to the Coushatta Tribe of Louisiana's Tribal Council at the age of twenty-five in 2003. He has since been reelected to four consecutive four-year terms. From 2004 to 2012, he served as the Vice Chairman and played key roles in making tribal policy and helped lead the charge to create a Tribal Natural Resource Department and a Department of Commerce. He is also the architect of the tribe's outreach efforts to Israel and various other nongaming business ventures. Sickey was recently reelected to a fourth term in 2015 and is again serving as the tribe's Vice Chairman.

Seeking Prosperity and Self-Determination

The Poarch Band of Creek Indians (PCI) is a blessed tribe. However, these blessings of today have not come without years of struggles. There are many times when I reflect upon the history of this tribe as well as my years growing up in the Poarch community. I'm constantly amazed and humbled to think of where we have come from, where we are now, and where our plans for the future will lead us. Without a doubt, I am proud to say I am a Poarch Creek Indian whose predecessors left a legacy of survival, perseverance, and compassion.

When counting the many blessings we have as a tribe, I do include tribal gaming. Undisputedly, tribal gaming is a controversial subject matter; however, it has been instrumental in our people's present quality of life. The tribe's mantra for many years has remained "Seeking Prosperity and Self-Determination." While most associate prosperity with financial means, I suggest to you that prosperity is a much broader concept. A prosperous nation is one in which its people are flourishing, healthy, happy, and living sustainable lifestyles. To me, true prosperity is measured by the overall well-being of the people.

Indeed, the tribal gaming industry has had a remarkable impact on the quality of life for our tribal members. For example, in 1984, when our tribe received federal recognition, many of our people were indigent, received minimal health care, and possessed a rudimentary level of education, if any. By 2014, our members received a dividend of business profits, exceptional health care benefits, and a generous education scholarship.

Beginning in 2005, the tribe began making per capita distributions to its tribal members from revenue accrued through its business entities, including gaming. Per capita distributions are not guaranteed from year to year; as a result, tribal members are not solely dependent upon this source of revenue. However, these additional funds help our members provide a better life for themselves and their children.

Historically, the Native American population is more susceptible to specific health conditions than other ethnicities in the United States. Some of these health maladies include: diabetes, heart disease, cancer, stroke, and obesity. Of the 2,153 patients seen by the PCI Health Clinic,[5] 844 have been diagnosed with heart disease, 411 have diabetes, 12 patients have had strokes, and 37 patients suffer with cancer. Cognizant of this information, the Tribal Council has made health care a priority.

Not only do we provide basic health services at our health clinic, but we also provide either health insurance or a health benefits card to our tribal citizens. Dental and optometry services are also available through the tribe. Additionally, Poarch's Recreation Department, with the support of Tribal Council, has launched a wellness program in which members are encouraged to adopt healthy habits and are subsequently rewarded for doing so. Most recently, the tribe invested millions of dollars in the construction of a new facility, which includes a 68,430-square-foot health clinic.

Throughout the history of our tribe, you will hear stories told about the struggles our people endured in order to acquire an education. Our past and current leaders recognized that a quality education is essential to the future success and sustainability of the populace. Many of our tribal elders were not given the opportunity to advance past the junior high school level. As such, these elders have not only stressed the importance of getting a quality education to their children and grandchildren, but they have also unwaveringly supported their descendants' pursuit of education.

Another perspective regarding education is that, once acquired, no one can take it away from you. You see, today's blessings are not promised tomorrow, and we live in an uncertain environment. So, we as leaders are striving to "teach a man to fish" instead of just continually handing over the fish. A quality education helps ensure that our tribal members will be able to seek and gain employment anywhere they wish, and that they will be empowered to stand on their own two feet, without the tribe as a crutch.

Therefore, Tribal Council, the PCI Education Department, and the Education Advisory Committee worked closely and diligently together in implementing tribal scholarship programs. Now, any tribal member or first-generation descendant earnestly seeking an education has the opportunity to achieve that goal with the assistance of these tribal scholarships. I have personally worked with this initiative for five years as the Tribal Council liaison to the Education Advisory Committee. You cannot imagine the immense pride I feel when I hear of our many tribal members and descendants receiving bachelor's, master's, and even doctorate-level degrees.

Just over sixty-five years ago our people were refused a high school education. Now, our students are achieving unimaginable levels of education and doing remarkable things with their lives. These descendants of educationally deprived predecessors are becoming teachers, nurses, businessmen and women, doctors, college professors, and lawyers. The educational endeavors that have been accomplished in such a short amount of time are truly remarkable.

The tribe has a significant interest in providing housing for its members. There are several housing programs that are administered through the PCI Housing Department that provide a means for individuals to acquire housing. These initiatives range from home ownership to rental units and also make provisions for home rehabilitation and renovation as well. This department also administers a program specifically for tribal elders needing handicap renovations, as well as a heating and cooling program.

Safety is of the utmost concern to almost any community, and Poarch is no exception. We take pride in being able to maintain a safe and pleasant atmosphere for our community members. However, it would not be possible without our police officers, firefighters, and emergency management team. These men and women are there at a moment's notice when you most need them.

Tribal leadership has continuously supported cultural education efforts as well as a museum. Cultural education and language revitalization ensure that our successors understand what it really means to be a Poarch

Creek Indian. Also, our museum serves the vital purpose of breaking down barriers and dispelling stereotypes through the educational experience it provides about the PCI to the public. Some of the classes that have been taught on the Poarch Reservation include: Mvskoke Creek language, basket weaving, moccasin making, patchwork and traditional clothing, Mvskoke hymns, beadwork, and pottery.

While the tribe does believe in taking care of its own, it also firmly believes in taking care of others. Were it not for the compassion of others during our difficult times, we may not be as successful as we are today. It is with this philanthropic spirit that the tribe commissioned an Endowment Committee. In eight years, over $36 million has been bestowed upon various organizations and entities.[6] God has blessed us beyond measure, and we are humbled by the opportunity to be a blessing to others.

These examples of endeavors and benefits that the tribe is now able to provide simply would not be possible were it not for our gaming facilities. Certainly there are those who adamantly disagree with the gaming industry, and these feelings most often stem from either misunderstanding or personal convictions.

Gaming activities may be identified as Class I, Class II, or Class III. These classifications provide stringent guidelines regarding the types of gaming activities that are permissible. Class I is the most limited classification, and Class III gaming is the most unrestricted class. The Poarch Creek Indians currently operate three gaming facilities within which Class II electronic bingo machines are utilized. By definition, Class II gaming is:

(7) (A) (i) the game of chance commonly known as bingo (whether or not electronic, computer, or other technologic aids are used in connection therewith)

(I) which is played for prizes, including monetary prizes, with cards bearing numbers or other designations,

(II) in which the holder of the card covers such numbers or designations when objects, similarly numbered or designated, are drawn or electronically determined, and

(III) in which the game is won by the first person covering a previously designated arrangement of numbers or designations on such cards, including (if played in the same location) pull-tabs, lotto, punch boards, tip jars, instant bingo, and other games similar to bingo.[7]

Indian gaming is a highly regulated and frequently audited *entertainment* industry. First, our properties must abide by a plethora of rules designed especially for tribal gaming facilities. Because Native American facilities are strictly scrutinized, tribal leaders across Indian Country are highly motivated to maintain the integrity of the industry. I have personally served on the Indian Gaming Working Group where we spent countless hours developing and reviewing Indian gaming policies. Trust me, no one is more vested in maintaining an honest and above-reproach gaming business than the Indian tribes that depend upon it.

Second, individuals *choose* where to spend their discretionary dollars. I choose to spend my money at the movie theater, occasional shopping trips, vacation, and on my beautiful children and grandchildren. However, many people choose to be a guest at our luxurious properties and be pampered at the spa, lounge by the pool, have a fine-dining experience, listen to a live band, sleep in a four-diamond hotel, and wager their luck at a Class II electronic bingo machine.

Many individuals have a skewed perception of the types of establishments that PCI operates. They hear the word "bingo" and automatically think of daubers, bingo cards, cigarette smoke, and "B3, B3, do I hear a bingo?" However, our "bingo hall" is a luxurious, four-diamond resort equipped with a top-of-the-line air ventilation system, and was designed to help you relax and have a good time. We are changing the perception of gaming one guest at a time.

In conclusion, I want to recognize our many past leaders of the Poarch Creek Indians, both official and unofficial, who have made countless sacrifices so that we might have a better life today. These tenacious individuals built a strong foundation that we continue to build upon today. Suffice it to say, if it were not for their perseverance and relentlessness, we would certainly not be where we are today.

I also want to share a memory with you. Years of planning had taken place for Wind Creek Atmore, our first major gaming resort property. The ground had been broken, the building constructed, and the ribbon cut. Prior to this moment, I spent many sleepless nights wondering if I had made the right decisions on behalf of the people I loved so dearly. Would people really travel to Atmore, Alabama?

I thought about the dirt underneath the floor that was somewhere below me—it used to be a cotton field where some of our very people provided for their families by picking the white, fluffy substance. Now, a massive seventeen-story casino sat atop the old field, and I watched from the seventeenth floor as the cars continued to roll in. I could not believe my eyes. People, police, and cars were everywhere! Traffic was backed up all the way up Interstate 65. It was like a field of dreams: "Build it and they will come."

The "Grand Opening" night of Wind Creek Atmore was unlike anything I ever could have imagined. That is one moment in my life that I don't think I will ever forget. Wind Creek Atmore was a vision that materialized right in front of my eyes. It was a joyous moment with many tears.

That building represents so much more than just a building with games inside of it. It is a physical testament to our predecessors that those long years of fighting to reclaim their identity were not in vain. The Poarch Band of Creek Indians are still here. We are thriving, and we are humbly continuing a rich legacy left by our forerunners.

Stephanie Bryan is a lifelong member of the Poarch Band of Creek Indians community and is a proud wife, mother, and "Nana." Stephanie's love of helping others prompted her decision to run for the Poarch Creek Indians Tribal Council. She was elected to the Tribal Council in June 2006 and served as the Tribal Vice-Chair until 2014. She has taken an active role toward regulations within the gaming industry in Indian Country. In a historic election, she was elected as the first female Tribal Chair for the Poarch Creek Indians in June 2014 and is truly humbled to embark on this journey with her people. Her ability to help her tribe is the result of a lifetime commitment to community.

Defining Moments

Author's Note: The following is a keynote address that I gave at the convocation of the entering class of 2018 at the University of North Carolina (UNC) at Chapel Hill on August 17, 2014. I wanted to give the students—many of whom know nothing about Native Americans—an introduction to our history and values using Louise Erdrich's 2012 novel, *The Round House*. The UNC Summer Reading Program had selected *The Round House* for its 2014 program, and here I had an opportunity to reflect on the power of storytelling and the call to action that the novel represents for young people. My goal was to present a forward-looking approach to their education that recognizes the significance of the past and the questions that often go unasked as students proceed through college.

Today we commemorate and celebrate a defining moment. It's my daughter Lydia's seventh birthday. Last night we had a party at the Durham Bulls baseball game, dinner out with Grandma and Grandpa, presents of course, and an elevated level of princess status. For Lydia, this is a festival of individuality, and it marks one more step to getting bigger, to having more control (which she wants desperately). For you, class of 2018, this is a big day also. We celebrate you taking responsibility for your own education and for assuming control over your destiny.

To the adults here, this day celebrates a different kind of defining moment, a special day on which we release our children into the world to make up their own minds. We do that every single day, but some days are more memorable than others. A birthday is similar. Today I mark the day I gave birth to my daughter, and I can't overstate the joyful, daily astonishments of parenting, nor the utter tedium of what it involves. Being a parent is an exercise in resilience, in assuming responsibility for someone's life and then letting go of that person, but not the responsibility. I have begun to say things I never thought I'd say, like, "Quit touching your feet while you're eating!" or "Whining won't get you what you want!" I guess I figured Lydia would learn that stuff all on her own, but I was wrong. I have to teach her, and since I was a teacher long before I was a parent, I do know that every student learns differently, and the whole world, even the dinner table, is a classroom. Parents are far better teachers than professors are, because parents know what motivates their children to learn.

Today your parents celebrate a rebirth into this worldwide classroom, as they release you to maintain that motivation on your own, to empower yourselves. That is education—not just mastering a set of skills but empowering yourself to understand the consequences of your decisions at these defining moments of your life.

In the United States we believe education gives us some measure of control over an otherwise uncontrollable future. The Lumbee Indians, to whom Lydia and I belong, founded the very first institution of higher learning by and for American Indians in the nation, the University of North Carolina at Pembroke. I am the grandchild of a Lumbee college graduate, a position that unfortunately too few American Indians can claim. The pleasure of college, in particular, is that we can choose what we want to study, based on what excites, interests, or motivates us, and then we can harness what we learn to direct our future independence. Up above, my grandfather Wayne is probably pleased and astonished that I am speaking before you on a topic—education—that he was most passionate about.

Many of the most memorable moments, the ones that define us the most, occur because of forces completely outside our control. Things happen to us; unfair things, things that are not our fault—violence, abuse, abandonment, illness, death. In these moments we lose things that we cannot get back. Those losses—the random ones, the ones where we thought we did everything right, we did our best, and we still lost—transform us. Many of you have this kind of defining moment in your young lives already, and education makes you realize you are not alone with those moments. Lydia, in fact, lost her father after a long illness two years ago, a defining moment for her and me. And while over time the explanation for his absence may become more concrete, the mystery of her continued connection to him will never go away. His loss, and his continued presence in her life, will define her for years to come. (And all things considered, that's not a bad thing.)

If you haven't yet realized what your defining moment is, don't worry, I'm here to tell you again what you've heard since kindergarten, what Lydia hears every time she watches an episode of *SuperWhy*—"when we have a question, we can look . . . in a book!" It hasn't sunk in yet for her, but then each of us tends to look to our own understanding to solve our problems. For most of us it takes being a parent to look beyond our own understandings; being a parent teaches us that if we are to do the right things, we can't do them alone, and even when we do the right things, we can and will suffer. So where do we turn?

Your families and teachers have asked you to turn to education, and you've said, "okay." Education provides us with some tools to help us solve our problems when we can't solve them ourselves. It is the means to look beyond our own understanding. With education we begin to love the right questions, instead of the right answers.[8] So educate yourself for the resilience your life will require. Listen to someone else's story. Then, tell your own story.

The stories of American Indians in the United States are a good place to start. After all, you may believe that Indians have suffered more than any other group in American history. We're the biggest loser. We've supposedly lost our land, our cultures, our religions, our languages, our very lives, all due to forces outside our control. But what you may not yet understand is American Indian resilience. After all, I stand here before you, a member of the Lumbee Tribe, born and raised in North Carolina, the state with the largest American Indian population east of the Mississippi. Louise Erdrich did not tell the Lumbee story in her book *The Round House*, but she told a story of resilience that your fellow North Carolinians, the Lumbees, can relate to.

Start listening to someone else's story by asking, "Who is involved? What defines them? What are the important moments of their story, and the significant conditions they live with?" Erdrich tells us what does and does not define an American Indian: "You can't tell if a person is an Indian from a set of fingerprints. You can't tell from a name. . . . You can't tell from a picture. . . . From the government's point of view, the only way you can tell an Indian is an Indian is to look at that person's history." "On the other hand," Erdrich continues, "Indians know other Indians without the need for a federal pedigree, and this knowledge—like love, sex, or having or not having a baby—has nothing to do with government."[9] Being Indian has nothing to do with government but everything to do with the same kind of knowledge we depend on to make the miraculous decisions of life, like love, sex, and parenting. It's knowledge of self, but of community too. The decision to love, to have sex, to become a parent—each are defining moments with consequences we cannot predict. We cannot know the right answers, but we do love the questions. Yet we will often suffer unfairly, and we will also feel a clarifying joy. Erdrich describes Indian women as round and strong, so we can "move with dignity under the weight of all this tradition, and not collapse."[10] We are resilient. This quality, of course, is not unique to American Indians. My Jewish step-daughter-in-law expressed this principle better than anyone else I've ever heard; she used to say, "It's 10 percent what happens to you, and 90 percent how you deal with it."

Next, when listening to someone else's story, ask "what happens to them?" In everyone's life, some traumas are caused by random evil, while other painful defining moments are caused by the most insignificant-seeming "small-time hypocrites." Erdrich describes these people as having rigid "moral standards for the rest of the world" who are always "able to find excuses for their own shortcomings." We all know someone like this, or if you don't, you can find them easily on Facebook. Erdrich warns us that these hypocrites "may in special cases be capable of monstrous acts if given the chance."[11] Linden Lark, a shadowy but significant character in *The Round House*, defines this type of hypocrite, one who committed a monstrous act. There was nothing special about Linden Lark, about his failures or what had happened to him—he simply felt he had been cheated out of love, and he was consumed by jealousy, but had he ever given of himself for someone else? Can't remember the answer? Look it up and go to a reading discussion—tomorrow—to tell us a story that you know about hypocrisy.

We feel rage, remorse, resentment, and seek vengeance for wrongs committed against us or people we love, but that never brings peace. I ask you, be careful not to confuse vengeance and justice.[12] Neither have clear, absolute definitions, but if we are to exercise either, they must be untainted by hypocrisy. If we do not face the source of that evil, which is sometimes our own hypocrisy, we become *wiindigoo*, the monster who tries to destroy others for its own sustenance. We are not powerless against this monster, there is justice to pursue. But Erdrich tells us that *wiindigoo* justice must be pursued with great care—it requires a place where people can do things in a good way, with consensus, reciprocity, responsibility.[13] The Round House is such a place, the university is a such a place. You know the three R's are reading, writing, and 'rithmetic? Only one of them actually starts with R, by the way. So let's add two real R's to our goals for learning, and make it reading, reciprocity, and responsibility. There is wisdom here at UNC, libraries full of it, people in whom it shines like the sun; but there is also idiocy, injustice, and hypocrisy. That hypocrisy within ourselves extends out to how we treat others. The systems that constrain our opportunities, the evils of circumstance or intention, are nothing more than small-time hypocrisies. We have the power to stop those. And as your teachers, it is our job to show you examples of how to do it.

Finally, when hearing someone else's story, ask yourself "What should I do with this? How do I respond? What words will I use?" We read and we teach to learn empathy, to witness the consequences of other people's decisions, and to learn from their mistakes. We educate ourselves in order to understand the systems that we live in that constrain our choices, and constrain the choices of others. During your time here at UNC, you will find yourself deeply engaged with that learning, but then you will also feel unfairly treated, stressed, and like you can't get a break. Your resilience will have to kick in, and we, your teachers and parents, ask you to remember what the tribal judge in *The Round House* told his son Joe, the main character. He says, "What I am doing now is for the future, though it may seem small, or trivial, or boring, to you."[14]

In your life's defining moments, the listening you have done will pay off.

Faced with his defining moment in the novel, fear covers and shakes Joe, and dread overwhelms him. Yet when he gets up, he realizes he has learned something: "Now that I knew fear," he says, "I also knew it was not permanent. As powerful as it was, its grip on me would loosen. It would pass."[15] Resilience is gained when we learn our lesson and then tell our own story. Telling our stories, the way Joe does, allows that powerful fear to pass away.

We take fear seriously; the hypocrisy, the evil, that seems to suffuse our global community is traceable to small—and big—time hypocrisies. We could be immobilized in this wreckage of fear, but we can't let it wreck us.[16] We should take bravery as seriously as we take fear. When we are overcome with bravery, every day is an exercise in resilience. Fear will pass, and you can face hypocrisy with courage. Draw good from any evil situation, and if you are uncertain how to go about it, return to our three R's—reading, reciprocity, and responsibility.

Malinda Maynor Lowery is a member of the Lumbee Tribe of North Carolina. She is an Associate Professor of History at UNC-Chapel Hill and Director of the Southern Oral History Program. She is an author and documentary film producer.

Working Toward a Healthy Future for the Cherokee Nation

My name is Ahli-sha (pronounced Osh-ah, it's a Cherokee name) Littlejohn Stephens. I grew up on the Cherokee Reservation my whole life, with the exception of my college years. I was raised by my grandparents. They were in their late sixties when they adopted me. Therefore, I grew up in the traditional ways for the most part. We gathered greens and medicine in the mountains. We also raised a garden every year and killed our own chickens to eat. As a kid, I was always active outside playing in the mountains, by the river, or simply in the yard riding my bike. Once I was old enough, I played community sports like basketball and softball. As I got older I also played volleyball and ran track. I love to be active and stay fit.

I was young and just out of high school when the Cherokee Life Fitness Center opened. The tribal leaders wanted a fitness center for the community members to go to and exercise, so they renovated an old building and put in a pool, basketball court, walking track, weight room, and cardio room. Tribal members can use the facility free of charge. Nonmembers must pay a fee just like any other gym. The reason for a need of a fitness center is so we can combat the chronic diseases many tribal members have, such as diabetes and heart disease. It offers them a place to stay healthy or become healthy. There is also personal training available and classes free of charge. Different programs were also started, such as a cardiac rehab program. It is a phase 2 program that helps people after having a heart attack or surgery. After patients go through a Level 1 Cardiac Rehab Program at the hospital where they are monitored by physicians, they graduate to this program where they do light exercise, stretch, and are guided through the recovery process. The tools are here, so it is up to the people to utilize them. For the most part, a lot of them do.

Since health and fitness are important to me, I decided to go into a health-related field. I graduated with a degree in Health Information Administration from Western Carolina University. Then, I worked in the field of medical records for about two years and loved it. It was challenging, but I was stuck behind a desk all day. In 2008, a job came open with the Cherokee Life Fitness Center, and I jumped on it. I saw it as an opportunity to do something I enjoyed and hopefully influence others to live a healthy lifestyle.

As I got more into the job, I started several projects. For example, we have a Recreation Department that handles the sports, such as football, basketball, and baseball, but not much was being done to work with individuals on their skills. As a result, my staff and I began holding a "Little Dribblers" camp where we work one-on-one with kids to learn the fundamentals. I also started a F.I.T. (Fitness Individual Training) program where we work with at-risk kids with health problems, such as obesity, type 2 diabetes, or who are prediabetic. We work them three times a week after school to exercise and learn healthy lifestyle habits.

Here on the Cherokee Reservation we have an immersion academy, called the New Kituwah Academy, where the children speak the Cherokee language all day. Since we have our own school system, the immersion academy often draws upon the tribal system to fill in the gaps of missing staff, so I also serve as the Physical Education (P.E.) teacher. I cover classes that are kindergarten through fourth grade, with each year getting bigger. I coordinate the class objectives and help them meet the criteria in a fun and educational atmosphere. We also test them in the President Fitness Challenge. Two years ago I started the Cherokee youth track meet. It is an opportunity for kids ages three to eighteen to prepare and then race in a track meet. It usually happens at the end of the summer with a huge and successful turnout. I have seen many people get into staying fit and running. Most people start because they want to lose weight, but continue on for the peace and enjoyment of running. The races are organized, promoted, and run with the help of my staff, to whom I give full credit because I cannot do anything without their help.

Fortunately, the casino money that my community receives enables us to host races, health and wellness fairs, and other community events. Without the amount of money that goes into these events, I'm not sure they would happen or be as successful. The tribal programs pour a lot of money into these types of events, and, as a result, it draws more people to them.

I have two sons and a husband. My sons are one and four. We sign up for everything offered in our town, such as the one-mile fun runs, peewee basketball, karate, and the Smart Start Program. This is so my boys will hopefully find a passion and love for being active and healthy. This is the wish that I have for other young people in my community as well. My hope is to educate the youth and set them on the right path early on so that they have healthier lifestyles. Then we may see a decline in diabetes, hypertension, and drug use. We cannot necessarily change people's behaviors because they have to want to change, but we can create an environment for the youth to be able to make better choices.

Ahli-sha Stephens is the exercise physiologist at the Cherokee Life Fitness Center on the Cherokee Reservation in North Carolina, where she has been employed for the last six years. She enjoys living a healthy and active lifestyle and helping others reach their health goals.

Native Youth in Agriculture

> The land belongs to the future.
> Willa Cather

Walk into your local grocery store and look around at the many different products available. Immediately, you are in awe of the rows of colorful fruits and vegetables and are enticed by the aroma of fresh-baked breads and pastries. As you continue your journey, you begin to notice even more food items that are stocked high upon the endless rows of shelves and the vast number of freezers. As millions of people do this every day, most do not ever take the time to consider the answer to a few simple questions. Where do these foods come from? What processes are involved in getting the food harvested and to the consumer?

Being a young member of the Coushatta Tribe of Louisiana, I have been given the unique opportunity to learn the answers to these questions. As a young boy, I assisted my grandmother in caring for her garden and providing food for family meals. Consequently, I spent countless hours in the hot summer sun preparing the soil and reaping the rewards of a plentiful harvest. However, these items were not just blessings to my own family but were shared with our community as well. Today, this spirit of giving continues on within our tribe as a new generation is equipped with the tools to be respectful and responsible caregivers of the land.

In the summer of 2014, I was invited by the Intertribal Agriculture Council (IAC) to the first annual Native American Youth Agriculture Summit in Fayetteville, Arkansas, at the University of Arkansas. The IAC conducts multiple programs with the intent of improving Indian agriculture for the benefit of Indian people. Not only does the IAC promote the Indian use of Indian resources, but it also contracts with federal agencies to maximize resources for tribal members. Consequently, I was honored to be one of forty-four students selected to have an in-depth look at the agricultural industry.

This group of young people was comprised of fifteen different tribes, which included students from Alaska and Hawaii and stretched from Oregon to Louisiana. However, I was blessed to be the only student from Louisiana, or the surrounding area, to attend this summit. Thankfully, the hot and humid Louisiana weather prepared me for the blistery southern heat of Arkansas that many students were not ready for and negatively commented about.

Some topics discussed at the summit were how to start an agricultural-based business, the benefits of purchasing crop insurance, shipping merchandise to stores, and many more. One of the most memorable experiences of the summit was a field trip to the regional distribution center of Walmart and Sam's Club. First, students were given a brief history of Walmart's rise to fame and an understanding of how this financial giant has maintained its place in the market. Although Walmart is like many other corporations, it does have one particular voice in its company that others do not have. Walmart has brought together Native Americans who act as consultants and provide input into hiring practices, especially concerning minorities. Walmart also focused its tour on food logistics and distribution, food retail, and food safety. In addition to touring Walmart, we also visited the Discovery Center Food Processing and Food Development Center of Tyson Foods. There, we had a firsthand look into how foods were processed and prepared for distribution. I was even surprised to learn that Tyson is much more than just a chicken distributor. Ironically, most of the meat that Tyson processes annually is beef. Furthermore, I was able to watch an assembly line in action. First, the chicken tenders were breaded and seasoned. Then, they were moved down the line to the fryer. Once the frying was complete, the tenders were cooled and later prepared for packaging. In the end, my experiences at Walmart and Tyson taught me to have a greater appreciation for the men and women who work tirelessly to care for the food we eat both before and after it enters the factory.

Another lesson we learned at the summit was to buy as much groceries as one can locally. We were told to always try to buy the majority of your groceries at farmers markets if at all possible, or to shop at locally owned grocery stores for all of the other items. To help demonstrate, the leaders accompanied us on a field trip to one of the oldest farmers markets in the United States, which is located in Fayetteville, Arkansas. Fresh-picked blueberries, sweet yellow corn, luscious blackberries, juicy watermelons, and other items highlighted the many hours of labor that these men and women put into their gardens and fields. It was also a reminder of how the agricultural industry cannot only benefit the large corporations like Walmart and Tyson, but it can also be another tool to benefit our Native American population.

Similarly, at home in the Elton Coushatta community, my tribe works hard to invite both Native Americans and members of the surrounding communities to come out every first Saturday of each month and attend and participate in the farmers market. Due to this effort, the tribe is able to share its hospitality with neighboring towns while also sharing our customs. Native American jewelry, baskets, artwork, and food make this a successful cultural and family event. Furthermore, our farmers market also sells an abundance of produce, including lettuce and tomatoes that are grown in our tribe's own hydroponic gardens.

The tribe's hydroponic gardens have been quite successful and have received positive feedback from people all across the United States. Hydroponics involves a process of growing plants using mineral nutrient solutions in water, without the use of soil. Hydroponic gardens grow faster and last longer than those planted in the ground. These gardens also offer jobs for our Coushatta people—both young and old. Currently, we offer only hydroponic lettuce and tomatoes, but it is our hope that we will be able to expand our produce selection in the near future.

In addition to the work done by the Coushatta Tribe, our local schools also help to assure that agriculture is an integral part of our lives. The organization that fosters this idea the most, and assists the tribe in various events, is the Elton High School Future Farmers of America (FFA). Under the direction of Lana Myers, the Elton FFA teaches young people to be hard working, respectful, and responsible leaders of society. Students plant gardens, raise poultry, and receive certifications in both hunter and boater safety. Furthermore, members participate in various contests throughout the year, including parliamentary law, welding, small engines, livestock judging, dairy cattle judging, floriculture, forestry, soils, and nursery landscaping. They also participate in a number of community service events, such as the Veteran's Home Fishing Rodeo and the "Walk a Mile in Her Shoes" event against domestic violence. Students also recognize the work of local farmers by inviting them to a farmer's breakfast. By doing so, we are able to thank the farmers in our area for their undying support of our school and organization and for the contribution that they make through a lifetime of farming.

The future for generations of my fellow Coushatta people shines bright. Each day the tribe continually works hard to ensure that our culture is not only maintained but succeeds in providing education and stability for our elders and for future generations as well. Through my involvement in the Native American Youth Summit on Agriculture and the FFA, and my membership in the Coushatta Tribe of Louisiana, I feel that other young people may see that anything is possible if they are willing to put forth the effort needed to accomplish their goals. Therefore, I am thankful for my family, the many new friends, and for a community and tribe that support me in my journey.

Elliott Nichols is the eighteen-year-old son of Phyllis and Raymond Nichols and is a member of the 925-member Coushatta Tribe of Louisiana, a federally recognized tribe located in southwest Louisiana. He is a senior at Elton High School and plans to attend Louisiana Tech to pursue a career in veterinary medicine.

Notes

Introduction

1. Gilbert, "Surviving Indian Groups," 430.

2. For a complete list of tribal petitions for federal recognition, see "500 Nations: Petitions for Federal Recognition," http://500nations.com/tribes/Tribes_Petitions.asp.

3. Federally recognized tribes located in the Southeast include the Poarch Band of Creek Indians of Alabama, Miccosukee Tribe of Indians of Florida, Seminole Tribe of Florida (Dania, Big Cypress, Brighton, Hollywood, and Tampa Reservations), Chitimacha Tribe of Louisiana, Coushatta Tribe of Louisiana, Jena Band of Choctaw Indians (Louisiana), Tunica-Biloxi Indian Tribe of Louisiana, Mississippi Band of Choctaw Indians, Eastern Band of Cherokee Indians of North Carolina, the Catawba Indian Nation of South Carolina, and the Pamunkey Tribe of Virginia. A listing of the state-recognized groups can be found at the "National Conference of State Legislatures," http://www.ncsl.org/research/state-tribal-institute/list-of-federal-and-state-recognized-tribes.aspx.

4. From the mid-1940s to the mid-1960s, the United States instituted an Indian termination policy based on the notion that Native peoples would be better off if they were assimilated into the mainstream. As a result, Congress set out to end the government's trust relationship with tribal nations by encouraging Indian people to move away from their reservation homes to large cities, cutting off federal Indian services, shutting down Bureau of Indian Affairs schools, and placing Indian trust lands in private hands. Since this policy was meant to transition tribes, on an individual basis, toward this new status, not all tribes were impacted before federal Indian policy once again shifted. In the South, however, there were movements toward terminating the Seminole of Florida and the Coushatta of Louisiana. For additional information on the termination era, see Fixico, *Termination and Relocation*.

5. The Indian Self-Determination and Education Assistance Act of 1975 (Public Law 93-638) reversed the termination policy that intended to sever the federal government's obligations to tribes. Influenced by Indian activism—generated through the development and work of intertribal organizations—the policy emphasized tribal self-determination and authorized the secretary of the Department of the Interior; the secretary of Health, Education, and Welfare; and other governmental agencies to enter into contracts and offer direct grants to federally recognized tribal nations.

6. The body of scholarship on the pre-twentieth-century South is making great strides in demonstrating the important role that Indians made to the early development of the region, as well as the nation at large. For a good overview of the historiography, see Saunt, "Native South."

7. Paredes, *Indians of the Southeastern United States*; Bonney and Paredes, *Anthropologists and Indians*; Williams, *Southeastern Indians since the Removal Era*.

8. Some examples of publications focused on the Eastern Band of Cherokees include, but are not limited to, Finger, *Cherokee Americans* and *Eastern Band of Cherokees*; Beard-Moose, *Public Indians, Private Cherokees*; and Hill, *Weaving New Worlds*.

9. Some examples of publications focused on the Mississippi Choctaw include, but are not limited to, Kidwell, *Choctaws and Missionaries in Mississippi*; Osburn, *Choctaw Resurgence in Mississippi* and "Mississippi Choctaws and Racial Politics"; and Wells and Tubby, *After Removal*.

10. Some examples of publications focused on the Florida Seminoles include, but are not limited to, Covington, *Seminoles of Florida*; Kersey, *Assumption of Sovereignty* and *Florida Seminoles and the New Deal*; Weisman, *Unconquered People*; West, *Enduring Seminoles*; Wickman, *Warriors without War*; and Mechling, "Florida Seminoles."

11. Some examples of publications focused on the Lumbee include, but are not limited to, Lowery, *Lumbee Indians in the Jim Crow South*; Sider, *Lumbee Indian Histories*; Dial and Eliades, *Only Land I Know*; and Blu, *Lumbee Problem*.

12. Some examples of publications focused on the Poarch Band of Creeks include, but are not limited to, Paredes, "Emergence of Contemporary Eastern Creek Indian Identity," "Kinship and Descent," and "Federal Recognition and the Poarch Creek Indians"; and Vickery and Travis, *Rise of the Poarch Band of Creek Indians*.

13. Some examples include, but are not limited to, Bates, *Other Movement*; Bowman and Curry-Ropper, *Forgotten Tribe*; Cromer, *Modern Indians of Alabama*; Denson, "Remembering Cherokee Removal"; Hudson, "Catawba Indians of South Carolina"; Klopotek, *Recognition Odysseys*; Kniffen, Gregory, and Stokes, *Historic Indian Tribes of Louisiana*; Lerch, "State-Recognized Indians of North Carolina"; Matte, *They Say the Wind Is Red*; Miller, *Forgotten Tribes* and *Claiming Tribal Identity*; Neely, "Adaptation and the Contemporary North Carolina Indians"; Oakley, *Keeping the Circle*; Perdue, "American Indian Survival in South Carolina" and *Native Carolinians*; Rountree, "Indian Virginians on the Move"; Stanton, "Southern Louisiana Survivors"; and Taukchiray and Kasakoff, "Contemporary Native Americans."

14. Hobson, McAdams, and Walkiewicz, *People Who Stayed*.

15. Some examples include, but are not limited to, Crediford, *Those Who Remain*; Waugaman and Moretti-Langholtz, *We're Still Here*; Ferguson, *Contemporary Native Americans*; Carney, *Eastern Band of Cherokee Women*; Duncan, *Living Stories of the Cherokee*; Moore, *Feeding the Ancient Fires*; and Goins and Moore, *People Speak*.

16. Some examples include, but are not limited to, Nabakov, *Native American Testimony*; Hirschfelder, *Native Heritage*; Jaimes and Hu-DeHart, *State of Native America*; Nerburn, *Wisdom of the Native American*; and Calloway, *First Peoples*.

17. Matika Wilbur Photography, "Project 562," http://www.matikawilbur.com/.

18. Deloria in Nabakov, *Native American Testimony*, xvii.

19. Ernest Sickey, personal communication, September 22, 2014.

Chapter 1. Growing Up Indian in a Southern Context

1. For literature on systematically writing autobiographical essays or memoirs, see Roorback, *Writing Life Stories*; and Kramer and Call, *Telling True Stories*.

2. The contributions of southern Indian women are often addressed in literature; however, particular scholarly attention on this subject has been given to the Eastern Band of Cherokee. For more, see Carney, *Eastern Band of Cherokee Women*; and Perdue, *Cherokee Women*.

3. This is a reference to one of the most documented accounts of Indian people standing up to the Ku Klux Klan. In 1958, several hundred armed Lumbees broke up a Klan rally in Robeson County, North Carolina. The story was picked up by the news media and circulated nationally. See Landry, "Native History."

4. See Sunray, "From Social Reality to Legal Fiction."

5. Paredes, "Federal Recognition and the Poarch Creek Indians," 122; Miller, *Forgotten Tribes*, 187–188; Gregory, "Louisiana Tribes," 174; Curry-Roper, "History of the Houma Indians," 22; Taukchiray and Kasakoff, "Contemporary Native Americans," 84; Dial and Eliades, *Only Land I Know*; Blu, *Lumbee Problem*.

6. Much progress has been made in some southern states as it relates to acknowledging the impact that Jim Crow specifically, and racism in general, played on Indian people. For example, in 2010 Virginia public schools began implementing a curriculum (Virginia Standards of Learning) that offered a richer understanding of the triracial social system in place in Virginia and how this impacted Native people—who were not even considered citizens until 1924. See "Featured Lesson Plan: Jim Crow and Virginia Indians," *The Commonwealth: A Newsletter for Teachers and Education Professionals from the Library of Virginia* (August 2010), 1.

Chapter 2. The Politics of History and Identity

1. Perdue, "Legacy of Indian Removal," 36.

2. Groups like the Clifton Choctaw of Louisiana complained that they were prevented from being able to list "Indian" on their birth certificates. See H. M. Westholz Jr. (State Department of Human Resources) to Anna Neal, April 16, 1987, and Anna Neal to Dianne Williamson, [1987], Roemer Papers, Louisiana State Archives. Also, Indian people in places within Alabama were only given the racial identifiers of "white" or "colored" to list on their driver's licenses. Framon Weaver, personal communication, April 23, 2014.

3. By 1987, one-third (34) of the total petitions for federal recognition (104) had come from groups in the Southeast. Many groups found their federal petitions for acknowledgment challenged by earlier government reports from the 1930s and 1940s that were prepared by anthropologists, ethnographers, and geographers who were sent to the South to determine the authenticity of groups claiming an Indian identity. These reports tended to downplay Indian identity, thus making their later claims difficult. See Gilbert, "Surviving Indian Groups"; and Price, "Mixed-Blood Populations of Eastern United States." For a more recent discussion of this issue, see Taylor, *Reconstructing the Native South*.

4. See McClure, *Cherokee Proud*.

5. Klopotek, *Recognition Odysseys*, 1.

6. See Sweet, *Legal History of the Color Line*.

7. "Among the whites" is the terminology used in the Treaty of Fort Jackson.

8. DuBois, "Souls of White Folk," 497–498.

9. Wright, *Black Boy*.

10. Woodward, *Strange Career of Jim Crow*.

11. Hoelscher, "Making Place, Making Race."

12. From notes from an oral history interview with elder Sallie Kever for the "Scott Town-Scotts Ferry-Woods Community Oral History Project" as part of the Florida Tribe of Eastern Creek Indians' petition for federal acknowledgment, conducted at the Blountstown Indian Community Tribal Office, Calhoun County Courthouse, Blountstown, Florida, March 1996.

13. Orwell, *Nineteen Eighty-Four*.

14. Anderson and Kickingbird, *Historical Perspective*, 17.

15. Don Rankin to Chief Wilford Taylor, July 13, 1998.

Chapter 3. Cultural Grounding

1. Hill, *Weaving New Worlds*.

2. Tobias, "Billie Swamp Safari."

3. Hendrix, *If the Legends Fade*; Howard, "Off Alabama's Beaten Path."

4. See Goertzen, "Powwows and Identity"; and Mattern, "Powwow as a Public Arena."

Chapter 4. Moving Forward

1. Mike Parker, "Foreword" in Ferrera, *Choctaw Revolution*, 3.

2. Dement, *Mississippi Entrepreneurs*, 94–97.

3. Kersey, *Assumption of Sovereignty*; Pleasants and Kersey, *Seminole Voices*.

4. Shotton, Lowe, and Waterman, "Introduction," in *Beyond the Asterisk*, 1.

5. This number is based upon Poarch Creek tribal members and first-generation descendants seen by the clinic from January 1, 2013, through February 19, 2014.

6. This number is based upon contributions given from 2007 through 2014.

7. This definition is from the Indian Gaming Regulatory Act, commonly referred to as IGRA. 25 U.S.C. §2703(7).

8. Rilke, *Letters to a Young Poet*.

9. Erdrich, *Round House*, 29–30.

10. Erdrich, *Round House*, 274.

11. Erdrich, *Round House*, 50.

12. Erdrich, *Round House*, 260.

13. Erdrich, *Round House*, 187.

14. Erdrich, *Round House*, 231.

15. Erdrich, *Round House*, 264.

16. Erdrich, *Round House*, 300.

Bibliography

Anderson, Terry, and Kirke Kickingbird. *An Historical Perspective on the Issue of Federal Recognition and Non-recognition*. Washington, D.C.: Institute for the Development of Indian Law, 1978.

Bates, Denise E. *The Other Movement: Indian Rights and Civil Rights in the Deep South*. Tuscaloosa: University of Alabama Press, 2012.

Beard-Moose, Christina Taylor. *Public Indians, Private Cherokees: Tourism and Tradition on Tribal Ground*. Tuscaloosa: University of Alabama Press, 2009.

Blankenship, Bob. *Cherokee Roots*. Vol. 1, *Eastern Cherokee Rolls*. Cherokee, N.C.: Cherokee Roots, 1992.

———. *Cherokee Roots*. Vol. 1, *Western Cherokee Rolls*. Cherokee, N.C.: Cherokee Roots, 1992.

Blu, Karen. *The Lumbee Problem: The Making of an American Indian People*. Cambridge: Cambridge University Press, 1980.

Bonney, Rachel A., and J. Anthony Paredes, eds. *Anthropologists and Indians in the New South*. Tuscaloosa: University of Alabama Press, 2001.

Bowman, Greg, and Janel Curry-Roper. *The Forgotten Tribe: The Houma People of Louisiana*. Akron, Pa.: Mennonite Central Committee, 1982.

Calloway, Colin G. *First Peoples: A Documentary Survey of American Indian History*. Boston: Bedford/St. Martin's Press, 2004.

Carney, Virginia M. *Eastern Band of Cherokee Women: Cultural Persistence in Their Letters and Speeches*. Knoxville: University of Tennessee Press, 2005.

Covington, James W. *The Seminoles of Florida*. Gainsville: University Press of Florida, 1993.

Crediford, Gene J. *Those Who Remain: A Photographer's Memoir of South Carolina Indians*. Tuscaloosa: University of Alabama Press, 2009.

Cromer, Marie West. *Modern Indians of Alabama: Remnants of Removal*. Birmingham, Ala.: Southern University Press, 1984.

Curry-Roper, Janel. "A History of the Houma Indians and Their Story of Federal Non-recognition." *American Indian Journal* 5, no. 2 (February 1979): 8–28.

Dement, Polly. *Mississippi Entrepreneurs*. Jackson: University Press of Mississippi/Cat Island Books, 2014.

Denson, Andrew. "Remembering Cherokee Removal in Civil Rights-Era Georgia." *Southern Cultures* 14, no. 4 (Winter 2008): 85–101.

Dial, Adolph L., and David K. Eliades. *The Only Land I Know: A History of the Lumbee Indians*. San Francisco: Indian Historian Press, 1975.

DuBois, William Edward Burghardt (W. E. B.). "The Souls of White Folk." In *The Oxford W. E. B. DuBois Reader*, ed. E. J. Sundquist. New York: Oxford University Press, 1996.

Duncan, Barbara R., ed. *Living Stories of the Cherokee*, Chapel Hill: University of North Carolina Press, 1998.

Erdrich, Louise. *Round House*. New York: Harper, 2012.

Ferguson, Leland. *Contemporary Native Americans in South Carolina: A Photo Documentation Covering the Years 1983–1985*. Columbia: Department of Anthropology, University of South Carolina, 1985.

Ferrera, Peter J. *The Choctaw Revolution: Lessons For Federal Indian Policy*. Washington, D.C.: Americans for Tax Reform Foundation, 1998.

Finger, John R. *Cherokee Americans: The Eastern Band of Cherokees in the Twentieth Century*. Lincoln: University of Nebraska Press, 1991.

———. *The Eastern Band of Cherokees, 1819–1900*. Knoxville: University of Tennessee Press, 1984.

Fixico, Donald L. *Termination and Relocation: Federal Indian Policy, 1945–1960*. Albuquerque: University of New Mexico Press, 1986.

Gilbert, William Harlen, Jr. "Surviving Indian Groups of the Eastern United States." *Annual Report of the Smithsonian Institution*. Washington, D.C., 1948.

Goertzen, Chris. "Powwows and Identity on the Piedmont and Coastal Plains of North Carolina." *Ethnomusicology* 45, no. 1 (Winter 2001).

Goins, Will M., and Marijo Moore, eds. *The People Speak: A Collection of Writings by South Carolina Native Americans in Poetry, Prose, Essays, and Interviews*. Columbia, S.C.: Phoenix Publishers, 2002.

Gregory, Hiram F. "The Louisiana Tribes: Entering Hard Times." In *Indians of the Southeastern United States in the Late 20th Century*, ed. J. Anthony Paredes. Tuscaloosa: University of Alabama Press, 1992.

Hendrix, Tom. *If the Legends Fade*. Chapel Hill, N.C.: Professional Press, 2000.

Hill, Sarah H. *Weaving New Worlds: Southern Cherokee Women and Their Basketry*. Chapel Hill: University of North Carolina Press, 1997.

Hirschfelder, Arlene M., ed. *Native Heritage: Personal Accounts by American Indians 1790 to the Present*. New York: Macmillan, 1995.

Hobson, Geary, Janet McAdams, and Kathryn Walkiewicz, eds. *The People Who Stayed: Southeastern Indian Writing after Removal*. Norman: University of Oklahoma Press, 2010.

Hoelscher, Steven. "Making Place, Making Race: Performances of Whiteness in the Jim Crow South." *Annals of the Association of American Geographers* 93, no. 3 (2003): 657–686.

Howard, Jennifer Crossley. "Off Alabama's Beaten Path, Tribute to a Native American's Journey Home." *New York Times*, July 22, 2014.

Hudson, Charles M. "The Catawba Indians of South Carolina: A Question of Ethnic Survival." In *Southeastern Indians since the Removal Era*, ed. Walter L. Williams. Athens: University of Georgia Press, 1979.

Jaimes, M. Annette, and Evelyn Hu-DeHart, eds. *The State of Native America: Genocide, Colonization, and Resistance*. Boston: South End Press, 1992.

Kersey, Harry A. *An Assumption of Sovereignty: Social and Political Transformation among the Florida Seminoles, 1953–1979*. Lincoln: University of Nebraska Press, 1996.

———. *The Florida Seminoles and the New Deal, 1933–1942*. Boca Raton: Florida Atlantic University Press, 1989.

Kidwell, Clara Sue. *Choctaws and Missionaries in Mississippi, 1818–1918*. Norman: University of Oklahoma Press, 1995.

Klopotek, Brian. *Recognition Odysseys: Indigeneity, Race, and Federal Recognition Policy in Three Louisiana Indian Communities*. Durham, N.C.: Duke University Press, 2011.

Kniffen, Fred, Hiram F. Gregory, and George A. Stokes. *The Historic Indian Tribes of Louisiana: From 1542 to the Present*. Baton Rouge: Louisiana State University Press, 1987.

Kramer, Mark, and Wendy Call, eds. *Telling True Stories: A Nonfiction Writer's Guide*. New York: Penguin Books, 2007.

Landry, Alysa. "Native History: Ku Klux Klan Formed as Secret Fraternity in Tennessee." *Indian Country Today Media Network*, December 24, 2013.

Lerch, Patricia Baker. "State-Recognized Indians of North Carolina, Including a History of the Waccamaw Sioux." In *Indians of the Southeastern United States in the Late 20th Century*, ed. J. Anthony Paredes. Tuscaloosa: University of Alabama Press, 1992.

Lowery, Malinda Maynor. *Lumbee Indians in the Jim Crow South: Race, Identity, and the Making of a Nation*. Chapel Hill: University of North Carolina Press, 2010.

Matte, Jacqueline Anderson. *They Say the Wind Is Red: The Alabama Choctaw Lost in Their Own Land*. Montgomery, Ala.: New South Books, 2002.

Mattern, Mark. "The Powwow as a Public Arena for Negotiating Unity and Diversity in American Indian Life." *American Indian Culture and Research Journal* 20, no. 4 (1996): 183–201.

McClure, Tony Mack. *Cherokee Proud: A Guide for Tracing and Honoring Your Cherokee Ancestors*. Somerville, Tenn.: Chunannee Books, 1999.

Mechling, Jay. "Florida Seminoles and the Marketing of the Last Frontier." In *Dressing in Feathers: The Construction of the Indian in American Popular Culture*, ed. S. Elizabeth Bird. Boulder, Colo.: Westview Press, 1996.

Miller, Mark Edwin. *Claiming Tribal Identity: The Five Tribes and the Politics of Federal Acknowledgement*. Norman: University of Oklahoma Press, 2013.

———. *Forgotten Tribes: Unrecognized Indians and the Federal Acknowledgment Process*. Lincoln: University of Nebraska Press, 2004.

Mooney, James. *Siouan Tribes of the East*. St. Clair Shores, Mich.: Scholarly Press, 1970.

Moore, Marijo, ed. *Feeding the Ancient Fires: A Collection of Writings by North Carolina American Indians*. Candler, N.C.: Renegade Planets Publishing, 1999.

Nabokov, Peter, ed. *Native American Testimony: A Chronicle of Indian-White Relations from Prophecy to the Present, 1492–2000*. 1978. Reprint, New York: Penguin Books, 1999.

Neely, Sharlotte. "Adaptation and the Contemporary North Carolina Cherokee Indians." In *Indians of the Southeastern United States in the Late 20th Century*, ed. J. Anthony Paredes. Tuscaloosa: University of Alabama Press, 1992.

Nerburn, Kent, ed. *The Wisdom of the Native American*. San Rafael, Calif.: New World Library, 1999.

Oakley, Christopher A. *Keeping the Circle: American Indian Identity in Eastern North Carolina 1885–2004*. Lincoln: University of Nebraska Press, 2005.

Oberg, Michael L. *The Head in Edward Nugent's Hand: Roanoke's Forgotten Indians*. Philadelphia: University of Pennsylvania Press, 2011.

Orwell, George. *Nineteen Eighty-Four*. 1949. Reprint, New York: New American Library, 1981.

Osburn, Katherine M. *Choctaw Resurgence in Mississippi: Race, Class, and Nation Building in the Jim Crow South, 1830–1977*. Lincoln: University of Nebraska Press, 2014.

———. "Mississippi Choctaws and Racial Politics." *Southern Cultures* 14, no. 4 (Winter 2008): 32–54.

Paredes, J. Anthony. "The Emergence of Contemporary Eastern Creek Indian Identity." In *Social and Cultural Identity: Problems of Persistence and Change*, ed. Thomas K. Fitzgerald. Athens, Ga.: Southern Anthropological Society Proceedings, No. 8, 1974.

———. "Federal Recognition and the Poarch Creek Indians." In *Indians of the Southeastern United States in the Late 20th Century*, ed. J. Anthony Paredes. Tuscaloosa: University of Alabama Press, 1992.

———, ed. *Indians of the Southeastern United States in the Late 20th Century*. Tuscaloosa: University of Alabama Press, 1992.

———. "Kinship and Descent in the Ethnic Reassertion of the Eastern Creek Indians." In *The Versatility of Kinship: Essays Presented to Harry Basehart*, ed. Linda Cordell and Stephen Beckerman. New York: Academic Press, 1980.

Perdue, Theda. "American Indian Survival in South Carolina." *South Carolina Historical Magazine* 108, no. 3 (July 2007): 215–234.

———. *Cherokee Women: Gender and Culture Change, 1700–1835*. Lincoln, Neb.: Bison Books, 1999.

———. "The Legacy of Indian Removal." *Journal of Southern History* 78 (February 2012): 3–36.

———. *Native Carolinians: The Indians of North Carolina*. Raleigh: Division of Archives and History, North Carolina Department of Cultural Resources, 1985.

Pleasants, Julian M., and Harry A. Kersey. *Seminole Voices: Reflections on Their Changing Society, 1970–2000*. Lincoln: University of Nebraska Press, 2010.

Price, Edward Thomas, Jr. "Mixed-Blood Populations of Eastern United States as to Origins, Localizations, and Persistence." Ph.D. diss., University of California, 1950.

Rilke, Rainer Maria. *Letters to a Young Poet*. New York: W. W. Norton, 1993.

Roorback, Bill. *Writing Life Stories: How to Make Memories into Memoirs, Ideas into Essays, and Life into Literature*. Cincinnati: Writer's Digest Books, 2008.

Rountree, Helen C. "Indian Virginians on the Move." In *Indians of the Southeastern*

United States in the Late 20th Century, ed. J. Anthony Paredes. Tuscaloosa: University of Alabama Press, 1992.

Saunt, Claudio. "The Native South: An Account of Recent Historiography." Native South 1 (2008): 45–60.

Shotton, Heather J., Shelly C. Lowe, and Stephanie J. Waterman, eds. Beyond the Asterisk: Understanding Native Students in Higher Education. Sterling, Va.: Stylus, 2013.

Sider, Gerald. Lumbee Indian Histories: Race, Ethnicity, and Indian Identity in the Southern United States. New York: Cambridge University Press, 1993.

Stanton, Max. "Southern Louisiana Survivors: The Houma Indians." In Southeastern Indians since the Removal Era, ed. Walter L. Williams. Athens: University of Georgia Press, 1979.

Sunray, Cedric. "From Social Reality to Legal Fiction: The Indian Boarding School Legacy of 'Non Federal' Tribes in the East and South." Haskell Endangered Legacy Project, 2012.

Swanton, John. The Indians of the Southeastern United States. Washington, D.C.: Smithsonian Institution Press, 1979.

Sweet, Frank W. Legal History of the Color Line: The Rise and Triumph of the One-Drop Rule. Palm Coast, Fla.: Backintyme, 2005.

Taukchiray, Wesley D., and Alice B. Kasakoff. "Contemporary Native Americans in South Carolina." In Indians of the Southeastern United States in the Late 20th Century, ed. J. Anthony Paredes. Tuscaloosa: University of Alabama Press, 1992.

Taylor, Melanie B. Reconstructing the Native South: American Indian Literature and the Lost Cause. Athens: University of Georgia Press, 2011.

Tobias, Melvie. "Billie Swamp Safari Celebrates 12th Annual Flute Retreat." Seminole Tribune, March 26, 2010.

Vickery, Lou, and Steve Travis. The Rise of the Poarch Band of Creek Indians. Atmore, Ala.: Upword Press, 2009.

Waugaman, Sandra F., and Danielle Moretti-Langholtz. We're Still Here: Contemporary Virginia Indians Tell Their Stories. Richmond, Va.: Palari Publishing, 2006.

Weisman, Brent R. Unconquered People: Florida's Seminole and Miccosukee Indians. Gainsville: University Press of Florida, 1999.

Wells, Samuel J., and Roseanna Tubby, eds. After Removal: The Choctaw in Mississippi. Jackson: University Press of Mississippi, 1986.

West, Patsy. The Enduring Seminoles: From Alligator Wrestling to Ecotourism. Gainsville: University Press of Florida, 1998.

Wickman, Patricia R. Warriors without War: Seminole Leadership in the Late Twentieth Century. Tuscaloosa: University of Alabama Press, 2011.

Williams, Walter L., ed. Southeastern Indians since the Removal Era. Athens: University of Georgia Press, 1979.

Woodward, C. Vann. The Strange Career of Jim Crow. 1955. Reprint, New York: Oxford University Press, 1974.

Wright, Richard. Black Boy (American Hunger): A Record of Childhood and Youth. 1945. Reprint, New York: HarperPerennial, 1988.

Index

Denise E. Bates is an assistant professor at Arizona State University and the author of *The Other Movement: Indian Rights and Civil Rights in the Deep South*.

The University Press of Florida is the scholarly publishing agency for the State University System of Florida, comprising Florida A&M University, Florida Atlantic University, Florida Gulf Coast University, Florida International University, Florida State University, New College of Florida, University of Central Florida, University of Florida, University of North Florida, University of South Florida, and University of West Florida.

OTHER SOUTHERNERS

Edited by John David Smith, University of North Carolina at Charlotte

This series features rigorous, innovative scholarship that brings forward complex histories of the multiracial and multiethnic American South.

We Will Always Be Here: Native Peoples on Living and Thriving in the South, edited by Denise E. Bates (2016)

CPSIA information can be obtained
at www.ICGtesting.com
Printed in the USA
LVHW110557100123
736830LV00003B/57